CULTURES OF AMBIVALENCE
AND CONTEMPT

Parkes-Wiener Series on Jewish Studies
SERIES EDITORS: DAVID CESARANI AND TONY KUSHNER

The field of Jewish Studies is one of the youngest, but fastest growing and most exciting areas of scholarship in the academic world today. Named after James Parkes and Alfred Wiener and recognising the co-operative relationship between the Parkes Centre at the University of Southampton and the Wiener Library in London, this series aims to publish new research in the field and student materials for use in the seminar room, and to re-issue classic studies which are currently out of print.

The selection of publications will reflect the international character and diversity of Jewish Studies; it will range over Jewish history from Abraham to modern Zionism, and Jewish culture from Moses to post-modernism. The series will also reflect the multi-disciplinary approach inherent in Jewish Studies and at the cutting edge of contemporary scholarship, and will provide an outlet for innovative work on the interface between Judaism and ethnicity, popular culture, gender, class, space and memory.

James Parkes in Europe during the 1920s
working for the International Student Service

Rev Dr James Parkes, in the 1960s

CULTURES OF AMBIVALENCE AND CONTEMPT

Studies in Jewish–Non-Jewish Relations

ESSAYS IN HONOUR OF THE CENTENARY OF
THE BIRTH OF JAMES PARKES

Edited by

Siân Jones, Tony Kushner and Sarah Pearce

VALLENTINE MITCHELL
LONDON • PORTLAND, OR

First Published in 1998 in Great Britain by
VALLENTINE MITCHELL
Newbury House, 900 Eastern Avenue
London IG2 7HH

and in the United States of America by
VALLENTINE MITCHELL
c/o ISBS, 5804 N.E. Hassalo Street
Portland, Oregon 97213-3644

British Library Cataloguing in Publication Data

Cultures of ambivalence and contempt: studies in
Jewish–non-Jewish relations. – (Parkes-Wiener series)
1. Parkes, James 2. Church of England – Clergy – Biography
3. Antisemitism
I. Jones, Siân, 1968– II. Kushner, Tony   III. Pearce, Sarah
305.8'924

ISBN 0-85303-324-2 (cloth)
ISBN 0-85303-325-0 (paper)

Library of Congress Cataloging-in-Publication Data

Cultures of ambivalence and contempt: studies in Jewish–non-Jewish
relations / edited by Siân Jones, Tony Kushner and Sarah Pearce.
    p. cm. – (Parkes-Wiener series)
    "Essays in honour of the centenary of the birth of James Parkes."
    Includes index.
    ISBN 0-85303-324-2 (cloth) – ISBN 0-85303-325-0 (paper)
    1. Judaism – Relations – Christianity. 2. Christianity and other
religions – Judaism. 3. Parkes, James William, 1896–1981.
4. Christianity and antisemitism. 5.Antisemitism – Great Britain.
I. Parkes, James William, 1896–1981. II. Jones, S. (Siân), 1968– .
III. Kushner, Tony (Antony Robin Jeremy). IV. Pearce, Sarah.
V. Series.
BM535.H27   1997   97-5221
296.3'9–dc21   CIP
                                         r972

Printed in Great Britain by
Bookcraft (Bath) Ltd, Midsomer Norton, Avon

Contents

JEWS AND ANTISEMITISM

    Middle Ages   **Colin Richmond**   205

10. Reporting Antisemitism: The *Jewish
    Chronicle, 1879–1979*   **David Cesarani**   247

11. The Necessity of Antisemitism **Frederic Raphael**   283

12. Afterword: Liberalism and
    Toleration   **Raymond Plant**   307

    *Select Bibliography of Major Works
    Referred to in this Volume*   313

    Select Bibliography of James Parkes   315

    Index   317

Preface

The Daily Telegraph in its obituary column of 10 August 1981 commented that:

> Dr James Parkes, who has died aged 84, was one of those independent scholarly Anglican clergymen who enhance the ministry by their gifts and graces, provided they are allowed to use their freedom in their own way.

Although highlighting the unfettered nature of Parkes' thinking and action, this understated comment did little to indicate the vision and importance of a truly great man of the twentieth century. Closer to the essence of Parkes was the tribute made to him when presented with his Doctor of Letters by the University of Southampton in 1969: 'James Parkes is a scholar in an age of unreason, an individualist in an age of conformity, a tolerant man in an age of intolerance.'

James Parkes' connection to the University of Southampton came late in his career. In 1964 he decided to transfer his unique library devoted to Jewish–non-Jewish relations throughout the ages to the University. Since then it has continued to expand and is now embarking on an exciting period with the formation of a Parkes Centre which, through teaching, research, publications and outreach work, will focus on areas within the broad scope of Jewish–non-Jewish relations that James Parkes pioneered. In 1989, as part of its increased commitment to mark the twenty-fifth anniversary of the transfer of the Parkes Library, the University instituted an annual Parkes Lecture, the first of which was delivered by the novelist and writer Frederic Raphael. Since then a series of distinguished lectures have been given as part of this programme. These are brought together in this volume and supplemented by other lectures given as part of the Parkes Seminar Programme, including the 1996 Montefiore Lecture by Nicholas de Lange and the Karten Lecture of 1995 by the first Karten Fellow, Sarah Pearce. Together we hope that these lectures represent a tribute to James Parkes' life's work and achievements on the occasion of the centenary of his birth.

We would like to take the opportunity of thanking all those who have contributed essays to this volume for the generosity of their time and energy when giving the lectures and their genuine interest and concern for the well-being of the Parkes Library. Particular mention should be given to Karen Robson and Jenny Ruthven, of the University Library Special Collections, who helped edit some of the essays when published as Parkes Library pamphlets. Chris Woolgar, Christine Ninness and Valerie Barron provided much welcome help and support from the University Hartley Institute. Thanks also to *The Seventeenth Century* for permission to reprint the essay by Claire Jowitt and to Robert Easton, Rachel Joseph and Frank Cass at Frank Cass and Vallentine Mitchell Publishers for their enthusiasm for this project and Sybil Lunn for providing the index.

Siân Jones, Tony Kushner and Sarah Pearce

Notes on Contributors

Paolo Bernardini is Human Capital and Mobility Fellow at the University of Essex. He is author of *La sfida dell'uguaglianza. Gli ebrei a Mantova nell'età della Rivoluzione Francese* (1994) and is editor of a number of projects on Jewish history.

David Cesarani is Parkes–Wiener Professor of 20th Century European Jewish History and Culture at the University of Southampton and Director of the Institute of Contemporary History and Wiener Library. He is the author of *The Jewish Chronicle and Anglo-Jewry, 1841–1991* (1994) and editor of *The Final Solution: Origins and Implementation* (1996).

Siân Jones is an Honorary Parkes Fellow at the University of Southampton where she is working on a project concerning the formation of ethnic groups in ancient Palestine. She has recently published a book on *The Archaeology of Ethnicity: Constructing Identities in the Past and Present* (1997).

Claire Jowitt has been a Visiting Fellow at the Hartley Institute, University of Southampton (1995–96) and now lectures in the English Department of the University of Wales at Aberystwyth. Her doctoral thesis looked at Renaissance fantasy voyages and she is currently working on a project which explores Jewish–Christian relations in the 1650s.

Tony Kushner is Marcus Sieff Senior Lecturer and Director of the Parkes Centre. He is the author of *The Holocaust and the Liberal Imagination: A Social and Cultural History* (1994) and other books on race, immigration and Jewish history.

Nicholas de Lange is Reader in Hebrew and Jewish Studies at the University of Cambridge and a former Parkes Fellow. He is the author of *Judaism* (1986) and *Origen and the Jews: Studies in Jewish–Christian Relations in Third Century Palestine* (1976).

Elisabeth Maxwell has worked extensively in the area of Christian–Jewish dialogue and has organised the two major international Holocaust conferences 'Remembering for the Future' I and II.

Sarah Pearce is the Parkes Lecturer and Former Karten Fellow at the University of Southampton where she lectures and researches on Jewish history in the Graeco-Roman period. She is currently writing a book on *Jewish Law from Bible to Mishnah*.

Raymond Plant is the Master of St Catherine's College, Oxford and former chairman of the Parkes Library Committee, University of Southampton. He is the author of *Hegel* (1973) and *Modern Political Thought* (1991).

Frederic Raphael is a Patron of the Parkes Library. Apart from his novels, television, cinema and newspaper work, he has written several literary biographies.

Colin Richmond is Professor of Medieval History at the University of Keele. He is the author of two volumes on the Paston Family in the Fifteenth Century (1990 and 1996).

James Shapiro is Professor of English and Comparative Literature at Columbia University. He is the author of *Rival Playrights: Marlowe, Jonson, Shakespeare* (1991) and *Shakespeare and the Jews* (1996).

1

Introduction

Interdisciplinary Approaches to James Parkes

SIÂN JONES, TONY KUSHNER AND SARAH PEARCE

JEWISH–CHRISTIAN RELATIONS

The field of Jewish–Christian relations is, as Nicholas de Lange remarks in this collection, one with which James Parkes is 'uniquely associated' and in which 'he made his enduring contribution'.[1] The scope of Parkes' work here is enormous, encompassing scholarly and popular studies tracing the history of Jewish–Christian relations, demonstrating the unique Christian contribution towards modern antisemitism, and urging a reformation in Christian attitudes towards the Jewish people. A comprehensive view of the many achievements and the legacy of James Parkes is provided here in de Lange's tribute delivered in honour of the centenary of Parkes' birth. He suggests that Parkes' early works, *The Jew and His Neighbour: a Study of the Causes of anti-Semitism* (1930), and *The Conflict of the Church and the Synagogue: a Study in the Origins of anti-Semitism* (1934), should be regarded as the 'foundation' of his subsequent writings on Jewish–Christian relations. Moreover, de Lange stresses that Parkes showed an extraordinary consistency throughout his writings in his arguments for the recognition of the roots of antisemitism in Christian teaching, and in his rejection of conversionism, and discusses in further detail the enduring significance of his teaching on these questions. The essays in this volume, covering the ancient, mediaeval, early modern and modern periods, take up themes central to Parkes' concerns in these areas revealing change as well as continuities throughout the ages.

Much of Parkes' great contribution was in the historical aspect of theology, concerning both Jewish and Christian history, based on his principle that 'bad history cannot be the foundation of good theology'.[2] This remark was made specifically in relation to the distorting influence of Christian anti-Jewish ideology on the representation of the Judaism of the period after the Babylonian Exile as 'Late Judaism'. The last 20 years have seen many important developments in the modern study of ancient Judaism, some of which inevitably render Parkes' earlier work in this field somewhat dated. One of the great triumphs, however, to which Parkes undoubtedly made a significant (if rarely acknowledged) contribution is in the modern recognition of the ideological distortion of early Jewish history. This has involved a decisive move away from the predominantly denigratory portrayal of ancient Judaism in earlier Christian scholarship, and the abandonment of Christian scholarly efforts to prove 'that Christianity was the legitimate and authentic expression of all that was good and enduring in the Hebrew Bible ... that the triumph of "the Law" was a relatively late development in Israelite religion ... and that the Judaism Christianity left behind was a sterile ... and legalistic religion'.[3] Scholars now commonly refer to the Judaism of the post-Exilic period as 'Early Judaism' in complete contrast to the notion of 'Late Judaism'. A striking embodiment of the new approach is represented by the revised edition of Emil Schürer's classic work, *The History of the Jewish People in the Age of Jesus Christ*, which not only up-dated the nineteenth century study, but removed from it 'purely polemical material'.[4]

Parkes' pursuit of the origins of modern antisemitism produced one of his most enduring works in his *The Conflict of the Church and Synagogue*, published in 1934. Nicholas de Lange emphasises that Parkes' argument, which attributed a substantial and unique responsibility for modern antisemitism to the Christian Church, was shocking to Parkes himself:

> I was completely unprepared for the discovery that it was the Christian Church, and the Christian Church alone, which turned a normal xenophobia and normal good and bad communal relations between two human societies into the unique evil of antisemitism.[5]

Furthermore, it represented a 'complete revolution in thinking about the origins of antisemitism', that is, in his distinction between 'normal good and bad communal relations between two human societies' such as typified ancient pagan hostility towards the Jews, and that hostility against the Jews which was based on religious ideology, and which he located in the early Church and no earlier. De Lange draws attention here to the appearance of recent works which, in his view, and against Parkes' thesis, minimise or deny the novelty of the distinctive Christian propaganda against the Jews, by their emphasis on the significance of pagan hostility towards the Jews. Crucially, however, Parkes' thesis gains support from the evidence of the monumental collection on pagan attitudes towards Judaism in antiquity edited by Menahem Stern, which demonstrates clearly that it is incorrect to portray ancient paganism as uniformly hostile towards Judaism. The evidence illustrates rather the variety of attitudes which existed towards the Jews in pagan antiquity – hostile, neutral, and admiring.[6] Sarah Pearce's contribution to this volume builds on Parkes' distinction between pagan hostility towards Jews in antiquity and the fundamentally different nature of the early Christian expressions of hostility towards the Jews.

A further, very important, development in the modern study of ancient Judaism, also pioneered by Parkes, is the widespread acceptance, both in academic and Church teaching, that earliest Christianity and the figure of Jesus must be understood in the context of ancient Judaism. Moreover, influenced particularly by the evidence of the Dead Sea Scrolls, modern scholarship increasingly reconstructs both early Judaism and early Christianity as diverse phenomena. The situating of early Christianity within Judaism does not contradict Parkes' insistence, which has been developed by many others, that 'the basic root of modern antisemitism lies squarely on the Gospels and the rest of the New Testament'.[7] Taking these factors into account, Sarah Pearce attempts to place early Christian anti-Judaic polemic within the context of family quarrels within Judaism, arguing that this became dangerous later because of being read out of context.

Parkes' concerns with the endurance of theologically constructed anti-Judaic themes in later periods are represented throughout this volume. In the mediaeval context, Colin Richmond, following Bob Moore, argues that the twelfth century saw the birth of 'a culture of contempt', that is, 'a persecuting, a victimising culture'.[8] He contends that 'it is the development of university education in the twelfth and thirteenth centuries which inaugurates antisemitism'.[9] It is the scholarly class of that period who 'coming to believe in a God of love on the one hand, and in Christianity as a rational faith on the other, characterise Jews as unreasonable in not responding to what God did out of love on the Cross'. The representation of the unreasonableness of Jews and their deliberate rejection of Christian doctrine is to be connected with the intensification of Christian hatred of Jews and a readiness to believe in 'irrational' Jewish behaviour, exemplified by the ritual murder charge.[10]

Paolo Bernardini's chapter in this volume shows how the persistence of prejudice affected scholarship on Judaism and Jewish history in early eighteenth century England. Such attitudes are seen to be exemplified in Prideaux's history of the Second Temple period, *The Old and the New Testament Connected* of 1718, in which he asserted the redundancy of the Jews from the time of the coming of Christ and the necessity, inspired by millenarian teaching, of their conversion. They are present in the approach of the English translator of J. Basnage's *Histoire des Juifs* of 1708, which deals with Jewish history in the Christian era, who regarded that history as 'a standing evidence of divine vengeance upon Unbelief, and an indelible Monument of the Truth of Christianity'. Bernardini maintains, however, that this was also a period in which some scholars began to produce works about Judaism and Jewish history with fewer anti-Jewish prejudices, and in some few cases to correct misrepresentations of Jews and Judaism. For instance, Bernardini describes the works of the French scholar Calmet, the illustrator Picart, and Tovey D'Blossiers as constituting 'a decisive step towards the propagation of a more positive view of the Jews in England'.[11]

Revealing, however, the persistence of earlier, unreconstructed attitudes and behaviour into the modern period, Elisabeth Maxwell explores the silence of indifference which characterised the climate in which Parkes sought to raise concern for the Jews on the continent of Europe during, and immediately following, the Second World War. She argues that at the root of this indifference was the fact of the contemporary Christian world's profound, if unconscious, anti-Jewishness,[12] a reality demonstrated by the evidence of statements from representatives of the Church and State, which illustrate the currency of the view that Jewish suffering was merited on account of the killing and rejection of Christ.

Parkes' early exhortations for a fundamental change in Christian thinking about the Jews and Judaism were controversial in his own time in the Christian world, to the extent that, as several contributions show, he represented a very isolated voice. That many of his demands no longer appear remarkable and have to a large extent been adopted, at least in the Christian west, points to his status as 'the pre-eminent historian–prophet of the Christian– and–Jewish worlds'.[13] The second part of Elisabeth Maxwell's chapter traces developments up to 1990 in the rethinking of Christian attitudes towards Jews, and isolates four elements which have been 'almost totally concealed from Christian teaching' until recently, the widespread acceptance of which represents a fundamental trans- formation 'in the traditional position of the Church *vis à vis* the Jewish people'.[14] Namely, the continuing validity of the Old Covenant; the Jewishness of Jesus[15] and the pluralistic Jewish society in which he lived; the existence of Rabbinic Judaism; and the fact that certain controversies in the Gospels may reflect relations between Christians and Jews after the time of Jesus. Maxwell concludes that 'complete understanding of the common root must be the starting point and springboard for the way forward to reconciliation'.[16]

Tony Kushner's chapter raises the question of two key areas in Jewish–Christian relations in which Parkes' stand was almost unique, and which remain today one of the greatest sources of difficulty, namely Christian missions to the Jews, and Christian attitudes towards the State of Israel, especially the city of Jerusalem. Parkes' own attitudes towards conversionism are reviewed also by de Lange: Parkes' first work, *The Jew and his Neighbour*, was 'a strong statement of the need for Christians to listen to Jews

and understand them, instead of trying to convert them'. [17]
Parkes was later to describe the disapproval he received
from the World Council on account of that book: 'I, a
Christian priest, had discussed the situation of the Jews,
and what to do about it, and had not made it clear that they
should all become Christians.'[18] Tony Kushner's
examination of Christian attitudes in Britain,
contemporary with Parkes' writing, shows that Parkes
represented a tiny minority in his rejection of
conversionism.[19] He makes clear that Parkes' stance was
based on his respect for the integrity of Judaism as a living
faith. Parkes regarded the creation of the modern State of
Israel as legitimate and necessary on the grounds of
historical continuity, legality, and the moral obligation to
'make the world safe to be a Jew'. Kushner illustrates the
pervasiveness and influence of a contrasting Christian
attitude which opposed, in particular, Jewish control of the
holy places in Jerusalem, arguing that 'for the Christian
world in Britain, the ideological legacy of the Crusades
lasted well into the twentieth century'.[20] Yet, whilst Parkes
concentrated so much of his energies into the
understanding of the specific dynamics of Jewish–
Christian relations, his life's work has considerable
significance beyond this specific, troubled area, which is
reflected in the contributions to this volume.

JEWISHNESS AND THE CONSTRUCTION OF 'RACIAL' AND NATIONAL IDENTITIES

Just as Judaism has been fundamental to the definition of
Christianity,[21] so the notion of Jewishness has been central
to the construction of national and 'racial' identities. It is
now widely recognised that such processes often involve
the categorisation of Jews as 'other' or 'alien' in opposition
to a particular national or 'racial' group.[22] In this manner,

the 'nation' or the 'race' becomes constructed in terms of what it is not, rather than what it is. However, the situation is also more complex than a simple 'insider'/'outsider' dichotomy. For Jewishness has frequently been taken as a metaphor through which the ambiguities of different identities are explored in changing social and historical contexts.[23] As a number of chapters in this volume show, the 'Jew' or the 'Israelite' are not only 'other', but also on occasion inflected in the definition of 'self', and used as a means of classifying other non-Jewish groups within various hierarchical schemes.

Throughout much of James Parkes' life, in fact up until the mid 1960s, such processes were not widely recognised. Group identities, whether national, 'racial' or ethnic, were considered to be fixed and stable, each group being a distinct, cohesive whole with a linear and continuous history.[24] Such groups were also assumed to be sharply delineated from one another, and although it was acknowledged that contact resulted in diffusion and acculturation, these processes were ultimately expected to lead to the reformulation of bounded and homogeneous units. In the human sciences, considerable attention was devoted to defining different groups through the identification of cultural, linguistic and physical characteristics, and to tracing the relationships between groups as they marched through time, setting the course of history.

Whilst identity was not a central theme in Parkes' work, much of it implicitly embodies similar assumptions about the nature of ethnic groups or peoples.[25] In his writing on the history of the 'peoples' of Palestine, Parkes treated each group, whether the Jewish people, Christians, Samaritans or Muslim Turks, as a discrete individual actor moving across an historical stage.[26] Moreover, whilst he acknowledged that most of the peoples of Palestine were the product of an amalgamation of cultures at some point in their history, he represented them as homogeneous, bounded wholes; an approach which is epitomised in his periodisation of the history of the region in terms of particular ethnic and religious groups: 'Jewish: the children of Israel'; 'Jewish: Judea under the Romans'; 'Pagan and Christian: Rome and Byzantium'; 'Muslim: the Arab conquest', and so on.[27]

Yet at the same time, some of Parkes' writing incorporates ideas which echo more recent theories of identity and multiculturalism. For instance, he paid particular attention to the way in which interaction between groups shaped their character, and argued that the role of Palestine as a cultural crossroads in the ancient and modern worlds is an important element in the development of its peoples and religions.[28] Moreover, his definition of the Jewish people is characteristic of recent approaches to the definition of ethnic groups, being based on self-definition and definition by others: '. . . even when they were scattered in a thousand ghettos in innumerable different Christian and Muslim countries, the Jews recognized themselves as, and were universally recognized by others to be, a single people'.[29]

Recent theories of ethnicity in the human sciences expand on these basic elements. Since the late 1960s ethnic and national groups have been defined in terms of self-identification and definition by others rather than on the basis of fixed, objective cultural characteristics.[30] Research has shown that, rather than being a product of social or physical isolation, group identities are constituted in the process of social interaction between people of diverse cultural and religious backgrounds.[31] This aspect of identity construction is taken still further by theorists who argue that rather than being based on 'objective' cultural differences, ethnicity involves a subjective dichotomisation between 'us' and 'them'.[32] Here, the construction of an 'other' or 'others' plays a central role in self-definition of the group; the group is defined in terms of what they are not, as much as what they are. Moreover, the construction of a minority group as 'other' by the dominant society may have considerable impact on the self-definition of that group.[33]

A number of chapters in this book both reflect and elaborate on these recent studies of group identity in considering the role of the notion of Jewishness in the construction of identities. Kushner considers the religious significance of Jerusalem and ambivalent attitudes to Zionism in the context of English conceptions of the Jews during the 1930s and 1940s. In examining these areas he uses the work of James Parkes himself as a marginal viewpoint through which to examine the reactions of mainstream religious leaders and politicians. Jowitt explores the attribution of Jewish/'Israelitish' identity to native Americans in the context of colonial expansion, and the economic and political interests associated with it. Shapiro interrogates the discourses of nation, gender and race which are negotiated in Shakespeare's *The Merchant of Venice*, and argues that the construction of the Jews was central to English conceptions of difference and national identity. In other chapters, issues of identity also emerge, although they are not the main focus of discussion, for instance in Frederic Raphael's exploration of the nature of antisemitism and Colin Richmond's discourse on attitudes towards the Jews in mediaeval England.

Although they are concerned with diverse social and historical contexts these chapters touch on a number of common themes. To begin with, very few of the authors are directly concerned with Jewish self-identifications, but instead focus on the ways in which other groups have attempted to define Jewish national and cultural identity. For instance, Shapiro and Richmond both reflect on the central place of the myths of blood libel, ritual murder and abduction in the construction of Jewishness in mediaeval and Renaissance Europe. Shapiro discusses Foxe's 1577

sermon on the conversion of Nathanial Menda which
provides a typical example of the way in which such myths
were used, condemning the 'circumcised Race' for their:

> intolerable scorpionlike savagenes, so furiously boyling
> against the innocent infants of Christian Gentiles: and the
> rest of their haynous abominations, insatiable butcheries,
> treasons, frensies and madness'.[34]

Such anti-Jewish discourses were later transformed into the
racial antisemitism of the nineteenth and twentieth
centuries which provided the broader context within which
attitudes towards Jerusalem and Zionism were
formulated in Britain during the 1930s and 1940s. Here, as
Kushner points out, the use of Jerusalem or Palestine as a
metaphor to refer to parts of Britain, such as the East End of
London, was used to emphasise the alien 'otherness' of the
Jews. Yet, in the context of debates surrounding Zionism,
considerable opposition was also expressed for the idea of
Jewish control over Palestine generally, and Jerusalem in
particular, due to their central place within Christianity and
consequently their relationship to British identity.

For the most part, these discourses illustrate a classic
tendency to denigrate and/or demonise the Jewish 'other'
which has been a central element in European history
since at the least the mediaeval period onwards.[35]
Nevertheless, they are complicated by philosemitic
discourses, demonstrating the ambivalent position which
ideas about the Jews play in the construction of European
identities. Thus, as Jowitt points out, the metaphor of
Jewish identity was awarded a special significance within
the seventeenth-century Puritan polemic concerning the
imminent end of the world due to the integral role which
Jewish conversion and their return to Palestine was
expected to play. Moreover, as Kushner notes, such
millenarian philosemitism can also be found in the
twentieth century in the form of the *British Association for*

the National Jewish Home in Palestine established in 1943.
Whilst such ideas are primarily concerned with Christian
expectations concerning the return of the Messiah rather
than with the Jews in themselves, they have nevertheless
played an important role in the conceptualisation of Jewish
people, their history and identity, by others.

It has been shown that such characterisations of the
Jewish people by other groups have influenced, if
indirectly, Jewish conceptualisations of their own identity.[36]
Consequently, the careful and critical analysis of
representations of Jewishness by others provides an
important context for understanding Jewish self-
identifications. However, it is clear that such representations of Jewishness say as much, if not more, about the
identity of those non-Jewish groups concerned than they
do about the Jews themselves.[37] As Shapiro states with
relation to late sixteenth-century England: 'Clearly even as
the Elizabethans have something to tell us about the Jews,
their obsession with the Jews tells us even more about the
Elizabethans'.[38] It is on the basis of such a position that a
number of the authors in this volume proceed in their
analysis of the role of Jewishness as a metaphor in the
construction of non-Jewish national and 'racial' identities.

Prior to the racial polygenism and the evolutionary
theories of the nineteenth century, ethnic and national
identities were invariably constructed on the basis of the
biblical framework, with genealogies being traced back to
various key biblical figures.[39] Inevitably, this required the
development of elaborate theories explaining present
human diversity, and the relationships between peoples,
such as those elaborated in Thomas Thorowgood's two
editions of *Jews in America* (1650 and 1660). In her analysis of
these texts, Jowitt observes that new and radical
appropriations of 'Israelitish' or Jewish identity were
emerging in the mid-seventeenth century. For instance,
Sadler and Winstanley attributed 'Israelitish' ancestry to the

English. In contrast, Thorowgood attributed Jewish identity to the newly discovered Native Americans, claiming that they were the descendants of one of the Lost Tribes of Israel. In doing so, Jowitt argues, he used the motif of Jewish identity as a mediating concept between the Protestant English, representing the highest pinnacle of civilisation and the Amerindians who he perceived as having degenerated to a mere shadow of the Hebrews. Thus, as Jowitt states:

> The description of native Americans as 'acceptable' Jews figured as a rhetorical strategy of a colonial discourse that was incapable of describing an alien culture in its own terms. Native American culture was translated into a Jewish culture so that it could be understood – as inferior of course – by the hegemonic discourse of Puritanism.[40]

Whilst Shapiro's chapter is not concerned with genealogical aspects of identity, his analysis of Shakespeare's *The Merchant of Venice* also reveals the way in which discourses about Jewish identity were implicated in constructions of race and nation, in this instance in Elizabethan England. He focuses specifically on the 'pound of flesh' narrative and the way in which myths of Jewish ritual murder, cannibalism and abduction are explored and often inverted within the play. For instance, Shapiro argues that the numerous references to Jewish cannibalism are used to offer an inversion of the Christian consumption of the blood and body of Christ. The act of ritual murder itself features strongly in Act Four where Shylock is seen sharpening his knife as Antonio stands with his bosom bared. The notion of 'flesh' is here, Shapiro suggests, laden with ambiguities, in particular being tied in with castration anxieties and an obsession with the Jewish practice of circumcision. Shapiro concludes that:

> In its resituation of the Jew in terms of various cultural myths, as well as within the nascent discourses of nation,

gender, and race, Shakespeare's play explores what may be described as a cultural identity in crisis, an insistence on difference that ends by undermining the very terms of identity by which that difference is affirmed: male, Christian, English.[41]

Thus, a number of chapters in this book indicate that the notion of Jewishness has at times been a central motif in the negotiation of group identities, both Jewish and non-Jewish. And yet their analyses do not end at this point. In contrast with traditional notions of identity as an inherent and essential characteristic divorced from social and political relationships, all of these authors proceed to unravel the ways in which concepts of Jewishness and attitudes towards the Jews intersect with specific economic and political interests. For instance, Shapiro suggests that in exploring the issue of ritual murder and the ensuing retribution brought upon the Jew, *The Merchant of Venice* provides a fantasy solution to economic and political problems, such as the need to balance usury against venture capital. In her analysis of Thorowgood's texts, Jowitt suggests a more overt political purpose underlying his construction of a Jewish identity for Native Americans. Here she sees his arguments in terms of an attempt to legitimise English territorial claims in the Americas, and, particularly in the later edition, to justify and qualify his own political allegiance with Cromwell against the monarchy.

Whilst it is clear from these cases that the notion of Jewishness has been used as an instrument in the negotiation of economic and political interests, it is also apparent that such constructions of identity cannot be reduced to interests alone. This is evident in Kushner's analysis of attitudes towards Zionism, Jerusalem and the Jews in the 1930s and 1940s, where he identifies a number of contradictory tensions. On a practical, economic and political level the British public and state wished to disentangle themselves from the problem of Palestine. However, on the cultural and ideological level, Palestine could not be easily dismissed due to the significance of Jerusalem within the Christian tradition. Thus, in this case, economic and political interests were not readily supported by discourses of identity and symbolic association. In some instances, notably anti-alien discourses, the Jews were symbolically associated with Palestine and Jerusalem, but in the context of Zionism and potential Jewish control of Jerusalem attempts were made to dislocate such discourses of identity.

Taken together the chapters dealing with identity in this book demonstrate the fluid and ambiguous nature of both group identities and the pragmatic interests with which they intersect. They support recent theoretical positions in arguing that group identities are, to a large degree, based on a dichotomy between 'us' and 'them', and that conceptions of 'otherness' play a significant role in the construction of identity. Moreover, they suggest that the motif of Jewishness has been appropriated in the exploration of a myriad of anxieties surrounding cultural identity. Thus, Raphael, in his exploration of a hypothetical treatise on the *Necessity of Antisemitism*, makes the point that within European logic the Jews occupy a central and yet undefinable place in the conceptualisation of history and identity. They are represented as '... both like and unlike other men, both part of Europe and external to it, both assimilable and indigestible', they are, as his unknown author eloquently remarks, '... the margin which runs down the middle of the page'.[42]

In some ways, the chapters in this book concerning group identity may seem a far cry from the work of James Parkes, and yet in many ways they are consonant with the agenda he outlined with relation to the conflict between Palestine and Israel:

> ... neither economics, nor nationalism, nor propaganda will be enough without a foundation in a new conception of the independence and *the interdependence of communities*, and the discovery of this new foundation is a moral and spiritual agenda.[43]

Parkes sought such a foundation in the concretion of historical and religious arguments,[44] whereas the chapters in this volume draw on historical and literary analysis. Nevertheless, in providing new perspectives on the construction of Jewishness, and the construction of other identities through debates surrounding Jewishness, they take a step towards a new conception of '*the interdependence of communities*'. The final section of essays in this collection, however, deal with the various attempts to destroy or at best marginalise Jewish communities throughout history.

JEWS AND ANTISEMITISM

In his *Antisemitism* (1963), which covered its subject matter from the last quarter of the nineteenth century to its post-Holocaust manifestations, James Parkes explained:

> why so much of th[e] book ... discuss[es] the history and character of the Jewish community. The answer is contained in the phrase used: *Hitler has made the world Jew-conscious*. The general answer to the Hitlerian picture is to give the real picture of the Jewish world and its relation to its neighbours, not to chase after the accusations, one by one, and deny them.

Thus, although Parkes wanted to avoid writing anything that appeared to be in the form of an apology for the Jews, even as late as the 1960s he believed that it was crucial to counter 'ignorance of what the true story [wa]s'. To James Parkes, recounting Jewish history was part of his life's work, fighting against antisemitism and working for a genuine understanding between the Jewish and non-Jewish peoples.[45]

From the early 1930s onwards in the English–speaking world, but also well beyond (his work was translated into most European languages), Parkes was, for the more enlightened thinker, the major authority on the Jewish experience. In particular, his popular and academic work on the history of antisemitism was path-breaking and challenging.[46] Although many contemporaries in the liberal world had little difficulty in condemning Russian and other pogroms in the late nineteenth century or Nazi violence towards the Jews in the 1930s, few were willing to accept the starting point of James Parkes: that antisemitism was fundamentally rooted in non-Jewish (and specifically Christian) culture. Indeed, it took several decades after the Holocaust for his position to become widely accepted.[47] As the century draws to a close there is now widespread acceptance, in the scholarly world at least, of the idea that Jews are not responsible for the hostility that exists against them. Historians and others may debate whether the continuities or discontinuities in the history of antisemitism are more important, especially with regard to the development of 'scientific' racism in the nineteenth century. Indeed, the chapters in this volume continue this important debate. Furthermore, the impact of antisemitism on the Jews is now accorded more attention, although not perhaps as much as should be the case. But the idea of starting with the Jews themselves to explain the existence and persistence of antisemitism has lost the legitimacy and widespread appeal it had at the point at which Parkes started his researches.[48]

Rereading the scholarship of James Parkes as the twentieth century draws to a close, it is, on the one hand, striking how innovative and forward looking much of his work remains. On the other, it is a sad reflection of the times in which he wrote, when the rise and spread of political antisemitism at times seemed almost inevitable, that his tone, as Colin Richmond and Frederic Raphael in this volume suggest, was so *reasonable* when trying to outline the nature of the prejudice faced by Jews in the western 'civilised' world. Yet the defensive side of Parkes' writings never dominated and his work always forced the reader to consider that the solution to the 'Jewish problem' rested with the non-Jewish world. Writing in a context where the total destruction of European Jewry might well have been achieved, it is not surprising that Parkes, when considering modern forms of antisemitism, concentrated on Nazi or other blatantly politicised articulations of hatred. Antisemitism, as he wrote at the very end of the Second World War, was 'An Enemy of the People'; it was one of the major weapons of those who wanted not only to destroy the Jews but the whole of democracy. Parkes was anxious to expose the Christian origins of antisemitism in antiquity (later reinforced in the mediaeval period) and then make clear its political use in the nineteenth and twentieth centuries. He was aware that its centrality in western and other cultures meant that it was unlikely to disappear alongside the defeated Nazis – he believed its elimination through education and rethinking would take centuries rather than decades.[49]

Nevertheless, it was inevitable given the context of his life and the marginality of his own position even in liberal British society that he would focus on the more extreme manifestations of antisemitism in the distant and more recent past. Parkes, and other early scholars of the phenomenon, defined antisemitism in a straightforward manner as 'hostility to the Jews' – a conflict based on prejudice. Parkes was one of the first Christians to realise the threat to the Jews by the Nazis. Indeed, he was also one of a mere handful of public campaigners throughout the 1930s and Second World War to keep the fate of the Jews alive in the liberal democratic world where they were rarely, as Elisabeth Maxwell highlights, given any priority.[50] Nevertheless, as Colin Richmond suggests, Parkes after the war rarely confronted the horrors of the Holocaust directly. It must be suggested that Parkes' astute awareness of what had been lost (he documented their destruction in a series of campaigning documents and semi-official documents during the war), in conjunction with his humanistic and religious, pluralist determination that Jewish life must somehow continue, stopped him dwelling on the subject intensely.[51] Parkes was not particularly interested in the machinery of destruction itself or the internal dynamics of the Nazi state (as opposed to its ideology). But he raised in *Antisemitism* what is still one of the key issues with regard to the implementation of the 'Final Solution' and more broadly to the nature of the human experience in the modern world:

> Tens of thousands of men and women, armies of officials ... were mobilised for ... terrible acts of mass murder. And of the human beings involved in their organisation very few would have been considered mentally unbalanced or insane by any normal medical examination. ...

> It is said that of the Jewish victims a million were children and babies. Men and women like ourselves took these little ones, inflicted hideous sufferings of hunger, thirst, and fear upon them, and then murdered them in cold blood. They did so because they were told to do so by their Government. But it is still true that they could only do so because they had insulated themselves from feeling anything in common with their victims. These children did not, to them, appear identical with their own children. Something took the place of the innocence and defencelessness of children; and that something was, in some form or other, created by group prejudice.

In a world that was still reluctant to accept responsibility, Parkes forced home his message that there was:

> no break in the line which leads from the beginning of the denigration of Judaism in the formative period of Christian history, from the exclusion of Jews from civic equality in the period of the Church's first triumph in the fourth century, through the horrors of the Middle Ages, to the Death Camps of Hitler in our own day.[52]

The essays by Elisabeth Maxwell, Frederic Raphael and Colin Richmond all concentrate on the post-war world's struggle to come to terms with the Holocaust. Elisabeth Maxwell in 'Silence or Speaking Out' charts the painful steps towards recognition of Parkes' view in the post-war Christian world. She highlights more recent progress such as the statement at the time of the *Kristallnacht* commemorations in 1988 of the then Archbishop of Canterbury, Robert Runcie, that 'without the poisoning of Christian minds down the centuries, the Holocaust would have been unthinkable'.[53] Frederic Raphael is less sanguine about the acceptance of responsibility in post-war Europe. Antisemitism is too central to European culture (Christian and secular), he argues, for the Holocaust to be confronted. He talks of 'the nature of the necessity which makes antisemitism Europe's elastic, agile, weightless companion, as necessary to its articulations as is the negative to its vocabulary'.[54] Referring to the suffering of the Jews in the war, Parkes stressed that he was 'not writing these things to be sentimental. I am writing them because it is right that we who are not Jews – and especially we who *are* Christians – should know and remember these things that happened in our own day. It is only when we do remember them that Jews will be able to forget them.'[55] More bleak still, Colin Richmond comments with regard to the *Shoah* that when post-war culture is surveyed (including responses to James Parkes himself as late as his death in

1981): 'Had it happened, one is obliged (over and over again) to ask?' Richmond concludes that 'Parkes hoped the *Shoah* had made a difference. We know it has not.' Parkes himself acknowledged as much between the first and second versions of his history of antisemitism:

> In *An Enemy of the People: Antisemitism* the last chapter was entitled 'The Elimination of Prejudice'. The change in the present book [the equivalent chapter has the title 'The Sterilisation of Prejudice'] reflects a change in perspective. In 1945, with all the horrors of the Death Camps still present to our minds and imaginations, men felt that while the present generation lived there could be no danger of a recrudescence of the violent antisemitism of the Nazis. Even if there were people so perverted as to believe that Hitler's policy towards the Jews had been right, they would be prudent enough to keep the feelings to themselves. They could win nothing but loathing from others if they proclaimed their views ... . We believed then that the political malady had been exorcised by the kind of shock treatment which would be applicable to an individual psychosis. Today there can be no such optimism.[56]

Yet if nothing else, the sheer scale of the Holocaust has prompted at least a reassessment of the nature and history of antisemitism. Not all of this work has been marked by subtlety and sophistication. After the war it was perhaps not surprising that an attempt to chart a German 'exceptionalist' model of antisemitism – of Luther to Hitler – emerged. Less geographically restricted histories of antisemitism have emphasised continuities in ideas and behaviour towards Jews often at the expense of periods of tolerance and relative harmony. Moreover, not enough attention has been given to the ambivalences and ambiguities that have been perhaps the more typical responses of non-Jews to the Jewish minority than the pogrom or mass murder. For example, whilst the rise of philosemitism in the seventeenth century and beyond (highlighted in this volume by Jowitt and Bernardini) rarely led to contemporaries treating real Jews in a sympathetic manner, it did provide an intellectual and cultural framework within which more positive behaviours towards Jewish communities could develop in the future. In this volume, David Cesarani provides a starting point which typifies more recent approaches, especially relating to work on the liberal world and Jewishness in the modern era:

> it is preferable to speak of a discourse about the Jews which operates through stereotypes that can be either positive or negative depending upon the intention of the agent employing them, something which can be deduced by careful attention to the context in which they are used.[57]

Cesarani highlights the tensions that existed in Britain, a country regarded as one of the most hospitable to the Jews. Through the pages of the longest-established and most influential Jewish newspaper, the *Jewish Chronicle*, he shows the range of strategies offered by British Jews when confronting antisemitism at home and abroad. British Jewry, by stressing the alien nature of antisemitism in Britain, faced the dilemma of explaining its domestic manifestations. James Parkes himself from the 1930s was intimately involved in the *Jewish Chronicle*. The Jewish community realised that Parkes, as a Christian clergyman, could state publicly what would have been rejected as self-interested pleading if voiced by the Jews themselves. Again indicating the insecure nature of British Jewry, David Cesarani indicates how there was a lingering tendency within the columns of the *Jewish Chronicle*, which did not end completely until the 1950s, to blame specific Jewish behaviour for the existence of some forms of antisemitism. Parkes could also be defensive in such a manner, citing the oppression experienced by Jews to explain to a non-Jewish audience why the minority might not be perfect in its public behaviour which could lead to it being perceived as an 'irritant'. Even so, he would always return to his overriding position, that antisemitism was a problem ultimately for non-Jews to solve.[58]

Moreover, Parkes, following many of his Jewish contemporaries, was prone to explain the existence of antisemitism in Britain in terms of the power of Nazi influences, most clearly in the case of the British Union of Fascists (against which he was an active campaigner not only in his writings, but also in working out resistance strategies for the streets of East London where the Mosleyites concentrated their violence against the Jews). To Parkes, a political idealist who became, during the war, the chairman of the progressive 'Common Wealth Party', antisemitism was the enemy of liberal democracy. Yet the work of Cesarani and what has become known as the 'new school' of British Jewish historians suggests that liberal culture is not necessarily benign as far as the Jews, or other ethnic/religious minorities, are concerned. Pressures to assimilate, alongside more exclusive tendencies which have denied the Jews full entry into society, have not been conducive to the creation of positive, freely developing Jewish identities. It might be suggested that Parkes, who so desperately wanted to create a society where there would be no inducement, formal or informal, on the Jews to remove their distinctiveness (although his concern was with religious identity and he was less interested in broader concepts of Jewish ethnicity), would be sympathetic to this new, pluralistic approach.[59]

More generally, the study of antisemitism is important in understanding the wider perspective of James Parkes. In the 1920s, Parkes discovered not only the virus of antisemitism and racial nationalism on the continent of Europe, but also the Jews, and particularly young Jewish students, in many different countries who were suffering from it. His approach to antisemitism was always deeply humanistic because he saw its impact on the rich and diverse Jewish communities and their individual members he had met and helped on what it emerged was the dawn of the Nazi onslaught.[60] Yet as Claire Jowitt, James Shapiro and even, to an extent, Paolo Bernardini, stress in their contributions relating to the early modern period and beyond, antisemitism (as well as philosemitism) can and frequently does exist independently of the presence of Jews. The specific chronological, cultural and geographical context is critical if we are to understand the impact of antisemitism on the Jews and on general society. At the same time, a deep historical perspective is essential for, as Shapiro points out in his study of *The Merchant of Venice*: 'The social anxieties that circulated through Shakespeare's play have had an afterlife over the course of the next four centuries'.[61] All of the essays in this volume, whilst concentrating on particular eras from the ancient to the modern, are anxious to show the links, whatever the discontinuities, across time and space that give their subject matter, however seemingly remote, extreme relevance today. Covering the areas that James Parkes did so much to pioneer within the broad scope of Jewish/non-Jewish relations, the authors are aware that problems of prejudice, hatred and intolerance of many kinds have not gone away and have in many instances intensified. Indeed, all the contributors, whose essays are brought together at the centenary of his birth to commemorate and celebrate the life and achievements of James Parkes, accept the principle and his example that it is the duty of the scholar to embrace activism so as to 'make the world safe to be a Jew'.[62] For James Parkes, as Richmond suggests, 'thinking was not enough'.[63]

NOTES

1. N. de Lange, this volume, p. 31.
2. J. Parkes, *The Foundations of Judaism and Christianity* (London: Vallentine Mitchell, 1960), p. x.
3. S. Cohen, 'The Modern Study of Ancient Judaism' in S. Cohen and E. Greenstein (eds), *The State of Jewish Studies* (Detroit: Jewish Theological Seminary: Wayne State University Press, 1990), p. 56.
4. One striking aspect of this revision is that where the earlier work concluded its account of the period in question with Jerome's description of the Jews' lamenting over the destruction of the city and sanctuary 'from which they had once thrown James the brother of the Lord', the new edition adds 'Yet the tears of mourning concealed hope, and hope refused to die', cf. E. Schürer, *The History of the Jewish People in the Age of Jesus Christ*, Vol. 1, revised and edited by G. Vermes, F. Millar, M. Black (Edinburgh: T & T Clark, 1973), p. 557. The editors of the second volume 'endeavoured to clear the notorious chapter 28, *Das Leben unter dem Gesetz* – here restyled as "Life and the Law" – and the section on the Pharisees ... of the dogmatic prejudices of nineteenth–century theology', cf. E. Schürer, *The History*, Vol. 2, revised and edited by G. Vermes *et al.*, p. v. On the legacy of Schürer and nineteenth–century historiography in relation to the distortion of aspects of ancient Judaism, see S. Cohen, 'The Political and Social History of the Jews in Graeco–Roman Antiquity: the State of the Question' in R. Kraft and G. Nickelsburg (eds), *Early Judaism and its Modern Interpreters* (Philadelphia: Fortress Press, 1986), pp. 34ff.
5. J. Parkes, *Voyage of Discoveries* (London: Victor Gollancz, 1969), p. 123.
6. M. Stern, *Greek and Latin Authors on Jews and Judaism*, 3 Vols (Jerusalem: Israel Academy of Arts and Sciences, 1974–84); J. Gager, *The Origins of antisemitism: Attitudes Toward Judaism in Pagan and Christian Antiquity* (Oxford: Oxford University Press, 1983).
7. N. de Lange, this volume, pp. 37–8, citing J. Parkes, 'Preface', in A. Davies (ed.), *Antisemitism and the Foundations of Christianity* (New York: Paulist Press, 1979).
8. C. Richmond, this volume, p. 215, cf. R.I. Moore, *The Formation of a Persecuting Society. Power and Deviance in Western Europe, 950–1250*, (Oxford: Basil Blackwell, 1987).
9. C. Richmond, this volume, p. 236.
10. C. Richmond, this volume, p. 236.
11. P. Bernardini, this volume, p. 116.
12. E. Maxwell, this volume, pp. 85–6.
13. A. Roy Eckardt, 'In Memoriam James Parkes, 1896–1981', *Christian Jewish Relations*, 15, (1982), p. 45.
14. E. Maxwell, this volume, p. 87.
15. Cf. J. Parkes, 'For any modern student it may be obvious to say that "Jesus lived and died a Jew". Fifty years ago one might as easily have found a bishop to declare that Jesus was a communist!' in 'The Way Forward', *Parkes Library Pamphlet* No. 23 (Southampton: Parkes Library, 1977), p. 5.
16. E. Maxwell, this volume, pp. 85f.
17. N. de Lange, this volume, p. 32.
18. J. Parkes, 'The Way Forward', p. 6.
19. T. Kushner, this volume, pp.187–8.

20. T. Kushner, this volume, p. 183.
21. On Judaism and Christianity see, J. Neusner and E.S. Frerichs (eds), *"To See Ourselves as Others See Us"*. *Christians, Jews, "Others" in Late Antiquity* (Chico, California: Scholar's Press, 1985).
22. See, amongst others, T. Kushner, 'Heritage and Ethnicity: an Introduction', in T. Kushner (ed.), *The Jewish Heritage in British History: Englishness and Jewishness* (London: Frank Cass, 1992), pp. 1–28; D. Cesarani, 'Dual Heritage or Duel of Heritages? Englishness and Jewishness in the Heritage Industry', in T. Kushner (ed.), *The Jewish Heritage*, pp. 29–41; C. Richmond, 'Englishness and Medieval Anglo–Jewry', in T. Kushner (ed.), *The Jewish Heritage*, pp. 42–59; E. Grosz, 'Judaism and Exile: the Ethics of Otherness', in E. Carter, J. Donald and J. Squires (eds), *Space and Place: Theories of Identity and Location* (London: Lawrence and Wishart, 1993), pp. 57–71; J. Boyarin, *Storm from Paradise. The Politics of Jewish Memory* (Minneapolis: University of Minnesota Press, 1992), Chps 4 and 5; S.L. Gilman and S.T. Katz (eds), *Anti-Semitism in Times of Crisis* (London: New York University Press, 1991).
23. See A. Finkielkraut, *The Imaginary Jew* (London: University of Nebraska Press, 1994) for an interesting perspective on the appropriation of Jewish identity as a symbol of the oppressed by the Left in the 1960s and 1970s: 'Jewish identity was no longer for Jews alone.... Every child of the postwar era could change places with the outsider and wear the yellow star', p. 17.
24. For critical reviews of traditional approaches to ethnic and national groups in the human sciences see J. Clifford, *The Predicament of Culture* (Cambridge, MA: Harvard University Press, 1988); T.H. Eriksen, *Ethnicity and Nationalism: anthropological perspectives* (London: Pluto Press, 1993); S. Jones, *The Archaeology of Ethnicity: Constructing Identities in the Past and the Present* (London: Routledge, 1997).
25. See J. Parkes, 'The Jewish Conception of a Chosen People', *Chayenu*, 8, 7/8 & 9 (July–Aug., Sept. 1945), pp. 3–4, 4–6; *idem.*, *A History of Palestine from 135 A.D. to Modern Times* (London: Victor Gollancz, 1949); *idem.*, *Whose Land? A History of the Peoples of Palestine* (New York: Taplinger, 1971); *idem.*, *The Jew in the Medieval World* (New York: Sepher–Hermon Press, [1938] 1976).
26. See, in particular, Parkes, *Whose Land?*
27. Each of these ethno–religious periods represents a chapter in Parkes' book, *A History of Palestine*, and its completely revised edition, *Whose Land?*
28. Parkes, *Whose Land?*, pp. 16, 21, 30.
29. Parkes, *Whose Land?*, p. 137. It is important to note that Parkes also dismissed physical ancestry in favour of culture and language when discussing the origins of, and relationships between, peoples, see, for example, *Whose Land?*, p. 16, and *The Jew in the Medieval World*, p. 4.
30. For example, F. Barth, 'Introduction', in F. Barth (ed.), *Ethnic Groups and Boundaries* (Boston: Little Brown, 1969), pp. 9–38, 10; M. Chapman, M. McDonald and E. Tonkin, 'Introduction', in E. Tonkin, M. McDonald and M. Chapman (eds), *History and Ethnicity* (London: Routledge, Kegan and Paul, 1989), pp. 1–33, 1; Eriksen, *Ethnicity and Nationalism*, pp. 11–12.
31. For example, Barth, 'Introduction', in *Ethnic Groups and Boundaries*, pp. 9–11.
32. For example, Chapman *et al*, 'Introduction', in *History and Ethnicity*, pp. 17–18;
33. See, Eriksen, *Ethnicity and Nationalism*, pp. 18–35; J. Comaroff and J. Comaroff, *Ethnography and the Historical Imagination* (Oxford: Westview Press, 1992), especially Chps 2 and 9.
34. Shapiro, this volume, p. 131.

35. See Gilman and Katz (eds), *antisemitism in Times of Crisis*; Parkes, *The Jew in the Medieval World.*
36. See S.L. Gilman, *Jewish Self-Hatred: antisemitism and the Hidden Language of the Jews* (Baltimore: John Hopkins University Press, 1986), and *idem.*, *The Jew's Body* (London: Routledge, 1991).
37. A similar approach has been adopted in post-colonial theory over the last two decades. For instance, in his seminal work on Orientalism, Said explores western scholarly representations of the Orient in terms of the 'Western' world's construction of itself in opposition to an 'other', rather than for what such representations have to say about the identity and social reality of the Orient. E. Said, *Orientalism* (London: Routledge, Kegan and Paul, 1978).
38. Shapiro, this volume, p. 135.
39. See M.T. Hodgen, *Early Anthropology in the Sixteenth and Seventeenth Centuries* (Philadelphia: University of Pennsylvania Press, 1964).
40. Jowitt, this volume, pp. 175–6.
41. Shapiro, this volume, p. 135.
42. Raphael, this volume, pp. 302, 306.
43. Parkes, 'Judaism and Palestine', *Chayenu*, 10, 10 (Oct. 1946), p. 7, our emphasis.
44. See G.I. Langmuir, *History, Religion, and Antisemitism* (London: I.B. Taurus, 1990), pp. 26–8.
45. J. Parkes, *Antisemitism* (London: Vallentine Mitchell, 1963), p. x (hereafter *Antisemitism* [1963]).
46. In his *Voyage of Discoveries*, p. 117 Parkes wrote 'In the spring of 1930 I decided that, as I had not found a competent short study of antisemitism in English I would write one.' His *A History of the Jewish people* (London: Weidenfeld and Nicolson, 1962) was particularly widely translated and circulated.
47. On the ambivalent responses to the Russian pogroms, see D. Feldman, *Englishmen and Jews: Social Relations and Political Culture 1840–1914* (New Haven and London: Yale University Press, 1994), pp. 132–7 and T. Kushner, *The Holocaust and the Liberal Imagination: A Social and Cultural History* (Oxford: Blackwell, 1994) sections I and II for discussion of similar reactions in the Nazi era. For post-war Christian responses see M. Braybrooke, *Time to Meet: Towards a Deeper Relationship Between Jews and Christians* (London: SCM Press, 1990; E. Maxwell, this volume.
48. See Gilman and Katz, *antisemitism in Times of Crisis*, J. Katz, *From Prejudice to Destruction: Anti-Semitism, 1700–1933* (Cambridge, MA.: Harvard University Press, 1980) and G. Langmuir, *Towards a Definition of Antisemitism* (Berkeley: University of California Press, 1990) for debates about continuities and discontinuities. J. Reinharz, *Living with Antisemitism: Modern Jewish Responses* (Hanover: Brandeis University Press, 1987) is one of the few studies on the impact of antisemitism on the Jews.
49. Parkes' first attempt at a history of antisemitism, *The Jew and his Neighbour: A Study of the Causes of Anti-Semitism* (London: Student Christian Movement, 1930), pp. 195–7 is at pains to stress the need for Jews to find 'the right adjustment of their situation in the general body of the State'. It is clear that Parkes wrote such statements so as to appear 'balanced' to the non-Jewish reader; J. Parkes, *Antisemitism: An Enemy of the People* (Harmondsworth: Penguin, 1945); Parkes, *Antisemitism* [1963], pp. ix–xiii.
50. Parkes, *Antisemitism* [1963], p. xi.; T. Kushner, 'Ambivalence or Antisemitism?': Christian Attitudes and Responses in Britain to the Crisis of European Jewry During the Second World War', *Holocaust and Genocide Studies*, 5, 2 (1990), pp. 175–89.

51. J. Parkes, 'The Jewish World since 1939', *International Affairs*, 21, 1 (January 1945), pp. 87–99; idem., *The Emergence of the Jewish problem, 1878–1939* (London: Oxford University Press, 1946). See also his *Voyage of Discoveries*, pp. 178–80, although his autobiography when covering the post-1945 years is noticeable for the lack of attention it gives to the Holocaust.
52. Parkes, *Antisemitism* [1963], pp. 4, 60, much of which predicts recent debates on the motivation of the killers. But see also Parkes' review of R. Hilberg, *The Destruction of the European Jews* (Chicago: Quandrangle, 1961) referred to by Colin Richmond in this volume. For recent debates see C. Browning, *Ordinary Men: Reserve Police Battalion 101 and the Final Solution in Poland* (New York: HarperCollins, 1992) which downplays the importance of a tradition of antisemitism and D. Goldhagen, *Hitler's Willing Executioners: Ordinary Germans and the Holocaust* (New York: Little, Brown, 1996) which places much greater emphasis on its role in motivating those involved in carrying out mass murders.
53. Runcie quoted by Maxwell, this volume, p. 87.
54. Raphael, this volume, p. 305.
55. Parkes, *Antisemitism* [1963], p. 120. More generally, see G. Hartman (ed), *Holocaust Remembrance: The Shapes of Memory* (Oxford: Blackwell, 1994).
56. C. Richmond, this volume, p. 227; Parkes, *Antisemitism* [1963], p. 158.
57. W. McGovern, *From Luther to Hitler: The History of Fascist–Nazi Political Philosophy* (London: George Harrap, 1946). For a revival of this interpretation see P. Lawrence Rose, *Revolutionary Antisemitism in Germany* (Princeton: Princeton University Press, 1990). Although a succinct one volume history, R. Wistrich, *Antisemitism: The Longest Hatred* (London: Methuen, 1991) would have benefited from considering the wider range of responses to Jews throughout the ages; see Cesarani, this volume, *passim*.
58. D. Cesarani, *The Jewish Chronicle and Anglo-Jewry 1841–1991* (Cambridge: Cambridge University Press, 1994), pp. 197–8; Parkes, *Antisemitism* [1963], p.6; idem., *A Problem for the Gentiles* (London: Peace News, 1945).
59. Parkes, *Voyage of Discoveries*, pp. 143–4 on Mosley and pp. 182–4 on 'Common Wealth'. On the latter see also A. Calder, *The People's War: Britain 1939–45* (London: Jonathan Cape, 1969), Chp. 9. On the 'new school', see T. Endelman, 'English Jewish History', *Modern Judaism*, 11 (1991), pp. 91–109 and P. Stansky, 'Anglo–Jew or English/British? Some Dilemmas of Anglo–Jewish History', *Jewish Social Studies*, 2, 1 (Fall 1995), pp. 159–78.
60. Parkes, *Voyage of Discoveries*, pp. 59, 114–15.
61. Shapiro, this volume, p. 151.
62. Parkes, sermon given at Oxford University in 1939, Parkes' papers, University of Southampton archive, 17/10/1.
63. Richmond, this volume, p. 241.

CHRISTIAN–JEWISH RELATIONS

2

James Parkes:
A Centenary Lecture[1]

NICHOLAS DE LANGE

James Parkes wrote more than 20 books, and apart from those he published under the pen-name of John Hadham (which are about God) and his autobiography, *Voyage of Discoveries*, they are all concerned with one aspect or another of Christian–Jewish relations. This is the leitmotif that runs through his life and work, and gives a sort of overarching logic and coherence to his career. It is a subject with which he is uniquely associated, and it is here that he made his enduring contribution. In endeavouring to assess his achievement and to sum up his enduring legacy I shall therefore concentrate on this central aspect of his work, leaving aside his other contributions to knowledge and to the betterment of society.

Nothing in James Parkes' early biography explains why he should have come to be devoted to the study of the Jews. Since he was born and brought up in Guernsey, it must have been quite a while before he ever met a Jew. I do not know when that was: perhaps during war service in the army, or later on at Oxford. What is certain is that at Oxford he gave serious indications of his earnest preoccupation with international affairs by running the Oxford League of Nations Union. Immediately after leaving

Oxford, in June 1923, he joined the full-time staff of the
Student Christian Movement (SCM), and this in turn led
him to a seven-year stint in Geneva as Secretary of Cultural
Co-operation in the International Student Service (ISS)
between 1928 and 1935 (interrupted by a term at Oxford
when he did most of the research for his D.Phil). It was the
work with the SCM and later with the ISS, helping
European students during the rise of fascism, that brought
him face to face with antisemitism[2] and the so-called
'Jewish Problem'.[3]

While working for the ISS, James Parkes published two
books, *The Jew and His Neighbour: a Study of the Causes of
anti-Semitism* (1930)[4] and *The Conflict of the Church and the
Synagogue: a Study in the Origins of anti-Semitism* (1934),
which was his doctoral thesis. These two books, which in a
sense complement each other, constitute the foundation of
his later work. It is remarkable how consistent his
approach remained throughout his remaining career. *The
Jew and His Neighbour* was a strong statement of the need
for Christians to listen to Jews and understand them,
instead of trying to convert them to Christianity. *The
Conflict of the Church and the Synagogue* is an erudite and
very detailed study of the origins and development of an
anti-Jewish ideology in the Church, and the ways in which,
once the Church acquired power, it used its power in part
to isolate and persecute the Jews. This was an unusual and
dangerous topic at that time, and it is a tribute to Parkes'
talents as a scholar and a writer that, though the background to the book is turbulent, the subject disturbing, and
the argument passionately sustained, *The Conflict* is still
recognised today as being essential reading in the field
with which it deals. It has never been surpassed or rendered obsolete.

Parkes' subsequent books can be divided under several
headings, all closely inter-related. *Jesus, Paul and the Jews*
(1936)[5] and *The Foundations of Judaism and Christianity* (1960)

are both concerned with the scriptural roots of Jewish–Christian relations, while *The Jew in the Medieval Community* is a book of history that carries forward in time the study begun in *The Conflict*.

Parkes' aim was to continue the historical project with three further volumes on the Church and the People in the Middle Ages, the post-mediaeval developments (including the Reformation, Christian Hebraism,[6] the Protestant missions, Deism and the immediate background to antisemitism as it emerged in the nineteenth century), and finally the nineteenth century itself. This project was sadly interrupted by the war, and not resumed subsequently.[7] The more recent history, with special emphasis on the rise of political antisemitism, features in a series of books: *The Jewish Problem in the Modern World* (1939), *An Enemy of the People: Antisemitism* (1945), *The Emergence of the Jewish Problem, 1878–1939* (1946), and also in *Judaism and Christianity* (1948), and *Antisemitism* (1963). Standing somewhat apart are *A History of Palestine from 135 AD to modern times* (1949), revised as *Whose Land?* (1971), and *A History of the Jewish People* (1963). Meanwhile 'John Hadham' wrote *God in a World at War* (1940), *Good God: sketches of his character and activities* (1940), *Between God and Man* (1941), *God and Human Progress* (1944), and *Common Sense about Religion* (1961), while James Parkes contributed *God at Work in Science, Politics and Human Life* (1952). This may seem a lot (particularly the five books in the four years 1938–41), but in addition there are numerous pamphlets, a collection of lectures, *Prelude to Dialogue* (1969), and an autobiography, *Voyage of Discoveries* (1969).

To assess James Parkes' achievements in the area of the Christian understanding of Judaism we have to remember, first of all, the background against which he began his work. This is essential, because in some respects his success has been so complete that a good deal of what he says seems nowadays banal and obvious. Take for instance the thesis that the Christian Church ultimately bears a heavy responsibility for what we now call antisemitism. This idea has come to be very widely accepted since Parkes first put it forward in the early 1930s. At the time, however, it was revolutionary and scandalous. About his own reaction as he made his discoveries he wrote later: 'it is impossible to exaggerate the shock and horror I felt as the grisly picture of Christian hatred unrolled from New Testament times onward'.[8] He also wrote this:

> I was completely unprepared for the discovery that it was the Christian Church, and the Christian Church alone, which turned a normal xenophobia and normal good and bad communal relations between two human societies into the unique evil of antisemitism.[9]

These remarks reveal or underline a very interesting aspect of James Parkes' personal trajectory. Unlike any of his predecessors,[10] Parkes came to the study of Judaism not through contact with Jews, or through a scholarly interest in the background to the New Testament. His preoccupation with Judaism and the Jews, which became indistinguishable from the subsequent story of his life, arose directly out of his experience of antisemitism. It was that experience of antisemitism which brought him into contact with Jews, and it was that experience of antisemitism too which, interacting with moral and political concerns born of his experience of the First World War and his sincere Anglican faith, led him into maintaining views that provoked direct conflict with many of those around him, both elders and contemporaries. It is characteristic of James Parkes that, once he had formulated his historical questions and secured answers to them, he did not flinch from drawing the required conclusions, however awkward or even painful that might be. Whether one calls this eccentricity or courage is a matter of choice. Saints have been canonised for less.

A hundred years ago, there were two main views of the remote origins of antisemitism. Some, not all of them anti-semites, maintained that the Jews had always been hated by non-Jews: that it was in some sense a normal attitude.[11]

Others had begun to point out that this was not so, and to trace the existence of 'Jew-hatred' to the relations between Jews and their neighbours. A prominent exponent of this version of history is Bernard Lazare, whose ground-breaking book *L'Antisémitisme, Son Histoire et ses Causes*, was published in Paris in 1894.[12] The rise of Nazism favoured the dissemination of the former of these views, that hatred of Jews was a natural human instinct. Its opponents tended to stress that the Jews had only them-selves to blame by being cliquey, stand-offish and élitist. James Parkes' position represented a complete revolution in thinking about the origins of antisemitism, and the key to it lies in the words I have already quoted: the Christian Church 'turned a normal xenophobia and normal good and bad communal relations between two human societies into the unique evil of antisemitism'. In other words, instead of looking for examples of hatred of Jews before the beginning of Christianity, and using them in effect to relieve the Christians of blame, Parkes drew a distinction between hatred or antagonism that has a concrete cause in a specific situation ('normal good and bad communal relations'), and hatred or antagonism that has no immedi-ate cause and is pursued for purely ideological reasons. This key feature of Nazi hatred of Jews Parkes found could also be located in the early Church, and at no point in previous history.

Since the war other scholars have pursued similar lines, and in general their work has confirmed Parkes' insight. Books such as Marcel Simon's *Verus Israel* (1948), Léon Poliakov's *Histoire de l'Antisémitisme* (1955), and Jules Isaac's *Genèse de l'Antisémitisme* (1956), all of which are in agreement with his thesis, have achieved classic status. (All three have been translated into English.) *Faith and Fratricide* (1974) by the radical American Catholic theologian Rosemary Ruether has made even more impact in the English-speaking world, though it has aroused a good deal of controversy.[13]

If it is fair to say that whilst, by and large, the novel analysis that Parkes advanced with such courage in the 1930s is now generally accepted and constitutes the consensus, it is important not to overlook the 'backlash' which, so far as I can see, began in the mid-1970s, and represents a return to the earlier arguments making the Jews the cause of their own persecution.[14] The proponents of this tendency, who argue that the Jews were generally or universally disliked, ridiculed and hated in the Graeco-Roman world, discard or overlook Parkes' key distinction between the antagonism bred of normal social intercourse and ideological hatred far from any cause in real life, and the effect is to minimise or deny the novelty of the Christian propaganda against the Jews.

One of these writers, a distinguished professional historian, writes of the Jews in the Roman Empire: 'Their exclusiveness bred the unpopularity out of which anti-Semitism was born.'[15] This can be taken as an implicit denial of the Parkesian thesis. Another, a Roman Catholic professor in Canada, adopts a more 'balanced' view, criticising Rosemary Ruether for giving a one-sided presentation of the evidence. 'On the whole, the visible legacy of "classical" times was antisemitic in tone', he writes.[16] (I cannot think that James Parkes would be happy with this anachronistic and unhistorical projection of anti-semitism, a specifically modern ideology, back into the ancient world.) He also accuses Ruether of playing down the Jewish persecution of Christians as an explanation of Christian attitudes.[17] So far as I am aware there is no published study of what one might call the 'revisionist' history of the origins of antisemitism. There ought to be.

A specific issue which has come to occupy the foreground of research and scholarly controversy since Parkes began his work is the question whether, if the roots of modern antisemitism can be traced back to the early Church, blame must extend to the New Testament writings themselves. Controversy on this point has become particularly acute since the publication of Ruether's *Faith and Fratricide* in 1974. It is difficult to be specific in tracking Parkes' personal trajectory on this issue. In *The Conflict of the Church and the Synagogue,* he does not make much of the specific claim that the New Testament carries the blame for the spread of anti-Judaism, but nor does he particularly deny it, and by implication it emerges from his argument that the New Testament writings, even if misunderstood by later generations, did contribute to the spread of hatred. If we consider the special case of the Fourth Gospel, perhaps the latest of the New Testament writings and belonging, for Parkes, to the period after the crucial 'Parting of the Ways' between Church and synagogue, we can see that he certainly has no hesitation, even in this early work, in identifying elements of ideological hatred within it, and in categorising them as 'unreal, unattractive, and at times almost repulsive'.[18] He finds little difference between the attitude of St John's Gospel and that of Justin's *Dialogue with Trypho,* written a little later. Similarly in his next book, *Jesus, Paul and the Jews,* Parkes is primarily concerned to explain the background to the hostile image of Judaism that emerges from a reading of the New Testament, and it is not his aim in any way to attack the New Testament, let alone to suggest any radical remedy. Towards the end of his life, after the publication of Ruether's *Faith and Fratricide,* Parkes writes in quite a different vein, issuing a blanket condemnation of the whole of the New Testament: 'It is dishonest henceforth to refuse to face the fact that the basic root of modern anti-semitism lies squarely on the Gospels and the rest of the

New Testament.'[19] At that time Parkes traced the history of the recognition of this fact back to a work published in 1933, *The Christian–Jewish Tragedy*, by Conrad H. Moehlman, a work which unfortunately had very little impact. From Moehlman he traced a direct line to Ruether, via his own book of 1936, Jules Isaac's *Jésus et Israël* of 1948, and A. Roy Eckardt's *Elder and Younger Brothers*, published in 1967.[20]

An oft-repeated demand at this last stage of Parkes' career was for something to be done to remedy the harmful influence of the New Testament in the Church, to which he specifically attributed the silence of the Churches when Israel's existence was threatened in the Yom Kippur War of 1973.[21] On the other hand he did not come up with a specific answer; the antidotes he suggested were manifold and vague:

> I hope every reader will consider what we should do about it. The challenge to the whole Christian liturgical tradition is so profound, and for almost all Christians so unexpected, that resolutions and sub-committees of a single organisation are obviously inadequate. It wants individual writing and speaking, the publication of pamphlets, the relating of the Holocaust to the basic conflict between Biblical scholarship and Biblical lectionaries. It wants the challenge brought up at official synods and comparable bodies. And if all this is done, there is still the problem of what to substitute, and how to agree on it.[22]

I do not wish to imply that there is any straightforward or obvious solution to the problem. On the contrary, Parkes' broad-spectrum approach is undoubtedly justified. However, I cannot help feeling that if he had really identified the problem in this fashion back in 1936, he would have eventually, in his inimitable fashion, put forward at least a few basic, common-sense steps, and driven them home at every opportunity until something was done. I believe that Rosemary Ruether's book served to crystallise Parkes' views about this central issue of Christian-Jewish relations, and led him to realise more clearly the dramatic implications of the work he did in the 1930s.

Surveying what has been attempted or achieved in this area in the past 20 years, I must say that it seems very little. It is true that the declaration *Nostra Aetate* of Vatican II calls for a new attitude to the Jews on the part of Roman Catholics, and that this implies a different and more positive reading of the relevant New Testament passages. Subsequent documents have built on those foundations,[23] and there have been some helpful publications by theologians.[24] Nevertheless, the New Testament continues to be read in an uncritical way and so to induct new generations of Christians into the traditional attitudes of hatred and contempt, particularly at Eastertide, and the Christian liturgy and hymnals, too, continue to instil the poison.

Another large area of campaigning which deserves mention is that of the Christian mission to convert Jews. Here Parkes' attitude is quite explicit and consistent over several decades. In an article in *Theology* for October, 1944 (at the height of the Nazi genocide), entitled 'A Christian looks at the Christian Mission to the Jews', he made the following points. Firstly, the development of the ecumenical movement demands a reassessment of Christian attitudes to other groups whose beliefs they do not fully share. This reassessment should extend to the Jews. Secondly, modern research on Christian origins shows that Jesus, far from rejecting Judaism, was a Jew himself. Thirdly, in a continuous history of over 1,800 years the mission to the Jews has been utterly unsuccessful, putting into question God's own assessment of it. Fourthly, Christianity and Judaism are both incomplete. 'The Christian church has the person of Jesus, but only scraps of His religion. The Synagogue has the religion of Jesus, but only scraps of His person.' It is therefore futile for either side to attempt to 'convert' the other. Fifthly (I am not sure if this is really a separate point), the Torah is the religion of Jesus. 'To ask Jews to leave Torah, to abandon its Way, is as wrong as to ask a Christian to abandon Christ.' And finally, 'I am convinced that both [religions] have got the truth, and each needs the other'. The article in *Theology* was followed immediately by a reply from Fr Lev Gillet of the Christian Institute of Jewish Studies, rebutting his arguments from a traditional missionary perspective and reasserting the belief in the obligation on the Christian to bring all men to a knowledge of Christ.

Interestingly, Alec Vidler, in his Editorial, while out-wardly maintaining a balance between the two views, explicitly supports James Parkes' claim that the ecumenical movement is a proper context in which to consider the relationship between Jews and Christians. 'Christians and Jews belong together and are one people, in a way that Christians and Hindus or Buddhists are not.' And he comes down firmly on the anti-missionary side when he writes:

> It is at present more important and more fitting to establish dialogues between the Church and the Synagogue than 'missions' from one to the other ... . When the Church remembers her responsibility for the terrible treatment of the Jews in the past, and contemplates the more terrible sufferings which they are bearing in the present, she must be eager to draw as near as possible to them. And Christians certainly have much to learn from the Jews.

Vidler even quotes with approval a remark of Ignaz Maybaum, 'the fate of Christianity depends on how much or how little Judaism it contains'.[25]

Four years later, Parkes developed his argument against the mission to the Jews in his book *Judaism and Christianity* (pp. 168–74), adding the telling condemnation: 'I do not believe there is any other activity of the Church in which good men from deeply religious motives have done such wicked things.' He maintained his opposition steadfastly, on both theological and practical grounds, and expressed it at every opportunity. Had he been alive at the time he would certainly have spoken out against the then Archbishop of Canterbury's insistence on lending his patronage to the Anglican Church's Ministry among the Jews (CMJ: the initials used to stand for 'Church's Mission to the Jews') at a time when that previously moribund organisation was being revivified by the young and dynamic, American-trained leadership of the Jews for Jesus movement. He would have pointed out, I am sure, the inconsistency of the Archbishop being simultaneously a figurehead of the Council of Christians and Jews, an organisation which Parkes himself had done so much to found, and which was openly viewed by the leadership of CMJ as a convenient forum in which to meet sympathetically-minded Jews.

Re-reading Parkes today I am struck by the clarity and vividness of his writing, and by the force of his argumentation, even if the style and diction sometimes seem dated with the passage of time. For instance, the expression 'the Jew' (meaning Jews in general) which peppers *The Jewish Problem in the Modern World* in 1939, gradually fades out, and indeed it is contrary to Parkes' attitude, which is rooted in an ability to see 'the Jew next door' as a real, flesh-and-blood neighbour, to be loved because he is 'like yourself'.

Here and there are historical interpretations which, with the passage of time, seem to call for nuance or correction. That is only to be expected. Following in the footsteps of earlier Christian writers such as George Foot Moore and Travers Herford, Parkes insisted firmly that the period of the Second Temple was a period of creativity and progress and not, as often portrayed by Christian historians, one of barrenness and decline. Surely no one would now deny this. However, the latest scholarship would not endorse his claim, often found in older books, that the institution of the synagogue goes back to the period of return from Babylonian exile, if not to the exile itself.[26] The claim is not advanced baldly, but supported with scriptural citations and arguments, and the numbering among the achievements of post-exilic Judaism of public Torah reading and worship cannot be lightly written off. Nevertheless, I feel it is misleading to suggest that the synagogue, in any form that we might recognise today, existed already in the Persian period.

Nor can I follow James Parkes in that important part of his argument in *The Conflict of the Church and the Synagogue* that carries the expressive title 'The Parting of the Ways'. According to this argument, the key rift occurred towards the end of the first century, after the disastrous war against Roman rule in Judaea. The rabbis in Yavneh inserted a condemnation of Christianity in the daily worship of the synagogue, as a kind of creed or test intended to exclude Jews who accepted Jesus as Christ from the community. The 'Jewish Patriarch of Palestine' sent messengers to the Jewish communities round the world enclosing the text of the new prayer and warning them to have no dealings with Christians. Thus, the Judaeo-Christians, that 'tragic group' who 'might have been the bridge between the Jewish and the Gentile world',[27] were rejected by the synagogue, just as they soon also came to be rejected by the Church.

This argument is put forward with confidence and with a good deal of supporting detail. I regret to have to say I do not believe a word of it. In the first place, it relies mainly on Christian sources, of a rather later period (second to fifth century), even for the details of the internal Jewish developments, such as the test-prayer and the Patriarch's letter. Rabbinic sources are never quoted directly, for the simple reason that James Parkes, who was an infant prodigy when

it came to Latin and Greek,[28] never learned Hebrew.[29] He
was heavily dependent on books by Christian scholars, like
Travers Herford's *Christianity in Talmud and Midrash*,
published in 1903, or the anthologies of Strack-Billerbeck
and Bonsirven, representing scholarship that already
belonged to a previous generation, if not century. At one
point, on supposed rabbinic condemnation of the teaching
of Paul, he even cites as his authority Gerhardt Kittel, who
would be regarded nowadays as a very dubious guide in
the world of rabbinics.[30]

As a matter of fact, there is some warrant in rabbinic
texts for the formulation of a 'Benediction of the Minim' at
Yavneh, and also for the use of prayers as theological tests,
so Parkes' innocence of Hebrew is not the whole answer.
What really undermines his argument is the passage of
time. More recent research on the history of Jewish institu-
tions has raised serious questions about the real powers of
the rabbis at Yavneh, the existence of a fixed public liturgy
at this time, the existence of the Patriarchate with the wide
powers Parkes ascribes to it, and the relationship between
Diaspora and Palestinian Jewish communities.[31] As for the
'Benediction of the Minim' mentioned in the Talmud, even
if it existed, convincing proof that it was directed against
Christians has yet to be found.[32]

'The Parting of the Ways' also gives the impression of a
decisive and fairly complete rupture between Jews and
Christians from the late first century or at the latest the
early second century. Yet, as Parkes himself makes clear in
other contexts, Judaism and Christianity continued to be
closely intertwined long after that time, with a good deal of
positive interaction and mutual admiration. Moreover,
some texts complaining of close relations between
Christians and Jews, which he himself quotes as evidence
of hostility to Judaism, could also be cited on the other side,
to demonstrate the real-life interaction as opposed to the
theological hatred.[33] As John Gager pointed out with some

force in his book *The Origins of Antisemitism*, all the texts that have come down to us from the early Church, starting from the New Testament Canon, are the result of a selection operated by one side in the Church, the side that was most opposed to Judaism and the Jews. The voice of the other side, including the voice of the Jewish Christians (who may well have continued to exist for longer than Parkes was prepared to admit), was silenced. In the nature of the evidence, this is a difficult topic to handle, but in the light of more recent work it may be fruitful to revise Parkes' model now, in favour of a less stark and final rupture.

There is one other point that strikes me now as I re-read James Parkes' words about the relationship between Judaism, Christianity and Islam. Parkes insists on the need to recognise Judaism as the parent of the other two religions.[34] I think that this can be a misleading generalisation, even if in certain contexts it can be an effective insight. Of course both Christianity and Islam have Jewish roots, but the stark statement that 'Judaism is the parent religion of both Christianity and Islam' smacks of the historical solecism of identifying present-day Judaism with a Judaism that existed in the Middle East many centuries ago. There is progress, thank goodness, even in religions, and James Parkes himself frequently railed against misleading Christian representations of Judaism as something that existed at the dawn of Christianity and thereafter faded from view. He also drew attention on a number of occasions to the influence of the Christian environment on contemporary Judaism. Consequently, I would say that the image of a 'parent–daughter' relationship needs to be used with caution.[35]

I should like to put on record how much I personally owe to James Parkes. First of all as an author. His work, especially *Conflict*, had a formative influence on my own thinking about relations between the Church and the Jews in the early centuries, which were the subject of my doctoral thesis and have remained a central concern ever since. Secondly, he was a most stimulating conversationalist, and in particular it was always fascinating to go round the Parkes Library with him: one invariably came across a book with a special history, or received some unsuspected insight. Thirdly, I was fortunate to meet, directly or indirectly through James Parkes, other active Christian participants in the campaign for a better understanding of Judaism. I think particularly now of W. W. Simpson, Peter Schneider, Charlotte Klein, all of whom made a significant contribution in their own distinctive way, and also Carl Witton-Davies, who came to play a special place in my life for a while as my landlord in Oxford. But that is another story. Finally, James Parkes was a model of a Christian to whom a Jew can relate on the personal level without an iota of suspicion or distrust. He earnestly rebutted every imputation of 'philosemitism': I suspect in his book philosemitism was a crime only slightly less serious than antisemitism, since both rest on a similarly deformed image of 'the Jew' and his place in 'society'.

He was a true friend of the Jewish people. His friendship was not uncritical, but his criticisms could be taken because they were grounded in a deep and unshakeable loyalty. As he took great pleasure in explaining, he was a friend of the Jews not despite, but because of, his own faith as a Christian.

James Parkes has left us two kinds of legacy, one more concrete and the other abstract. The concrete legacy is the Parkes Library, which, after an initial period of uncertainty, is now establishing itself as a centre of research and publication in subjects which were at the centre of his own work, and the two organisations he founded, the Council for Christians and Jews (CCJ) and the International Council for Christians and Jews (ICCJ), which are still going strong, but (for various reasons) not quite as strongly as some of us would wish. The abstract legacy is the continuation of his life's work in research, controversy, and reform. Much has already been done by others building on the foundations he laid, although, as I have tried to suggest, there is still a long way to go in the eradication of prejudice, discrimination and contempt, and in the building of bridges of true understanding and fellowship. Christian-Jewish relations is a major area of publishing today. It struck me recently that, whereas up to a few years ago people who wrote about this subject generally paid tribute to Parkes' pioneering work and cited his many books in their footnotes, nowadays his name is often missing. At first I found this mildly irritating. On reflection, though, it struck me that it is really a kind of tribute. His work has not been rendered obsolete or cast aside, it has simply been institutionalised to the point that it is taken for granted. And that is a high form of praise.

Still, I do not think we should let it go at that. Those of us who continue to build on the foundations that he laid owe it to his memory to acknowledge his contribution, and to remain true to the vision that he nurtured so faithfully throughout a long working life, of Jews and Christians respecting each other, learning from each other, and labouring side by side for God's kingdom.

NOTES

1. This paper was first presented as the 1996 Parkes Lecture at the University of Southampton.
2. This is the spelling that Parkes championed, maintaining that the usual, spuriously scientific, spelling, 'anti-Semitism', is in itself antisemitic, since it implies that there is a contrary movement, 'Semitism', which it aims to combat. See, for example, J. Parkes, 'Christianity, Jewish History and Antisemitism' (Southampton: Parkes Library Pamphlet 22, 1976), p. 4; and J. Parkes, 'Preface', in Alan Davies (ed.), *Antisemitism and the Foundations of Christianity* (New York: Paulist Press, 1969), p. viii.
3. When did this interest begin? Parkes' own statements on the matter are frustratingly vague and somewhat inconsistent. In a talk given in 1959 he said, 'It is now more than thirty years since I was plunged unexpectedly into a close study of European academic antisemitism', J. Parkes, *Prelude to Dialogue*

(London: Schocken Books, 1969), p. 3. In a lecture dated 1966 he stated 'my concern with some aspects of the Jewish question goes back now for forty-five years, and ... it has been my central interest for more than thirty years', Parkes, *Prelude to Dialogue*, p. 188. In 1969 Parkes dates 'the beginning of my real involvement in the Jewish question' to 1929, J. Parkes, *Voyage of Discoveries* (London: Gollancz, 1969), p. 111. Subsequently, however, in an address to a Colloquium held in his honour in 1977 (privately printed as 'The Way Forward: an Offering to the Colloquium of July 1977', Iwerne Minster, 1977), Parkes pointed to an earlier involvement with the Jewish question, when he was asked by the National Union of Students to look into the claim of the new World Union of Jewish Students to membership of the (also new) Confédération Internationale des Etudiants. The date he gives is 1924–25. Cf. his preface to Davies (ed.), *Antisemitism*, p. vii: 'My own concern with anti-semitism began in 1925'.
4. 'It was a short work, meant for ordinary people', Parkes, 'Preface', in Davies (ed.), *Antisemitism*, p.vii.
5. 'It was, I believe, the first book by a Christian writer on Jesus and Paul which had a Foreword by an Orthodox Jew [Herbert Loewe]', Parkes, *Voyage of Discoveries* p. 126. 'It came out in 1936, but made no impression', Parkes, 'Preface', in Davies (ed.), *Antisemitism*, p. viii.
6. The material on this subject collected by Parkes bore fruit eventually in Raphael Loewe's article 'Hebraists, Christian (1100–1890)', in *Encyclopaedia Judaica*, 8 (Jerusalem: Keter, 1971), Cols 9–71. This remarkable study lists over 1,400 Christian Hebrew scholars. For Parkes' interest see *Voyage of Discoveries*, p. 200, and his article in *Studies in Bibliography and Booklore*, 6 (1962), pp. 11–28.
7. See Parkes, 'Christianity, Jewish History and Antisemitism', p. 8.
8. Parkes, 'Preface', in Davies (ed.), *Antisemitism*, p. viii.
9. Parkes, *Voyage of Discoveries*, p. 123.
10. Such as George Foot Moore, Travers Herford or Herbert Danby.
11. On this and what follows, see Nicholas de Lange, 'The Origins of Anti-Semitism: Ancient Evidence and Modern Interpretations', in S.L. Gilman and S.T. Katz (eds), *Anti-Semitism in Times of Crisis* (New York: New York University Press, 1991), pp. 21–37. Note the distinction I make there between the claim that antisemitism has ancient origins or roots and the claim that antisemitism as such existed in antiquity, which is manifestly false.
12. English translation: *Antisemitism, Its History and Its Causes* (London: University of Nebraska Press, 1967). On Bernard Lazare see Nelly Wilson, *Bernard Lazare: Antisemitism and the Problem of Jewish Identity in Late Nineteenth-Century France* (Cambridge: Cambridge University Press, 1978), esp. Chp. 5.
13. Parkes welcomed the appearance of the book, as the first testimony to the New Testament origins of antisemitism by a Roman Catholic theologian (personal remark), though he deplored the fact that 'as a book it is written too hastily, and as a scholarly work, it is too slipshod' (Parkes, 'Preface', in Davies (ed.), *Antisemitism*, p. xi; cf. Parkes, 'The Way Forward', p. 5, 'a much too hastily written book'). For an assessment of the importance of Ruether's work, set against the background of Parkes' achievement, see John Gager, *The Origins of Antisemitism* (New York: Oxford University Press, 1983).
14. See Nicholas de Lange, 'The Origins of Anti-Semitism', pp. 28f.
15. E.M. Smallwood, *The Jews Under Roman Rule* (Leiden: Brill, 1976), p. 123. The return to the 'pseudo-scientific' spelling 'anti-Semitism' is interesting (see above, note 3).

16. John C. Meagher, 'As the Twig Was Bent: Antisemitism in Graeco-Roman and Earliest Christian Times', in Davies (ed.), *Antisemitism*, pp. 1–26 (here p. 11, but the whole essay needs to be read as the argument is dense and complex; see also Ruether's reply, ibid, pp. 231–5).
17. John C. Meagher, 'As the Twig Was Bent', pp. 20–2. On a completely different tack, Parkes, along with others, is blamed for making too much of the memory of Jewish persecutions in patristic writings by Miriam S. Taylor in *Anti-Judaism and Early Christian Identity. A Critique of the Scholarly Consensus* (Leiden: Brill, 1995), pp. 99–104.
18. J. Parkes, *The Conflict of the Church and the Synagogue* (London: Soncino, 1934), p. 60.
19. Parkes, 'Preface', in Davies (ed.), *Antisemitism*, p. xi.
20. See Parkes, 'Preface', in Davies (ed.), *Antisemitism*, pp. viii–x.
21. Parkes, 'Christianity, Jewish History and Antisemitism', p. 6; 'The Way Forward' p. 9.
22. Parkes, 'The Way Forward', p. 6. Compare the even vaguer and more limited suggestions advanced in 1948: 'It is not possible to rewrite the Bible; it is only possible to a limited extent to omit wholly from public use sections of the Bible which are repellent to modern Christian feeling... . What is wanted is something more fundamental ...' (J. Parkes, *Judaism and Christianity*, London: Gollancz, 1948, p. 175).
23. For example, Bishops' Committee on the Liturgy, *God's Mercy Endures Forever: Guidelines on the Presentation of Jews and Judaism in Catholic Preaching* (Washington DC: USCC, 1988). Cf. E.J. Fisher, 'Official Roman Catholic Teaching on Jews and Judaism: Commentary and Context', in E.J. Fisher and L. Klenicki (eds), *In Our Time: The Flowering of Jewish–Catholic Dialogue* (Mahwah NJ: Paulist Press, 1990) , pp. 1–26; R. Neudecker, SJ, 'The Catholic Church and the Jewish People', in R. Latourelle (ed.), *Vatican II: Assessment and Perspectives, Twenty-Four Years After (1962–1987)*, Vol. 3, (New York: Paulist Press, 1989), pp. 282–383.
24. For example, Franz Mussner, *Tractate on the Jews: the Significance of Judaism for the Christian Faith* (Philadelphia: Fortress Press, 1984); J.T. Pawlikowski and J.A. Wilde, *When Catholics Speak about Jews* (Chicago: Liturgy Training Publications, 1987); J. Willebrands, *Church and Jewish People: New Considerations* (Mahwah NJ: Paulist Press, 1992).
25. From Ignaz Maybaum, *Synagogue and Society* (London: James Clarke, 1944), p. 49.
26. J. Parkes, *Foundations of Judaism and Christianity* (London: Vallentine Mitchell, 1960), pp. 5f., 12ff.
27. Parkes, *Conflict*, p. 92.
28. Parkes, *Voyage of Discoveries*, p. 15.
29. Parkes, *Voyage of Discoveries*, p. 114.
30. Parkes, *Conflict*, p. 77.
31. On the last two points, see now Martin Jacobs, *Die Institution des Jüdischen Patriarchen* (Tübingen: Mohr, 1995), esp. pp. 346f.
32. In my opinion too much weight has been attached to versions of the prayer recovered from the Cairo Genizah. These are of mediaeval date, and probably stem from Byzantine liturgies where the prayer for the overthrow of the Roman empire is naturally linked to a wish for the end of Christian rule. I have suggested that they go back ultimately to an anti-Roman prayer instituted at the time of the Hadrianic persecution. See Nicholas de Lange, 'Jews and Christians in the Byzantine Empire: Problems and Prospects', in

D. Wood (ed.), *Christianity and Judaism* (Studies in Church History, 29) (Oxford: Blackwell, 1992), pp. 15–32 (esp. pp. 27f.). The great variety in the wording of the various Genizah texts testifies to the lack of an established tradition, perhaps as much as a millennium after the time with which Parkes is concerned.

33. See Wolfram Kinzig, '"Non-Separation": closeness and co-operation between Jews and Christians in the fourth century', *Vigiliae Christianae: a Review of Early Christian Life and Language*, 45 (1991), pp. 27–53.

34. J. Parkes, 'Continuity of Jewish Life in the Middle East' (London: Anglo-Israel Association Pamphlet No. 2, n.d.), pp. 3f., 13.

35. 'Perhaps it would be more realistic to view the three as brothers or sisters rather than as parent and children', Nicholas de Lange, *Judaism* (Oxford: Oxford University Press, 1986), pp. 2f.

3

Attitudes of Contempt:
Christian Anti-Judaism
and the Bible[1]

SARAH PEARCE

> The Christian public as a whole, the great and overwhelm-
> ing majority of the hundreds of millions of nominal
> Christians in the world, still believe that 'the Jews' killed
> Jesus, that they are a people rejected by their God, that all
> the beauty of their Bible belongs to the Christian Church
> and not to those by whom it was written; and if on this
> ground, so carefully prepared, modern antisemites have
> reared a structure of racial and economic propaganda, the
> final responsibility still rests with those who prepared the
> soil, created the deformation of the people, and so made
> these ineptitudes credible.[2]

These are the words of James Parkes in the final page of his
pioneering thesis, *The Conflict of Church and Synagogue*,
published in 1934. This work was the first major study of
the history of the Christian Church which attempted an
objective description of relations between the Church and
Jews from the first century until the seventh century of the
Common Era (CE). A considerable part of this was devoted
to uncovering the role played by the Christian interpretation of Scripture in producing and perpetuating a climate
of hatred and contempt for Jews and Judaism.

What Parkes had said before the genocidal events of the Second World War about the dangers of Christian contempt for Jews, based on their traditions about Scripture, found confirmation in one of the first meetings of the *International Council of Christians and Jews*. This met in 1947 at Seeligsberg, and its purpose was to make urgent recommendations to different areas of society about the prevention of the spread of antisemitism. In the case of the Council's 'Address to the Churches', the emphasis of the recommendations was entirely related to the interpretation of Scripture, and can be summarised as follows: that it must be taught that One God 'speaks to all through the Old and the New Testaments'; that Jesus and his disciples were Jews and that 'his everlasting love ... embrace(s) his own people and the whole world'; that Christians should avoid disparaging biblical and post-biblical Judaism with the object of extolling Christianity; that they should avoid using the word 'Jews' in the exclusive sense of the enemies of Jesus; and that they should refrain from representing all the Jews as responsible for the death of Jesus, or promoting the superstitious notion that the Jewish people is reprobate, accursed, and reserved for a destiny of suffering.[3]

It was not until some considerable time later, however, that any significant numbers from the Christian world, either in the Churches or in the university faculties of theology, began to engage seriously with the question of the role of Christian tradition, and especially Christian teaching on Scripture, in fostering hatred of Jews and in preparing the ground from which the Nazis were to draw some of their ideological ammunition against the Jews.

What is the root of the Christian problem about 'the Jews'? This has been a much-debated question. Some have argued that there is no link between modern antisemitism, which arises in a political and racial context, and Christian tradition. However, while it is true that Nazism was essentially anti-Christian, it nevertheless drew heavily on

centuries-old practice and teaching about the Jews, and
was successful in persecuting Jews in countries of Christian
tradition (where bystanders were receptive to propaganda
based on ancient prejudice). Others have argued that antisemitism is essentially alien to earliest Christianity and was
taken over from ancient pagan prejudice against Jews. In a
sense, as I will argue later, antisemitism has nothing to do
with earliest Christianity as represented by the New
Testament; but neither has it anything to do with ancient
paganism. It *is* a term which belongs to the modern era,
and refers to pseudo scientific racial theories. It is anachronistic, therefore, to describe either earliest Christianity or
ancient paganism as antisemitic. Ancient pagan criticism of
Jews was not based on racial prejudice.[4] In many cases, it
was related to the cultural elitism of Greeks and Romans.
To be a Greek or a Roman was to belong not to a race but
to participate in a culture distinguished from the rest of the
world of barbarians. Jews will have been found as
members of each group. Much of the contemptuous
description of Judaism in ancient Greek and Latin writings
does single out their peculiar religious practices, especially
circumcision, food laws, and Sabbath. The apparent social
separatism of some Jews, based on their religious practices,
also drew allegations of Jewish misanthropy and sinister
acts against the non-Jewish world. In times of Jewish
rebellions against Rome, there was a marked increase in
literary expressions of hostility towards the rebellious Jews
– the writings of Tacitus after the first Jewish Revolt
provide a notable example – but, in context, that was hardly peculiar. There is also evidence of good relations
between Jews and non-Jews, and intellectual admiration
for Jewish monotheism and the Jewish philosopher–
nation, as it was seen by some pagan intellectuals in
Graeco–Roman antiquity.[5] Furthermore, the refusal of the
Jews to be incorporated into the pagan religious system
received official legal support, by exemptions from

activities that might be considered idolatrous or contrary to the observance of Jewish religious practices.

While some of the hostile attitudes of early pagan writers may have influenced Christians of pagan background in a general way, this does not explain the most characteristic basis on which hostility towards Jews was formulated in Christian writings,[6] a point to which I will return shortly. To go back to the question of the root of the problem – some have suggested that the New Testament itself is antisemitic, a judgement based on passages of extreme hostility, which seem to make blanket condemnations of 'the Jews' such as Mt. 27:25, 'All the people answered, "His blood be on us and on our children"'; or Jn. 8:44, 'You are of your father the devil, and your will is to do your father's desires'; or the parable of the wicked tenants in Mt. 21:45, which is addressed to the 'chief priests and the Pharisees', and according to which 'the kingdom of God will be taken away from you and given to a nation producing the fruits of it'.

Leaving aside the question of anachronism in the term 'antisemitism', this raises a very important point about the place of the New Testament, especially the writings of Paul, the Gospels and Acts, in relation to first-century Judaism. All the books of the New Testament were almost certainly written by Jews who had 'become Christian', that is who believed Jesus to be the Messiah. Although some books of the New Testament (especially the Pauline letters, and Luke–Acts) express openness to gentiles, there is no conclusive evidence for gentile authorship: where it is asserted by modern scholars, this is usually based on very limited notions of what the possibilities within first-century Judaism were. The writers of the books of the New Testament, who themselves differed widely in their assessment of Jesus and of other Jews, can be described as Jews according to what we know about definitions of Jews in antiquity.

Jewish self-definition in antiquity is a complex area.[7] At its most simple, a Jew was one who saw himself or herself as being in continuity with the people of Israel described in the Torah, who had received the teachings of the Torah from Moses, and who observed those teachings. The observance of those teachings was, however, a matter of interpretation and debate among Jews, and was essentially what gave rise to the many varieties of Judaism in the first century and before, to the extent that some scholars now prefer to speak of Judaisms rather than an abstract Judaism to which no particular reality corresponded.[8]

This period was a time in which many groups within the Jewish people were disaffected to varying degrees with the ruling Jewish elite which controlled the Temple cult, and they expressed this in different ways. Some, like the Pharisee party, developed religious practices which tried to sanctify life outside the Temple, especially in the home. Although they did not reject the Temple, neither was it fundamental to their religious practice: it was this that appears to have made Pharisaic teaching an important foundation for the reorientation of Jewish religious life after the Temple was destroyed.

Other movements within Judaism objected more strongly to the Temple establishment and its priesthood, and regarded it as an illegitimate and false leadership. The group about whom we know the most are represented by some of the documents recovered from Qumran earlier this century. Some of these writings express an extreme sectarian position, according to which a Jewish group has separated itself from the rest of the world including the rest of the Jewish world, and especially its leaders, who are denounced in violent, polemical language for their profanation of the Temple and the Holy City. It claims to represent the true embodiment of the parent body from which it has broken away, and distinguishes itself from all others by the adoption of special practices and beliefs.[9]

Much of the sectarian self-definition is based on the use of Scripture: especially important is the group's self-identification with the repentant or faithful group which returned from the Babylonian exile to Judah, and the identification generally of the community and its leader with those loyal to God in Scripture, and of their opponents with the wicked described in Scripture.[10]

Apart from the New Testament, some of the sectarian Qumran writings provide us with our best evidence for the claims of a movement within Judaism to represent the true Israel, and the rejection of outsiders as, at best, an Israel which has gone astray, at worst, the 'sons of darkness' predestined by God to damnation and the lot of the devil, and to destruction in the final age of this world which is expected soon. They represent a group which has distinctive beliefs about the awaited Messiah or Messiahs, about the Temple which is rejected completely, about the interpretation of Mosaic Law which only the group understands correctly; they even keep their Jewish festivals and fasts, such as the Day of Atonement, according to a different calendar than the rest of the Jewish world. They are, nevertheless, Jews.

For a Jew to explicitly abandon Judaism was very rare in antiquity as far as we are able to judge. Apostasy required the complete abandonment of Jewish practices, and paganising acts which demonstrated rejection of Judaism, such as are described in the Books of Maccabees during the persecution under Antiochus IV Epiphanes.[11]

Even a gentile from an entirely non-Jewish background on becoming a Christian would have opted into a very large measure of Jewish religious culture in the early centuries of Christianity, and tensions between Jews and Christians in that period would have appeared more like tensions between types of Judaism than tensions between natives and complete aliens. If we consider the case of Paul brought before the Roman proconsul Gallio at Corinth, it is clear that there the pagan official sees the Jews and Christians as types of Jew quarrelling about what he sees as trivial differences: Paul was accused of 'persuading men to worship God contrary to the law' (Acts 18:13); Gallio responds '... since it is a matter of questions about words and names and your own law, see to it yourselves ...' (18:15). Gallio regarded the quarrel as an inner-Jewish dispute: this was no doubt a frequent pagan reaction for some time to come. Consider also the angel's command to the seer in the Book of Revelation: 'And to the angel of the church in Smyrna write: "The words of the first and the last, who died and came to life. I know your tribulation and your poverty (but you are rich) and the slander of those who say that they are Jews and are not, but are a synagogue of Satan"' (2:8–9). What does this suggest about the addressees? Surely that they too are Jews, Christian Jews.

In talking about the New Testament, we are considering writings which reflect events over a period of about 70 years, in which a new movement in Judaism is showing an increasing tension with representatives of the Jewish leadership, or local leaders, and some Jewish teachers, but is still broadly a Jewish movement. The bitter polemic in the Gospel of Matthew against Pharisees and Sadducees is very much an inner-Jewish quarrel and may be compared with the very bitter polemical language of some Qumran writings. The latter certainly condemn the priestly establishment which included members of the Sadducees. They may also polemicise against precisely the Pharisees, who in some of the Qumran writings are referred to by symbolic names (derived from Scripture) of the group led by 'the Liar', the 'Seekers of Smooth Things'. The Fourth Gospel, though coloured by very bitter quarrels which seem to have begun with the community having been thrown out of local synagogues, represents an extreme sectarian form of Christian Judaism, whose conflict with other Jews is focused very precisely on the claim that Jesus was divine in some sense.[12]

Can writings such as the New Testament which are almost certainly Jewish writings expressing hostility towards other Jews be usefully described as antisemitic or anti-Jewish? Certainly, they come to be perceived as such when read in a new situation from the original, family context of the quarrels represented in the New Testament. But in their original context, the writings of the New Testament arise from Christian movements within Judaism, though in some cases expressing a strong sense of sectarian alienation and hostility towards the rest of the Jewish people.[13]

It is very difficult to be precise about when it was that Christians came to be increasingly of non-Jewish origin rather than Christian Jews, in contrast to Jesus, his family, followers, Paul and the writers of the Gospels. When some Christians of gentile background who had absorbed little of Jewish culture read the conflicts recorded in the New Testament, many did so in a situation quite different to that of the original writers. For many, 'the Jews' were no longer members (however much hated) of the family – they became, instead, a more alien and unknown opponent. When, for example, it is said that Jesus was executed by the Romans on the instance of action by 'the Jews' or some Jewish leaders, if this is said by a gentile, it has the seeds of antisemitism; but if it is spoken by what we may call disaffected Jews, such as disciples of John the Baptist who accepted Jesus as the Messiah, it would not be so. The same kinds of things said about Jesus and his fate, if said first by Jews and then repeated by gentiles in a later time who had not been in the original quarrel, would sound very different in the new context.[14]

The second century produced a crisis in the early Christian Church, centring on the teachings of Marcion, generally thought to have been a gentile Christian. In face of the problem of evil, he could not accept that the

Christian Old Testament was inspired by the supreme deity: it was, rather, the work of the God who created this evil world, who punished humanity, and had given a Law which Christians of his tradition did not keep. In his view of things, Jesus' revelation had brought freedom from that God and his Law. Accordingly, Marcion rejected the Old Testament as religiously authoritative and also most of the New Testament which he saw as inextricably bound to its sources in the Old Testament. Marcion's teaching was countered by the leaders of the early Church, who rejected his purifying reductionism of Scripture. His opponents sought not to cut off Christianity from Judaism, and the God of their Old Testament from the God of the New Testament, and began to develop arguments for the retention of the Old Testament which asserted the continuity of Christianity with the teachings of the Old Testament. Many of these arguments drew on passages in the New Testament, which claimed that the key to the true interpretation of Jewish Scripture was Christ and his Church, that Christ was predicted by the Prophets, and that the Old Testament was evidence of the truth of Christian claims. It was asserted that the portrayal of the God of the Old Testament, to whom Marcion objected, was not unjust when he punished the Israelites: according to Tertullian and others, it was Israel's *hardness of heart* which demanded punishment; and because of that hardness they had rejected Christ.[15]

Arguments stressing the continuity of Christianity with Judaism were also important for Christians before Constantine and the establishment of Christianity as the official religion of the Roman Empire. Under the Roman Empire, Judaism was a legal, officially tolerated religion for the most part. Once Christianity became seen as distinct from Judaism, it was exposed to the charge of being an illegal 'innovation' and subject to persecution by the State. It needed to assert its antiquity, and its claim to the Old

Testament supported this.[16] It is from the context of the Marcionite crisis that there developed credal statements about the relationship of Christianity to what it claimed as its own Old Testament, which asserted that God's Spirit spoke through the prophets, and that God is author of both Testaments.

It is from this time and onwards to the fourth century, that some early Christians elaborated teachings of hostility about the Jews. By about 400 CE, after almost a century in which Christianity was established as the official religion of the Roman Empire in which so many Jews lived, individual teachers within the Christian community had developed the main elements of Church teaching about Jews and Judaism that would continue until this century.

That teaching was not presented in one official pronouncement. Instead, individual writers from the early second century on repeated and developed inherited formulae relating particularly to the theme of supersessionism – that is, the idea that the Christian people has replaced the Jewish people as the Chosen People of God. The formulae were put together from sequences of quotations – *testimonia* – taken from the books of the Old Testament to prove this supersessionist claim.[17]

The teaching of early Christian writers on Jews and Judaism yields the following set of ideas: that the Jewish people have lost their status as the Chosen People of God because of their failure to recognise Jesus as the Messiah, the Christ; that failure, and especially alleged Jewish responsibility for the death of Christ, is seen as the final act in a long series of rebellions and rejections of God on the part of the Jewish people; Jews did not understand the true, spiritual meaning of their own Scripture which, read properly, would lead them to Christ; and the recent catastrophes of 70 CE (the destruction of the Temple) and 135 CE (the expulsion of Jews from Jerusalem and its vicinity) represented the divine punishment of the Jews for the killing of Christ. However, based on the teaching of Augustine, it was affirmed that there was divine sanction for the Jews to continue to exist because they had a special role to fulfil: firstly as a witness to the truth of Christianity prefigured in the Old Testament, and as evidence of God's punishment for their sin – shown in their enforced state of degradation – and to show that they had been superseded as the Chosen People by the new people, the true Israel, the Christians. Such ideas should not be seen as representative of the understanding of all early Christians, but, as Gavin Langmuir has stated,

> [this teaching] decisively influenced ecclesiastical teaching, preaching, and legislation about Judaism and Jews in the long run because it was elaborated by individuals who came to be considered Fathers of the Church.[18]

Anti-Jewish teaching began to have a material effect on Jews as early as the fourth century, as Church leaders influenced the Christian Roman Emperors to develop legislation discriminating against Jews socially, and gradually limiting relations between Jews and Christians.

If we think back to the kind of objections expressed about Jews from pagan antiquity, the early Christian hostility is essentially of a very different kind. It is basically theological. As early as Melito in second-century Sardis, the death of Jesus is objectionable precisely because he is believed to be God, the divine Messiah:

> O lawless Israel, what is this unprecedented crime you committed, thrusting your Lord among unprecedented sufferings, your Sovereign, who formed you, who made you, who honoured you, who called you 'Israel' .... . Listen, all you families of the nations, and see! An unprecedented murder has occurred in the middle of Jerusalem. – And who has been murdered? ... Who is this? To say is hard, and not to say is too terrible. Yet listen, trembling at him for whom

the earth quaked. He who hung the earth is hanging; he who fixed the heavens has been fixed; he who fastened the universe has been fastened to a tree; the Sovereign has been insulted; God has been murdered; the King of Israel has been put to death by an Israelite right hand.[19]

Much of the hostility was shaped by the interpretation of Scripture: that same Scripture was unknown to almost all pagans. It was not a social or a cultural judgement about Jews; nor was it a racial judgement. This distinct type of hostility towards Jews has been increasingly characterised by modern scholars as anti-Judaism, meaning hostility towards Jews in so far as they are perceived to embody the religion of Judaism, which represents unbelief in Christ, and rejection of Christ.

I now want to look a little more closely at how some of the early Church Fathers employed Scripture in such a way that it produced very negative images of the Jews which were to become so influential later on. It is still a matter of considerable debate as to what extent the severe denunciations of the Jews in these writings have anything to do with a situation involving real, contemporary Jews. One very influential view, developed by Marcel Simon in his study *Verus Israel*, contends that, while certainly such passages do not describe real, contemporary Jews, they arise in a context where Christians, such as Melito in Sardis or John Chrysostom in Antioch, are competing with the local synagogue for converts, and their vitriolic language really expresses their anger against Christians attracted to the local Jewish community and its practices.[20] A recent study published by Miriam Taylor argues that the depiction of Judaism in these writings cannot be assumed to be connected with Christian perceptions of Jews in day-to-day life.[21] For the most part, their 'Jews' are symbolic, they are the Jews of the New Testament who do not accept Christ, and their role is as a symbolic opposition within the intra-Christian theological process of self-definition. Though Taylor's thesis is, in important respects, not supportive of Parkes' model of early Jewish–Christian relations, Parkes also recognised that the early Church Fathers did not attempt deliberately to denigrate the contemporary Jew; the Jews who are the subject of their rage are imaginary Jews, whose portrayal depends on that of the people of Israel in Scripture.[22]

In their interpretation of Scripture, the early Church Fathers drew on a number of methods of interpretation which are closely paralleled in the New Testament and in other Jewish literature known from the first century. Some of the writings from Qumran include examples of biblical interpretation: many of these are very complex and include the rewriting of Scripture on a large scale. There is one particular type of interpretation which modern scholars refer to as *pesharim*, writings which give the *pesher* or hidden meaning of a biblical passage. The *pesher* on the prophetic *Book of Habbakuk* explains that the prophet did not understand the meaning of God's words which he wrote down for future generations: the true meaning was not revealed until the arrival of the Teacher of Righteousness 'to whom God has disclosed all the mysteries of his servants, the prophets'.[23] The *pesharim* interpret the words of some of the Prophets and Psalms in terms of their predicting future events and personalities, including the Teacher and his followers and their opponents. The Qumran writings also provide evidence of the method of proof-texting: the collection of scattered passages from the Old Testament to be used as testimonies – to prove a particular point. Proof-texting underlies much of the New Testament, and is certainly important in the writings of the early Church Fathers. Other characteristic methods of biblical interpretation employed by the Church Fathers are typology and allegory. Both are represented especially by the Jewish philosopher Philo of Alexandria who in many works offered symbolic interpretations, mostly of the Pentateuch. In the case of the Laws of Moses, he argued against some other Jews that the literal interpretation of the laws also mattered, that, for example, circumcision and Sabbath were not merely symbols, but should be observed in practice:

> For all that the Seventh Day teaches us the power of the unoriginate and the nonaction of created beings, let us by no means annul the laws laid down for its observance. ... And though it is true that circumcision indicates the excision of pleasure and all passions and the removal of the godless conceit under which the mind supposed itself capable of engendering through its own powers, let us not abrogate the law laid down for circumcising.[24]

A striking example of typology in early Christian writings was to consider any piece of wood occurring in the Old Testament in relation to a significant figure or event, for example, the rod of Moses or the tree of life, and to see in it a prefiguring symbol of the Cross.

So much for the methods of interpretation and use of Scripture and their origins. We now turn to consider the results of such processes. Here I shall focus only on the formation of negative pictures of Jews and Judaism. It has been noted already that the new people of God claimed to be the sole legitimate guardians and interpreters of the sacred writings of the former people of God. Justin referred in his famous literary debate with a Jew named Trypho to 'Your scriptures, or rather, not yours but ours. For we believe in them: but you, though you read them, do not catch the spirit that is in them'.[25]

The New Testament writings characteristically explained the life and death of Jesus and the history of his followers as prefigured in Scripture. This interpretative process was developed more fully, so that, according to Augustine's formula – 'In the Old Testament, the New

Testament lies hidden; in the New Testament, the Old Testament becomes clear'.[26]

Some statements in Paul's letters stress that Jewish Law is not necessary for Christian salvation. His statements are complex and there is a wide-ranging debate on what he means in different places. It appears to be the case, however, that he says different things according to different situations, and that what he says about the Law as having no further purpose is addressed only to Christians not born as Jews. He may also not be making clear that he is not speaking globally when he refers to the Law: for example in Galatians, he is mainly speaking about circumcision; in 1 Cor. 8–9 about food laws. When he asserts that the Law is not necessary, but is speaking only about matters such as circumcision or dietary requirements, it is not clear that he is undermining or rejecting the whole Law, especially when he insists strongly on other distinctive aspects of Jewish Law – such as the prohibition of idolatry or sexual immorality. In his last letter, addressed to the Romans, his explanation of the value of the whole Law is more subtle than in earlier letters. Here he evaluates the Law as holy and good (Rom. 7:12), and states:

> For we hold that a man is justified by faith apart from works of law. Or is God the God of Jews only? Is he not the God of Gentiles also? Yes, of Gentiles also, since God is one; and he will justify the circumcised on the ground of their faith and the uncircumcised through their faith. Do we then overthrow the law by this faith? By no means! On the contrary, we uphold the law.[27]

Based, however, on some of the most negative things Paul says about the Law, many of the early Christian writings are very critical of elements of the Jewish Law – and especially of the ritual law – though they continue to use what they distinguish as the moral parts of the Law, but side-line the Jews in their interpretation. Justin (c. 160 CE), for example, argued that the requirement of circumcision was punishment for Jewish infamy (to be committed long after Abraham, in the killing of the prophets and Christ)[28] and to mark Jews out for exclusion from Jerusalem after 135 CE. The rest of the ritual law was given by God as punishment for the Israelites' apostasy when they worshipped the Golden Calf at Mount Sinai. Moses, enraged, broke the first set of tablets containing the Law; the second set was intended to punish. Each law is seen to be related to a particular sin: food laws serve to suppress natural Jewish gluttony; the laws of the sacrificial cult to suppress the Jewish tendency to idolatry.[29] The central symbol of Judaism in this time, the teaching of Moses, as far as it was understood and practised by Jews, was depicted in such writings largely in negative terms.

The early Fathers used Scripture to explain the relationship of the old and new peoples of God. Tertullian writes on the interpretation of words spoken to Rebekah the mother-to-be of Jacob and Esau (Gen. 25):

> 'Two nations are in your womb, and two peoples born of you shall be divided; the one stronger than the other, the elder shall serve the younger' – Beyond doubt, the older and greater people, that is, the Jewish, must necessarily serve the lesser, and the lesser people, that is, the Christian, overcome the greater.[30]

Tertullian was writing to refute Marcionites, and to show the inextricable relationship of Judaism and Christianity; but the emphasis on the 'overcoming' of the Jewish people by the Christian people evolved into standard Christian doctrine.[31]

Other arguments portrayed Christianity as from the beginning the only true Israel, seeking to show that the Old Testament relates the history of the Church before the Incarnation, that Christ has always been the agent of divine revelation (to Abraham, Moses, etc.), and that the message has always been addressed to the Church.[32] This is illustrated in a passage from the *Didascalia* from Syria (which is markedly less anti-Jewish than many of the writings of the Church Fathers), '... Hear, thou Catholic Church of God that was delivered from the ten plagues, and did receive the ten words, and did learn the Law, and hold the faith .... '[33]

Negative portrayals of the people of Israel in the Christian Old Testament were treated in much early Christian exegesis as representations of non-Christian Jews.[34] Condemnations addressed to the people of Israel in Scripture were interpreted as referring to 'the Jews' of Jesus' time and later. Most commonly 'the Jews' are the 'stiff-necked people', berated so often by Moses.[35] Some of the most constantly quoted *testimonia* were drawn from Deut. 32, especially vv. 19–21:

> The Lord saw [their idolatry], and spurned them, because of the provocations of his sons and daughters. And he said, 'I will hide my face from them, I will see what their end will be, for they are a perverse generation, children in whom there is no faithfulness. They have stirred me to jealousy with what is no god; they have provoked me with their idols. So I will stir them to jealousy with those who are no people; I will provoke them with a foolish nation'.

Hos. 1:9 also received a significant treatment: the name of the last child of the prophet's unfaithful wife, who is called 'Not my people, for you are not my people and I am not your God', is applied to the Jews, but the passage of hope immediately following is not so applied:

> Yet the number of the people of Israel shall be like the sand of the sea, which can be neither measured nor numbered; and in the place where it was said to them 'You are not my people', it shall be said to them, 'Sons of the living God'.

Augustine developed the typological explanation of Cain

in the Genesis story as the type of Jew, who sinned against God by the murder of his brother Abel (a type of Christ), and was sentenced to wander the earth, rejected by God, but marked as a sign that he should not be killed, but preserved as witness to the judgement of God and the truth of Christianity.[36]

John Chrysostom urges his readers that Jews should be shunned 'like filth and a universal plague' because in the words of Deut. 32:17, 'They sacrificed their sons and daughters to the demons ... .' The same writer accused Jews of cannibalism, on the basis of the prophesied behaviour of the people of Israel, should they reject the teachings of Moses (Deut. 28:53). Every kind of crime portrayed in Scripture was attributed to the Jews, to show that their murder of Christ was foreshadowed in their history. All prophecies of failure and disaster were allotted to the Jews, and all those of success and prosperity to the Church. It is not certain whether this was motivated by hatred of actual Jews, or rather as many commentators suggest, the language of extreme persuasion addressed to Christians or those who were not full Church members because early Church discipline was so severe, and many were more attracted to the local synagogue.

Nevertheless, the approach I have just outlined was to prove very influential over time in identifying the Jews with all things bad in the Old Testament. The page headings of the Authorised Version on Isaiah allot all pleasant passages for 'the Church' and all unpleasant passages to 'the Jews'. In relation to Isa. 41:8, 'But thou, Israel, art my servant, Jacob whom I have chosen' – the page heading reads 'God ... about his mercies to the Church'; and referring to Isa. 65:2, 'I have spread out my hands ... unto a rebellious people' – the heading indicates 'the Jews rejected'.[37]

The teaching of supersessionism was effectively to write real post-biblical Jews out of history, perceived only as the

Jews of the Old Testament and New Testament, with selec-
tive and distorting emphasis on the negative images.
Judaism in the time of Jesus came to be understood as 'late
Judaism', a religion in its dying throes. The Jewishness of
Jesus and earliest Christianity was ignored and they came
to be contrasted strongly over against Judaism, a tendency
still present in some theological writings. Negative statements in the New Testament about Jewish Law or the
alleged legalism of the scribes and Pharisees, or Jesus'
interpretation of the laws of Sabbath, for example, were
emphasised in the depiction of Jewish Law, and Jewish
religion in the time of Jesus was portrayed as one of empty,
arid, anti-spiritual legalism. The most dire effect is
summarised by Marcel Simon: the Jew was the Jew whom
God had condemned in the past and denounced by the
prophets, whose words were taken out of context and

> combined into a single portrait, provided all the evidence
> that could be wished for of the utter depravity of the
> people of God. Thus was created the picture of the eternal
> Jew.[38]

Today we have come to a point very much further on in
a horrible history. Looking back we can see that the roots
of what became a whole tradition of contempt and rejection of relationships between Christians and Jews are in
the period reflected by the New Testament, and that that
period, as may perhaps surprise many, is a time when the
Christian movement was still within Judaism. Looking at
some of the modes of argument with hindsight, Christians
may feel horrified and ashamed at finding there the roots
of persecution, forcible conversion, unjust civil laws
against the Jews to which eventually the Nazis appealed.
Yet for all that, careful study of the New Testament and the
earliest period of the Church, as well as of early Judaism,
shows that many of the kinds of argument are paralleled in
the writings of disaffected Jews such as the sectarians

behind the writings found at Qumran, who attack the Jewish leadership in Jerusalem and other groups within Judaism. A lot of the controversial tone of the New Testament which with hindsight we see as ugly is still part of its Jewish context. It did not have to become the expression of antisemitism. But as the Church became more and more composed of people who never had been Jews, old accusations and criticisms came to be read differently.

It has taken the Holocaust to jolt Christian consciences thoroughly. It took the horror of it to open Christian eyes, and many Christians are now convinced, as Parkes was more than 60 years ago, when much that is now known of early Judaism was still undiscovered, that the New Testament must be read with fresh eyes without the perspective of confessional, exclusivist bias, and with a concern for the original context of expressions of hostility. Many Christians, including the official teachers of the Catholic Church, are expressing a sense of being commanded by God to teach differently about the New Testament, and about the relation of the Jewish people in general and the Jesus-centred Judaism of the first century. There are perhaps traditionalists who will say this is to abandon plain accusations and judgements recorded in the New Testament. On the contrary, I am convinced that it is to liberate the real sense of the New Testament, to realise that Jesus lived and died as a Jew, and so did the Apostles.

NOTES

1. This paper was presented as the first Karten Lecture at the University of Southampton in 1995.
2. J. Parkes, *The Conflict of the Church and the Synagogue* (London: Soncino Press, 1934), p. 376.
3. 'The Task of the Churches', in *Reports and Recommendations of the International Conference of Christians and Jews, Seeligsberg* (Geneva: The International Council of Christians and Jews, 1947), pp. 14–16.
4. S. Cohen, 'Anti-Semitism in Antiquity: the Problem of Definition', in D. Berger (ed.), *History and Hate: the Dimensions of Anti-Semitism* (Philadelphia: Jewish Publication Society, 1986), pp. 44f.

5. M. Hengel, *Judaism and Hellenism* (London: SCM Press, 1981, ET of *Judentum und Hellenismus* (Tübingen: J.C.B. Mohr, 1973), p. 255.
6. Rejecting attempts to prove that in antiquity antisemitism inevitably accompanied 'the Jew', James Parkes emphasised that the reasons for the tragedy of the Jews in the Christian era 'have nothing to do with the old enmities. They are to be found only in the conflict of Christianity with its parent religion', see J. Parkes, *The Conflict*, p. 26.
7. See, for example, M. Goodman, 'Identity and Authority in Ancient Judaism', *Judaism*, 39 (1990), pp. 192–201.
8. On the varieties of first-century Judaism, see M. Smith, 'Palestinian Judaism in the First Century', in M. Davis (ed.), *Israel: its Role in Civilisation* (New York: The Seminary Israel Institute of the Jewish Theological Seminary, 1956), pp. 67–81; R. Kraft, 'The Multiform Jewish Heritage of Early Christianity', in J. Neusner (ed.), *Christianity, Judaism and Other Graeco–Roman Cults*, Vol. 3 (Leiden: E.J. Brill, 1975), pp. 174–99; J. Dunn, 'Judaism in the Land of Israel in the First Century' in J. Neusner (ed.) *Judaism in Late Antiquity*, Part 2 (Leiden: E.J. Brill, 1995), pp. 229–61.
9. See, for example, the sectarian rules of 1QS (the Community Rule) and CD (the Damascus Document). For an English translation of the Qumran material, see G. Vermes, *The Dead Sea Scrolls in English*, 4th. ed. (London: Penguin Books, 1995).
10. Such ideas are found frequently in CD and the so-called *Pesharim*.
11. See also, for example, Josephus, *War* 7.50–51 describing the actions of a renegade Jew in Antioch in 67 CE . Cf. M. Goodman, 'Jews [referring to the late first century CE] could not conceive of an ethnic Jew ceasing to be part of the nation with which God's covenant had been made, and they might readily claim as one of them a non-observant ethnic Jew if only out of spite' (cf. Josephus, *Ant.* 20.100 on Tiberius Julius Alexander), 'Nerva, the Fiscus Judaicus and Jewish Identity', *Journal of Roman Studies*, 79, (1989), p. 41.
12. This is not the place to pursue in detail the question of the meaning of the expression 'the Jews' – *hoi Ioudaioi* – in the Fourth Gospel (or Acts). There are several important factors, however, which suggest that the condemnatory passages of 'the Jews' in these writings should not be read straightforwardly as 'anti-Jewish'. In the case of the Fourth Gospel, references to 'the Jews' as opponents occur in the context of the specifically religious and ideological dispute over claims to Jesus' divine status. One of the most important studies of recent years suggests that 'the Jews' who reject Jesus are to be identified with the 'alliance of chief priests and Pharisees' which was trying to establish its authority in the aftermath of the destruction of the Second Temple, see J. Ashton, *Understanding the Fourth Gospel*, (Oxford: Clarendon Press, 1991), pp. 131–59; see also J. Dunn, 'The Question of Anti-Semitism in the New Testament', in J. Dunn (ed.), *Jews and Christians: the Parting of the Ways A.D. 70 to 135* (Tübingen: J.C.B. Mohr (Paul Siebeck), 1992), pp. 177–211.
13. On the polemical language of the New Testament, see L. Johnson, 'The New Testament's Anti-Jewish Slander and the Conventions of Ancient Polemic', *Journal of Biblical Literature*, 108, 3 (1989), pp. 419–41.
14. See P. Cunningham, 'The Synoptic Gospels and their Presentation of Judaism', in D. Efroymson, E. Fisher and L. Klenicki (eds), *Within Context: Essays on Jews and Judaism in the New Testament* (Collegeville, MI: The Liturgical Press, 1993), p. 44.
15. For a detailed account of the significance of Marcion's challenge for the development of 'anti-Judaic themes', see D. Efroymson, 'The Patristic

Connection', in A. Davies (ed.), *Antisemitism and the Foundations of Christianity*, (New York: Paulist Press, 1979), pp. 98–117.

16. For Parkes, the real disaster in early Jewish–Christian relations was centred on the Christian apologetic claim to the antiquity of Christianity, which it could claim 'only on the basis of the possession, as exclusively part of its own history, of the story of Israel as revealed in the Old Testament', cf. J. Parkes, *Anti-Semitism: a Concise World History* (Chicago: Quadrangle, 1963), p. 62.

17. See, for example, the evidence for early patristic use of 'Testimonia that the Gentiles have Replaced the "Nation"', in R. Murray, *Symbols of Church and Kingdom* (Cambridge: Cambridge University Press, 1975), Table 1.

18. G. Langmuir, 'Faith of Christians and Hostility to Jews', in D. Wood (ed.), *Christianity and Judaism* (Studies in Church History, Vol. 29) (Oxford: Blackwell, 1992), p. 81.

19. S. Hall (ed.), *Melito of Sardis on Pascha and Fragments* (Oxford: Oxford University Press, 1979), pars. 582–8, 693–5, 709–16.

20. M. Simon, *Verus Israel: a Study of the Relations between Christians and Jews in the Roman Empire (AD 135–425)* (Oxford: Oxford University Press, 1986, ET of French edition, Paris: E. de Boccard, 1964).

21. M. Taylor, *Anti-Judaism and Early Christian Identity: a Critique of the Scholarly Consensus* (Leiden: E.J. Brill, 1995).

22. J. Parkes, *The Conflict*, especially pp. 191ff., 374.

23. 1Qp Habbakuk, 7.1ff.

24. Philo, *De Migratione Abrahami*, 89ff.

25. Justin Martyr, *Dialogue with Trypho*, 29.2.

26. Augustine, *Contra adv. Leg. et Proph.*, 1.17.35 (PL 42,623).

27. Rom. 3:28–31.

28. Justin, *Dialogue*, 16.2–3.

29. See further M. Simon, *Verus Israel*, pp. 165ff.

30. Tertullian, *Adversus Judaeos* (PL, 2.636).

31. See further M. Simon, *Verus Israel*, pp. 77f.

32. See M. Simon, *Verus Israel*, pp. 76ff.

33. R.H. Connolly (ed.), *Didascalia Apostolorum* (Oxford: Oxford University Press, 1929), XXV, pp. 8–10.

34. See H. Maccoby, 'Antisemitism', in R. Coggins and J. Houlden (eds), *A Dictionary of Biblical Interpretation* (London: SCM Press, 1990), pp. 32–4.

35. This interpretation is found in its earliest Christian form in Acts 7:51.

36. Augustine, *Enarrationes in Psalmos*, 58.1.22.

37. Despite the official teaching of the Roman Catholic Church since the Second Vatican Council which repudiates the presentation of the Jews 'as rejected or accursed by God, as if this followed from the Holy Scriptures' (*Nostra Aetate*), the 'theology of substitution' reappeared recently in the French edition of 'The Bible of the Christian Communities' 1994. This was intended as a popular, pastoral edition of Scripture. It showed beyond doubt that the teaching of contempt for Judaism was alive and well in some quarters. A few examples will suffice: the title given to Psalm 48 reads 'The Church Zion, mountain of God'; the note accompanying Psalm 47 reads, 'The Church is today the new Jerusalem' ('L'Eglise est aujourd'hui la nouvelle Jérusalem, la ville imprenable, centre du monde et colonne de la vérité. C'est au sein de l'Eglise que Dieu nous a communiqué le meilleur de ses grâces'), cf. *La Bible des Communautés Chrétiennes* (Paris: Médiaspaul, 1994), pp. 1046f. The Imprimatur of this edition has since been withdrawn.

38. M. Simon, *Verus Israel*, p. 215.

4

Silence or Speaking Out[1]

ELISABETH MAXWELL

> It was by seeking, by probing silence that I began to discover the perils and power of the word.[2]

I have often reflected upon silence, and became aware of its many-faceted depths, especially as I read the works of Wiesel. Wiesel lies at the origin of my scholarly interest in the Jewish people and the new theology and some of his books were seminal to my studies, as were those of many of the pioneers in that field.

Samuel Johnson once dismissed a book with the withering comment that it was both good and original, but that which was good in it was not original and that which was original was not good. Many in my audience will discover, no doubt, that that which is good in my lecture is not original. I will not apologise for this, for my present knowledge about the Christian–Jewish dialogue, biblical Judaism, early Christianity and the Holocaust was learnt through the pioneers of today: the Eckardts, Franklin Littell, John Pawlikovsky, Father Dupuy, Paul van Buren, Emil Fackenheim, Norman Solomon, Yehuda Bauer, Irving Greenberg, Geza Vermes, the Sisters of Zion and from those survivors who have dedicated their lives to remembering, through their teaching, the six million Jews murdered by the Nazis: Yisrael Gutman, Elie Wiesel, Saul Friedlander and many others.

It was also my good fortune to have known two of the original pioneers: Jules Isaac and Bill Simpson. All these friends helped to shape my new thinking about Christianity through their writing, their lectures and our many talks. My one regret is that I did not manage to meet James Parkes himself, but I am honoured to speak today in memory of his life's work on my chosen topic of:

SILENCE AND SPEAKING OUT

Against Silence was the title given to the collection of Wiesel's lectures, addresses, articles and interviews and it was this compilation which really set me thinking about the many different types of silence. 'In the beginning there was silence – no words' wrote Wiesel.[3] That was the great silence that preceded creation, the primeval silence which frightened the French philosopher, Pascal: 'Le silence éternel de ces espaces infinis m'effraye[4] (the eternal silence of infinite space frightens me)'. Then there is the silence of solitude – the peaceful silence of the monastic cell and the silence of nature you encounter in the high mountains or anywhere you can actually hear silence in the depths of the country.

There is also the powerful dignity of silence in the face of moral or physical aggression, the silence with which martyrs of all faiths confronted persecution. That form of silence is equally powerful when it is the silence of contempt – a crushing silence that will not be moved, a silence which underlines the unworthiness of the one to whom it is directed.

Then there is the agonising silence of prison or the concentration camp – the unending silence of abandonment, equal to the silence of death.

Common to all these types of silence is a power and strength which should not be underestimated. Listen to Wiesel's forceful anecdote illustrating the power of silence:

On 15 May, 1967, Arab nations began daily broadcasts of their intention to destroy Israel. Their statements were clear, unashamedly open. Day after day, hour after hour, Cairo radio broadcast in Hebrew: 'Jews of Israel, be prepared, we are coming. We shall burn your cities and kill your children. And before killing your women we shall use them. Jewish women be prepared. ...' Imagine the effect these statements had in Israel and on World Jewry too. As soon as the crisis erupted, the Jews in Kiev met in the only synagogue still open and said: 'We must do something for Israel.' What could they do? Only this. Yonah Gindelman, the president of the synagogue, was a bad Jew and a bad human being. He was a collaborator who was appointed by the secret police. On Friday evening he came to the synagogue. It was crowded. He ascended the *bimah* and said to the *hazzan* (cantor), 'Let us begin *Maariv* (the evening) service', but the *hazzan* did not move. Gindelman shouted, but with no result. He asked others to conduct the service. No one answered. Then the oldest man in the synagogue stood up and said, 'Comrade Gindelman, according to Jewish *Halakhah* (Law), it is forbidden for Jews to pray together with informers'. You can imagine the effect of such a statement in Kiev, the most antisemitic city in Russia. Gindelman answered, 'All right. In that case, no one will pray.' The older man said, 'All right. No one will pray.' They stayed there an hour, two hours, in absolute silence and did not pray. They came back for many days. Always they remained silent and did not pray. They did not open the ark. They did not read the Torah. They did not say a word. They all came together and did not pray. *Shavuot* (a holy period) followed after Israel's victory, when the president of the congregation finally conceded and said, 'All right. You win.' And he left. The report that reached me ended:

'...And this is how we Jews in Kiev helped Israel win the war.'[5]

Perhaps the worst form of silence is that of indifference, the silence of the coward. This is the form of silence I wish to explore with you today: it is the one which haunts me and which is the driving force for my action towards Jewish–Christian dialogue.

James Parkes himself was certainly not guilty of this silence of indifference. He was a man of courage and was once on the Nazi wanted-list for his pro-Jewish activities. But when Parkes expressed his perception of what was happening to German Jews, when he examined where responsibility lay and appealed for help, he was no prophet in his own country. In fact he was preaching in the desert, the desert of those who were worse than deaf, because they refused to hear. 'The worst sin towards our fellow creatures is not to hate them, but to be indifferent to them: that is the essence of inhumanity.'[6] George Bernard Shaw's words depict the ultimate example of this form of silence – indifference – which is epitomised in the silence of the world during the Holocaust. For the purposes of this lecture, the word Holocaust does not encompass the eleven million people murdered in the camps by the Nazis, but those six million Jews amongst them, who were earmarked for complete annihilation after the decision taken at the Wannsee Conference in January 1942. The word now gaining acceptance for the genocide of the Jews is the *Shoah*.

So the world was silent – a silence so widespread and so complete that being aware of it should make almost every Christian of my generation unable to look into the eyes of a Jew. Repeatedly in the 1930s, James Parkes had warned this country and America about the treatment being meted out to the Jews:

> The law offers them the minimum of protection and even then the 'Party' can achieve what the legal apparatus of the

State would hesitate to apply. No Christian and no honourable or civilised man can accept this situation.[7]

Yet if we look at the action and reaction of the world at large, what we find is a catalogue of deception, designed to ensure that nothing would be done to save them.[8] The Bermuda Refugee Conference, for instance, convened in the spring of 1943, declared that: 'it would be unfair to put nationals who professed the Jewish Faith on a priority list for relief'. The Allies were not only reluctant to describe the destruction of the Jews in simple, blunt language but for five months (August to December 1942) they held back official confirmation of the exterminations after they had been reported. During these five months, one million Jews were murdered. All that the Allied governments declared was that 'the perpetrators of the exterminations shall not escape retribution', but no plans were suggested to put an end to the exterminations.

The Americans acted in an even worse manner. Listen to the Secretary of the Treasury, Henry Morgenthau Jr.:

> We knew in Washington from August 1942, that the Nazis were planning to exterminate all the Jews of Europe. Yet, for nearly 18 months after the first reports of the Nazi horror plan, the State Department did practically nothing. Not only did officials dodge their responsibility and procrastinate when concrete rescue schemes were placed before them, but they even suppressed information about atrocities.[9]

This suppression of information was not only the prerogative of the Americans. Listen to James Parkes, writing a memo for a peace conference at Chatham House:

> While the section on the Nazis was being written, news was filtering in of the reality of the Final Solution. In the first draft, I had written that there had been 50,000 Jews murdered in cold blood. The Foreign Office crossed off a nought. More news came in. In the second draft, it was half

a million – and the FO crossed off a nought. When they did the same for 5 million, I gave it up and no figure is mentioned in the book.[10]

On 1 August 1942, the Chief of the Geneva office of the World Jewish Congress, Dr Gerhart Riegner, heard from a German industrialist 'that a plan had been discussed in Hitler's headquarters for the extermination of all Jews in Nazi-occupied lands'. Dr Riegner sent this information via the American and British consulates to Dr Stephen Wise, President of the American Jewish Congress, who in turn passed it to the Under-Secretary of State, Simon Wells. The latter asked Dr Wise not to release the information until it could be confirmed. Another three months was spent checking Dr Riegner's report. Bombarded with demands for urgent action, the State Department spent more time trying to stem the flow of information at source.

In 1943, any real opportunities to rescue 70,000 Jews in France and Romania were ignored from March until December, when the war authorities issued the first licence for the payment of *francs* and *lei* to evacuate persons in danger. By then, of course, matters had worsened and rescue had become more difficult.

In December 1943, the State Department at last called the Treasury Department to clear the financial phases of refugee relief in Geneva. This was then sent to the British Legation who decided they needed specific advice from London. What do you think the answer from London was? They wrote to the American Embassy:

> The Foreign Office is concerned with the difficulty of disposing of any considerable numbers of Jews should they be released from enemy territory. For this reason they are reluctant even to approve of the preliminary financial arrangements.[11]

Even the US State Department read the British answer with astonishment.

I could continue with chapter and verse about the abysmal failure of the Allies and the British complicity in the destruction of the Jews. We only have to look at the response of the British Foreign Office. Viewed from the lofty heights of Whitehall, the suffering of the Jews counted for little against the mounting slaughter of worldwide war. 'Why should the Jews be spared distress and humiliation when they have earned it?' reads one minute. And another: 'In my opinion, a disproportionate amount of the time of the Office is wasted on dealing with these wailing Jews.' And another: 'What is disturbing is the apparent readiness of the new Colonial Secretary to take Jewish Agency "sob-stuff" at its face value.'[12]

It was only in January 1944 that an independent agency, the United States War Refugee Board, was created, with the power to negotiate. By then millions of Jews had perished.

On the British Government side, a White Paper had been issued in 1939 restricting Jewish immigration to Palestine, although it is true that Britain agreed to take in and re-settle 10,000 Jewish children at that time. In late 1939, a second White Paper dealt with the barbarous treatment of Jews by Germany, but regrettably the British Government maintained an official silence until December 1942 when another White Paper described the German plan to exterminate European Jewry.

By contrast, at that time, the Press in Britain continuously told the British people what was happening and was full of one story after another detailing the slaughter of the Jews. By July 1942, the chronicle of massacre and details of the new Zyklon-B gas were matters of current reporting. The governments of Britain and the United States made a declaration of solemn protest. The deliberate plan to exterminate all the Jews under Nazi rule was now widely recognised, but no efforts were made to stop the process.

Why were no genuine large-scale rescue efforts attempted? Why were there no threats of retaliation and reprisals for Nazi prisoners? Postwar punishment meant little at a time when Germany was fully confident of military victory.

Comparison with another situation is very telling: when Japan was accused of using gas against the Chinese, the President of the US issued a solemn warning threatening to retaliate against the Japanese with gas warfare. Yet as millions of Jews were suffocated in lethal gas chambers, no one threatened any retaliation, for during the war the rescue of Jews interfered with the principle of victory first. Yet, at the eleventh hour in May 1944, when the war offensive had passed to the Allies, had the tracks to Auschwitz been bombed, 400,000 Hungarian Jews might have been saved, among them almost every member of my late husband's family.

Reflecting on the list of 'legitimate' enemy targets, one stands aghast at a civilisation that readily bombs chemical-producing factories but assiduously avoids disrupting the operations of those that produce human corpses. If, as the British said, bombing the death camps posed 'certain technical difficulties', these have never been clarified. It is difficult to avoid the conclusion that the Allies had written off the Jews as casualties of war. Although they promised to punish the perpetrators, the victims were not to be saved.

After the war, the liberation of Jewish survivors was a fortuitous by-product of military victory which taxed many Allied officers with sticky problems, for which they had neither time nor taste. The ghostly remnant of the Jewish people returned to the cemeteries which their old communities had become and had to endure the last ignominy, a new form of persecution: Hitler had been defeated but not anti-semitism. Just as there had been no Allied plan to rescue Jews during the war, so there was none to give surviving Jews any security in Europe afterwards.

If we turn to the role of the International Red Cross, the great humanitarian agency from which the Jews could justifiably expect help during the Holocaust, the reaction was also passive. It certainly made no rumpus about the Jewish question, although its position was slightly redeemed by co-operation with Raoul Wallenberg in Hungary. Admittedly, there were some Christian voices that spoke out fearlessly against this un-Christian condition; many were silent, however, while others made baptism the sole criterion of protest and rescue. In Germany itself, instead of giving a lead after Kristallnacht, a German cardinal sent a letter to his clergy telling them that this nationwide attack on Jewish places of worship, businesses, homes and persons was *not* a matter for Church concern.

The Church of Rome held sway over nearly 80 per cent of the population of German-invaded Europe, yet it did not condemn the exterminations outright. The Vatican remained silent, although it is patently clear, from letters of the French episcopate, that the Catholic Church knew what was happening as early as June 1940. In September 1942 it was urged by US State diplomatic representatives to condemn the mass executions, but in October 1942 the Vatican replied that up until then, it had not been possible to verify the accuracy of the reports and assured the US Government that 'everything possible was being done behind the scenes to help the Jews'.

When the Berlin correspondent of *L'Osservatore Romano* asked Pius XII if he could not protest about the extermination, the Pope is reported to have answered: 'Dear friend, do not forget that millions of Catholics serve in the German armies. Shall I bring them into conflicts of conscience?' The President of the Polish Government in exile implored the Pope to break his silence, but no protest came. Had a lead been given by the Vatican, had the myth of 'wandering', 'travelling' and 'resettled Jews' been publicly exposed and excommunication applied, it is likely that many more

Christians would have helped and sheltered Jews.

By contrast, the Orthodox Patriarch of Constantinople wrote to all his bishops in the Balkans and Central Europe, urging them to help Jews and affirming that to conceal them was a sacred duty. Bulgaria was one of the countries which acted with effectiveness and did not surrender its Jewish nationals to the Nazis.

Denmark gave the world the perfect example of what could have happened if governments had shown the courage of King Christian X who, when asked by the Nazis about the Jewish question, replied: 'There is no Jewish question. These are my people.' And the leader of the Danish Christians also spoke out forcefully and – more importantly – *he spoke in time.* So the Danes were fully aware of the persecution of the Jews and were therefore conditioned to act to save them when the Nazis struck. Thus 92 per cent of Danish Jews survived.

In France, Pasteur Boegner, the President of the French Reformed Church, made several trips to Vichy to urge Maréchal Pétain to protest against the deportation of the Jews. He also preached against antisemitism from his pulpit in Paris, until he was threatened with arrest and had to flee to Unoccupied France. Several French bishops did likewise and thereby encouraged people around them to save Jews.

However, the guilt of the leaders and people of occupied Europe who, by and large, collaborated with the Nazis, either directly by aiding or abetting, or by remaining indifferent bystanders, cannot be assuaged by the heroism of a comparatively small number of righteous gentiles.

My very sketchy outline of the Allies' lack of response to what Churchill called 'the greatest and most horrible crime ever committed in the whole history of the world', prompts us to probe this silence further. In the words of David Bronstein, editor of *The Hebrew Christian Alliance Quarterly*: 'Too long have we Christians been silent. Our voices of protest should have been heard long before this happened.'[13]

What was the nature of this silence? It was not a silence of ignorance or lack of information. As I have just made clear, the persecution that culminated in the Final Solution was reported in the American and British Protestant press from the very beginning and governments were informed. About this there can be no question. The information was just not sufficiently persuasive to prompt governments or large groups of influential people into any significant action or intervention to slow down or stop the extermination of six million European Jews. It was therefore firstly a silence of failure to persuade.

And there was a second silence of failure. Some prominent churchmen and leaders of denominations, editors, officers in the Federal Council of Churches of Christ in America and clergymen did attempt to enlist the support of Protestant Christians on behalf of the Jews, but they were basically unsuccessful. It was a silence caused by failure of concerted efforts.

Yet a third silence of failure ensued, the failure of modest action. People gave monies, wrote letters, approved protests, sent representatives to Germany, petitioned President Roosevelt, but neither this activity nor any part of it was ever sufficient. Hitler's calculation of the risks involved proved correct. The Nazis carried out these actions for years, with no fear of interference from the nations of the West.

An intergovernmental conference held at Evian les Bains in 1939 to discuss the future reception of refugees was a total failure, if not an outright farce. *The Herald Tribune*'s leading article declared: '650,000 Exiled Jews Refused at Evian'. Refused by the world. As for the German papers, one headline read: 'Jews for sale ... Who wants them?' When Winston Churchill was asked by one of the Nazi leaders in July 1938 whether Hitler's anti-Jewish measures would create obstacles to a German-British pact, the British politician answered, 'No, not at all'.[14] How can we explain that?

The international community, which at Evian had been presented with an opportunity to keep open the gates of refuge, chose that moment, so desperate for the Jews already under Nazi rule, to signal its own hesitations and reluctance. It was a neutral stance, not a hostile one, but this neutral stance was to cost a multitude of lives.[15]

Even the one great intervention, the Second World War, did nothing for the Jews and those classed as subhuman by the Nazis. The war effort was against Hitler and Nazism, against Mussolini and Fascism, against the Japanese and their Imperial Army and Navy. The Second World War was not *for* the saving of Jews who were being gassed or shot in massive numbers, it was not *for* the bombing of the rail lines that led to Auschwitz, Chelmno, Treblinka, Buchenwald and Sobibor, the known 'death factories'; it was not *for* the bombing of the great Buna factory system or the aircraft and missile factories of Doranordhausen or the slave-labour-run quarries near Mauthausen (that is, it was not against the slave-labour system of the Nazis). The purpose of the Second World War, as stated by President Roosevelt and by the military leaders, was to win the war and in this way only help the Jews and others held prisoner in the slave-labour system and in the concentration camps. The concern for Jews as victims of German–Nazi persecution receded into the larger and inarguably correct need to win the war.

When the Allied troops finally entered the death camps, all they found was a remnant of cholera- and typhus-riddled living corpses. By the time they finally occupied Europe, thousands of Jewish communities had been annihilated and six million Jews murdered. It was therefore another silence of failure – failure as an intervention for Jews.

So you may say, what else could we have done? The question is a haunting one. Clearly, many projects could have been energised. A few propaganda broadcasts or leaflet raids directed at the camps might have made a great difference, for if there is anything more crushing than the burden of atrocious captivity, it is the sense of being forgotten in that captivity. The effects of propaganda by print media, both in a positive and in a negative sense, were known and used, but the device was not used to sustain the inmates of the Nazi camps. My own experience in occupied France is pertinent here: I would often find batches of Allied propaganda leaflets on my walks. I would carefully conceal a few of them, take them home to read in the secrecy of my own room and then spread the news by word of mouth. Surely something of this sort could have been tried for the Jews?

The fourth dimension of silence, then, is the failure of the Second World War as an intervention for Jews, the failure to do anything specifically aimed at informing Jews held in the concentration, slave-labour and death-camp system that they had not been forgotten. The masses of Jews and others held in these camps never received such a sign.

And now we come to another aspect of silence, the failure to speak in 'moral passion'. After Majdanek was overrun by the Russians in July 1944 and the world received the first eye-witness account of an actual 'death factory', not told by an escaped survivor, even the authentic accounts of chaplains, service personnel, military officers of high rank, motion pictures and photographs were still not sufficient to arouse moral passion.

The reaction was one of shock, horror, disbelief and silence. There was no indignation or moral passion, no words of moral outrage at such evidence of human degradation and utter disregard for human life. Few words were specifically addressed to Jews in sign of atonement. The world, particularly the Christian world, had 'passed by on the other side', in the classic sense of the parable of the good Samaritan. It was silence, silence all the way. 'Let's face it', to use the words of Wiesel, 'the world did not care, humanity was unconcerned ... .'[16] An article in a Jewish monthly magazine may have come closest to the truth in the spring of 1945:

> The most shocking [aspect] of the war, indeed of all history, is the extermination of close to five million European Jews. Almost equally shocking is the indifference of the civilized world. If the Nazis had murdered five million dogs or cats under similar circumstances, the denunciations would have risen to the high heaven, and numerous groups would have vied with one another to save the animals. Jews, however, have created hardly a stir! Hitler certainly has scored a superlative success in at least one field in the war on the Jews![17]

If you read the world press through the late spring, summer and autumn of 1945, on into 1946 and 1947, you look in vain for the profound soul-searching, searing condemnation–confession of a man of Christian faith or any Christian leaders stepping forward to say: In our blindness, in our preoccupation with ourselves, we have failed at the very heart of the most fundamental of all Christian commandments, to love our neighbour as ourselves. By ignoring the most basic of Christian responsibilities, we have sinned against our elder brother. No such statement was found.

Yet there was an outpouring of moral indignation when atom bombs were dropped on Japanese cities, with some 200,000 casualties. Articles such as: 'Atomic Bomb shocks World', 'The Ultimate in Violence' appeared. Editorials discussed 'The Church's responsibility in the light of the apocalyptic end of the war' if 'the abyss into which [man] has stared in horror is not to engulf him'. There was a deluge of protest but with hardly a reference to the extermination of the Jews under Hitler.

My lecture so far begs the question, Why? Why was the world silent on the Holocaust? The unpalatable truth is that at that point in time the Christian Western world was profoundly, if unconsciously, anti-Jewish. Any State documents, Foreign Office correspondence, intergovernmental exchanges that you care to read of the period, will demonstrate plainly by the attitudes, tone and vocabulary adopted the prevailing opinion: the Jews had brought upon themselves what had happened to them, i.e. they deserved it.

In 1942 when Jews were pleading with Archbishop Kametko of Nietra to intervene against the deportation of Slovakian Jews, the Archbishop replied:

> It is not just a matter of deportation, you will not die there of hunger and disease. They will slaughter all of you there, old and young alike, women and children at once. It is the punishment that you deserve for the death of our Lord and Redeemer, Jesus Christ. You have only one solution. Come over to our religion and I will work to annul this decree.[18]

Why was the Christian world anti-Jewish? Because for nearly 2,000 years it had been taught lies about the Jews. 'For many centuries, primitive Christian Europe had regarded the Jew as the "Christ-killer"; an enemy and a threat to be converted or killed; to be expelled, or put to death with sword and fire.' The first exponent of the Reformation, Martin Luther, wrote thus in 1543, setting out his 'honest advice' as to how Jews should be treated:

> 'First, their synagogues should be set on fire, and whatever does not burn up should be covered or spread over with dirt so that no one may ever be able to see a cinder or stone of it.' Jewish homes, he urged, should likewise be 'broken down or destroyed'. Jews should then be 'put under one roof, or in a stable, like Gypsies, in order that they may realize that they are not masters in our land'. They should be put to work, to earn their living 'by the sweat of their noses', or, if regarded even then as too dangerous, these 'poisonous bitter worms' should be stripped of their belongings 'which they have extorted usuriously from us' and driven out of the country 'for all time'.[19]

Even in 1948 members of the German Evangelical Church could say that the Holocaust was God's punishment for the Jews' rejection and crucifixion of Christ and that they had only themselves to blame.[20]

In his 1988 Kristallnacht Memorial Address, the Archbishop of Canterbury, Dr Robert Runcie, voiced this unpalatable truth: 'without the poisoning of Christian minds down the centuries, the Holocaust would have been unthinkable'.[21] Admittedly, Europe was not made up entirely of committed Christians but, as Alice Eckardt says: 'millions of European Christians had the opportunity to suffer for Christ and the faith during the Hitler years, few accepted the challenge.'[22]

More aware today of the horrors of the Holocaust and the Church's share of responsibility, Christians are gradually revising their teaching and starting to grapple with the theological implications of this revision. This re-thinking requires a retracing of footsteps, a real determination to discover the roots of antisemitism which allowed the Holocaust to occur within Christendom. It is now generally accepted that 1,800 years of antisemitic teaching has done its treacherous work, a view admirably summed up by Franklin Littell:

> The cornerstone of Christian antisemitism is the superseding or displacement myth, which already rings with the genocidal note. This is the myth that the mission of the Jewish people was finished with the coming of Jesus Christ, that 'the old Israel' was written off with the appearance of 'the new Israel'. To teach that a people's mission in God's providence is finished, that they have been relegated to the limbo of history, has murderous implications which murderers will in time spell out.[23]

Where did the poison originally spring from? The traditional view of the Church was that the Jews rejected their Messiah and crucified him. God, therefore, punished them, by destroying Jerusalem and scattering them in exile. The Jews had forfeited the promises made to them in the old Covenant and these promises had been taken over by the Church, the new Israel, which lived by grace not law. Often Christians came to speak of the Jews as 'children of the devil',[24] invented infamous libels about them, made them wear distinctive dress and forced them to live in ghettos.[25] Christians today, however, increasingly recognise the tissue of falsehoods under which they have laboured, in particular that Jesus was not the Messiah of Jewish expectation and that the crime of deicide must be repudiated.

Over the millennia, what has been almost totally concealed from Christian teaching is fourfold:

1. The continued validity of the Old Covenant.
2. The Jewishness of Jesus and the pluralistic Jewish society in which he lived and preached.
3. The existence of Rabbinic Judaism, a religion whose roots we share and which developed in parallel with ours.
4. The origin of the Gospels: when and how they came to be written.

The continued validity of the old Covenant has been obscured by centuries of Christian teaching based on the theology of supersessionism, as developed by certain Church Fathers in the first to sixth centuries. According to this theology, God had abandoned his Covenant with the Jewish people because of the alleged crime of deicide, punishing them by destroying the Temple and putting the Christian Church in the place of the Jewish people as God's Chosen Ones. Supersessionism thus emphasised the division between the Testaments. The 'New' Covenant not only fulfilled the 'old' but replaced it completely, hence Christian triumphalism which asserted that the Church fulfilled all Israel's hopes.

The Holocaust was the catalyst which started the Churches rethinking their position, especially in regard to the validity of the Old Covenant. It will be to our eternal shame that it took 1,800 years to begin this process, and that the cost in human misery was so high, since for centuries, the Jews were the victims of large-scale pogroms and massacres.

On the initiative of the Ecumenical Council of Churches, a meeting took place in Stuttgart in 1945, between representatives of the Churches of countries which had been at war with Germany and the first reconstituted Council of the Evangelical Churches in Germany, whose many pastors had paid with their lives for their resistance to Nazism. It was headed by Pastor Niemöller only a few weeks after his release from 11 years in a concentration camp. An extraordinarily moving event occurred: the German delegation decided to withdraw for one day and they returned with a momentous statement now known as the Declaration of Culpability of Stuttgart. This was the very first step taken by a Christian Church in recognising its guilt towards the Jews and making an act of repentance.[26]

Gradually, the churches of the various denominations of the world produced more and more constructive declarations until in 1965, the Vatican Council, the authoritative body of the Roman Catholic Church in matters of faith, published a Conciliar Declaration called *Nostra Aetate*.[27] This was a fundamental declaration which, although weak, did provide a basis for building a new relationship with the Jewish people.

It was strongly reinforced when in 1974 Pope Paul set up a Commission for Religious Relations with the Jews which produced in the following year 'Guidelines' for the implementation of *Nostra Aetate*. In 1985, further 'Notes' were published to mark the 20th Anniversary of *Nostra Aetate*. These documents amounted to a recognition that the 'Old Covenant' has never been revoked, that the Gospels are the result of long and complicated editorial work and that certain controversies described by the New Testament writers reflect Christian–Jewish relations long after the time of Jesus.[28]

This statement was indeed momentous: it was the equivalent of removing the corner-stone of a building. From that day onwards, all the old theology started to collapse.

The Second Vatican Council emphasised the 'spiritual bonds' linking the Church to the Jewish people 'at the very level of their identity'.[29] This relationship, they commented, was a living relationship like two branches of a single olive tree. The image here used was St Paul's, from Romans, chapters 9–11. It expressed, alas, neither apology for erroneous teaching, nor confession, nor regret, but it did exonerate the Jews of the crime of deicide and it affirmed, with St Paul, God's continuing Covenant with the Jewish people. It openly condemned all persecution and displays of antisemitism but it did not confront the impact of the *Shoah*.

The Anglican Bishops in 1988 commended the document, *Jews, Christians and Muslims: The Way to Dialogue*. It was the first time the Anglican Commission had addressed the subject and marks a great step forward, although it will require strengthening just as *Nostra Aetate* did. The World Council of Churches, after many weak and incomplete statements, did, in 1988, declare the continued validity of the Covenant and the living tradition of the Jews. Other Churches, such as the Synod of the Rhineland Churches, made the most courageous statement to date, recognising the right of the Jews to the Promised Land.

And herein lies another problem which has to be confronted, that of the Land of Israel. For the Jews, the Promised Land is part of the Covenant God made with his Chosen People: it is part of their faith. By 1984 there were several documents in existence asserting that the Jewish people attached a religious significance to their bond with the Land of Israel, a bond which was rooted in biblical tradition. Although a pontifical letter has acknowledged the right of Israel to secure borders, to date the Vatican has

not recognised the State of Israel and conveniently leaves
to politicians and international pressure the problem of
determining the existence of these rights. Subsequent to
the time of writing, the Vatican formally recognised the
State of Israel in December 1993. The matter is very complex, as Marcus Braybrooke indicates:

> ... and the tragedy is that almost all involved are prisoners
> of history ... . The Christian is in no position to lecture or
> adopt a high moral tone ... . The Christian from outside
> must beware of inflaming passions, and the role, it seems to
> me, is that of conciliator, not advocate.
>
> Above all, the Christian needs to approach the tragic situa-
> tion with penitence, especially if the Christian is British.
> European antisemitism and Christian anti-Judaism have
> partly caused the problem and British policy was often
> self-serving.[30]

The second area of concealment in Christian teaching
has been the subject of a great deal of recent research: that
is the Jewishness of Jesus. What is emphasised now is that
Jesus cannot be understood except as 'fully a man of his
time and of his environment ... , the anxieties and hopes of
which he shared'.[31]

Jesus taught in the synagogues of his people fully as one
of them.[32] His message can be understood *only* as a Jewish
message addressed to Jews by a Jew. Any notion of presenting Jesus against, or in opposition to, Torah and Judaism,
therefore, will inevitably result in diminishment or even
corruption of his essential proclamation.[33] This is not to deny
the uniqueness of Jesus' contributions to Israel's witness, for
the Christian Testament is powerful evidence of the remarkable authority with which Jesus preached.

Jesus' 'Torah of Love' is a prime example of his
Jewishness.[34] When asked to give the 'first' or central commandment, he responded with the Bible's own answer, cit-

ing from the opening words of the *Shema* in Deuteronomy 6: 'Hear, O Israel! The Lord is our God, the Lord alone! Therefore, you shall love ... ' (Deuteronomy 6:4-5). In the time of Jesus, this passage was prayed at least twice daily by every practising Jew – and still is today. To understand this Torah of Love, therefore, Christians must be fully aware both of the role of the *Shema* in Jewish prayer life and of the Biblical passages to which Jesus refers: Deuteronomy 5 and 6 and Leviticus 19, with their warnings against revenge, bearing hatred for others (Leviticus 19:17) and the commandment to have 'the same love' for the alien as one has for one's own fellow citizens (Leviticus 19:34). For this is the Jewish depth in Jesus' saying so often missed by Christians who treat it as some sort of 'new' law of love, above or transcending God's word in the Torah.

Further evidence of Jesus' Jewishness can be found in the Our Father,[35] with its references to the Jewish Scriptures,[36] and striking parallels with Jewish liturgical tradition. Jesus' way of praying finds its original setting and full depth in synagogue prayer and this is a reality that should temper our Christian tendency to triumphalism.

As for Jesus' relations with the Pharisees – indeed, with most of his fellow Jews – a superficial reading of the Gospels can give the impression that they were always marked by conflict and polemics. The Vatican *Notes*, together with recent scholarship, however, should disabuse us of that idea, for they demonstrate clearly that many doctrines crucial to Jesus' teaching were distinctively pharisaic.

A third point of concealment in Christian teaching was the existence and parallel development of Rabbinic Judaism. The fact is that early Christianity developed historically alongside Rabbinic Judaism. The Church was originally perceived by the Graeco-Roman world simply as yet another Jewish sect. What is tragic is that in claiming its own inheritance, Christianity came to deny the inheritance of its sibling, thus forgetting its own roots and ignoring at its peril St Paul's counsel against 'boasting'.[37] Untold suffering was to ensue from this lapse, as well as an impoverishment of Christianity's self-understanding.[38]

Much recent research, however, has highlighted the common root, the similarities rather than the differences, for both Christianity and Rabbinic Judaism were shaped by their unique responses to the same great crisis of Jewish history, the destruction of the Jerusalem Temple in the year 70 CE. The links between the two faiths are clearly evident, even in specific sacraments such as Baptism, the Eucharist and the marriage liturgy. So, too, is Christian Pentecost, an adaptation of Jewish Pentecost (Acts 1–2), and the great Jewish cycle of Rosh Hashanah (New Year) and Yom Kippur (Day of Atonement) has remarkable parallels in theme and content to the beginning of the Christian year in Advent.

A final area of concealment in Christian teaching concerns the origins of the Gospels, for it is vital to emphasise that the Gospels were actually set down in writing only towards the end of the first century. Thus, they often reflect the concerns of their authors and communities at the time of writing. The Vatican reminds us that many of the Christian Testament's 'references hostile or less than favourable to the Jews have their historical contexts in conflicts between the Nascent Church and the Jewish community ... long after the time of Jesus', even if the Evangelists place the references on Jesus' lips.[39]

Such then are the broad areas of recent scholarship which have led to a reappraisal of Christian teaching, bringing significant progress in analysing the common root and the parting of the ways. What has happened to the Christian Church in the last third of the twentieth century is in every way as momentous as the Reformation in the first third of the sixteenth century. A transformation has been effected in fundamental Church doctrine, that is in

the traditional position of the Church *vis à vis* the Jewish
people and the interpretation of the Hebraic scriptures.

The two momentous events of the *Shoah* and the
creation of the State of Israel have brought Christians face
to face with Jews who were truly alive and steeped in their
own faith, a faith which our own tradition had proclaimed
extinct for more than 19 centuries. Although St Paul had
explained that God had not rejected his people and did not
repent of his gifts, it was almost as if the Church needed
the shock of the *Shoah* or the birth of Israel or meeting
living Jews to hear them clearly for the first time.[40]

But having experienced the shock, we must make sure
that we learn from it, that we can now approach another
viewpoint with an open mind. This key to another realm of
religious knowledge, this exciting new insight into the
inheritance of God's Covenant through the miracle of Jesus
Christ, this is good news indeed. What a wonderful
opportunity to be disciples of Jesus Christ without the
treacherous implications that were attached to former
Christian teaching.

Clearly, we as Christians need to develop the virtue of
humility: we are not alone in the world in proclaiming and
preparing the way for God's reign on earth. We have a sister tradition at our side – the Jewish people – a people who
also stand in strict continuity with biblical Israel, and who
fulfil Israel's promise in their own unique way.
Reconciliation, the reforging of our bonds with Judaism,
requires firstly profound repentance on the part of
Christians and an acknowledgement of the theological
validity of the Jewish 'Other' in our midst.

For Jews, reconciliation will require something perhaps
even more difficult – a rebuilding of trust and an acknowledgement that the Christian Church, despite the heinous
sins of its members over the ages, is related in its essence to
the essence of Jewish witness in and for the world.
Complete understanding of the common root must be the

starting point and springboard for the way forward to reconciliation.

Had we Christians been more willing to recognise this fundamental bond 50 years ago, events could possibly have been very different. What we have to accept is that during the war, nearly all of us in Christian Europe were antisemitic, or rather anti-Jewish.

There were, of course, a few notable exceptions, those courageous people who refused to persecute the Jews overtly, those who refused to be bystanders, those who refused to be silenced, most of the time at the cost of their own lives. To this rare breed of bravery, Israel has given the highest accolade, the title of Righteous Gentiles. But how many Righteous Gentiles were there? My own research led me to the conclusion that it is impossible to give an approximate figure, let alone an accurate one, since the numbers given range from about 10,000 recognised by Yad Vashem to one million according to the American historian, Philip Freedman. Even if this figure of one million is accurate, it would still only represent 0.27 per cent of the several hundred million people who called themselves Christians and who remained indifferent.[41]

So, what is the way forward for us? Progress in scholarship is admirable, but we have to ensure that its findings are used for positive ends and that its message filters down from the academics to the grass roots. This is the moment for speaking out, for shouting loudly from the rooftops to spread this new teaching. We must not stay silent again. We must ensure that our theologians pursue the new theology and that it is taught in our seminaries, universities and schools.

As James Parkes himself told us:

> On the Christian side, no fundamental change was possible until modern scholarship had opened a door to a new interpretation of the inspiration of the Scriptures.[42]

and he too focused on the supreme role of education:

> So far it extends academically but it scarcely affects the sermon in the parish church. There is an enormous amount of education to be done, as well as the need to continue intellectual and spiritual pioneering.[43]

> May it not be said by our generation that we have shut up the Kingdom of Heaven against men, when it was our task both by our lives and our teaching to reveal it.[44]

Nothing will change until we can educate the masses. It will take a long time to eradicate 1,800 years of murderous teaching, for antisemitism is still rampant today.

Hayim Pinner, Secretary General of the Board of Deputies of British Jews, wrote a courageous article in The *Evening Standard*, entitled 'The Nightmare that never ends'. His salient points were that antisemitism exists and seems to have taken on a new lease of life, fuelled by the extreme right wing, by some left-wing elements disguising their antisemitism as anti-Zionism and by a small section of the Muslim community: the Islamic fundamentalists. But even more disturbing, is a latent antisemitism which rises to the surface in people who ought to know better. Thus Lord Denning was quoted in *The Spectator* as having described Sir Leon Brittan as 'a German Jew telling us what to do with our English law'.[45]

Rabbi Bayfield's Editorial in *Manna* entitled 'Still the Church stays silent'[46] indicates another case in point: a spokesman for *Pamyat* – the Russian National Front – appearing on the nation's television screen, feigning reluctance before telling his interviewer that the Jews had destroyed the Russian people by inflicting Communism upon them, even as they had murdered Jesus Christ. Surely a responsible TV producer would have been well-advised to introduce an English historian or theologian to counter this man's argument and prevent him polluting our screen with his antisemitic diatribe?

Once again, James Parkes' comments, as early as 1938, are of the utmost relevance: 'The Jewish problem will never be solved until antisemitism, as we know it today, disappears.'[47] And, 'the battle with antisemitism is the battle for decency and fellowship in communal life and this is not a battle which concerns Jews only.'[48] You may well say, what can we do, what can I do? I'll tell you. We all know the cost of silence; let us speak out. We must not allow antisemitic statements to go unchallenged; we have to be vigilant and openly denounce them. Speaking out has to be our prime concern: this is the wisdom we have gained from our past sins of omission. We must be prepared to learn from the rich history of the Jews and the permanence of their existence as well as from the sombre pages of our Christian history. We must resist the temptation to turn our backs on the problem and have the courage to face it head-on. As for myself, I can never be the same Christian as I was before Auschwitz and I can truly say with Johannes-Baptist Metz that:

> There is no truth for me which I could defend with my back turned toward Auschwitz.
>
> There is no sense for me which I could save with my back turned toward Auschwitz.
>
> And for me there is no God to whom I could pray with my back turned toward Auschwitz.[49]

Notes

1. This paper was first presented as the 1990 annual Parkes Lecture at the University of Southampton.
2. A. Rosenfeld and I. Greenberg (eds), *Confronting the Holocaust: The Impact of Elie Wiesel* (Bloomington & Indianapolis: Indiana University Press, 1978), p. 200.

3. Elie Wiesel, *Against Silence* (New York: Holocaust Library, 1985), Vol. I, p. 56.
4. Blaise Pascal, *Pensées*, Oeuvres Complètes — Ed. L'Intégrale (Paris: Editions du Seuil, 1963), p. 528.
5. Elie Wiesel, *Against Silence*, p. 238.
6. Bernard Shaw, 'The Devil's Disciple', in *The Complete Plays of Bernard Shaw* (London: Hamlyn, 1965), Act II, p. 230.
7. James Parkes, *The Jew and his Neighbour* (London: Student Christian Movement Press, 1938), p. 166.
8. Most of the information concerning the Allied governments' attitude to the Nazis' Final Solution and quotations which follow are taken from, Nora Levin, *The Holocaust: The Destruction of European Jewry 1933–1945* (New York: Schocken Books, 1973 [1968]).
9. Nora Levin, *The Holocaust*, p. 669.
10. James Parkes, *Voyage of Discoveries* (London: Victor Gollancz Ltd., 1969), p. 180.
11. Nora Levin, *The Holocaust*, p. 671.
12. Rex Bloomstein and Piers Brendon, 'Auschwitz and the Allies', *The Listener*, 16 Sept. 1982, pp. 2–3.
13. Robert Ross, *So it was True: The American Protestant Press and the Nazi Persecution of the Jews* (Minneapolis: University of Minnesota Press, 1980). This quotation and others which follow are taken from the above book, particularly from the chapter, 'Too Long Have We Christians Been Silent', pp. 285–301.
14. Elie Wiesel, *Against Silence*, p. 150.
15. Martin Gilbert, *The Holocaust: The Jewish Tragedy* (Glasgow: William Collins, 1986), p. 65.
16. Elie Wiesel, *Against Silence*, p. 55.
17. Robert Ross, *So it was True*, p. 293.
18. Marcus Braybrooke, *Time to Meet: Towards a Deeper Relationship between Jews and Christians* (London: SCM Press, 1990), p. 46, quoted by Irving Greenberg in *Auschwitz: Beginning of an Era*, by Eva Fleischner (New York: Ktav, 1977), pp. 11ff. I strongly recommend Marcus Braybrooke's book. It is an excellent résumé of the present state of theological research and of Jewish–Christian dialogue. I have quoted unashamedly from it: the best compliment I can pay the author!
19. Martin Gilbert, *The Holocaust: The Jewish Tragedy*, p. 19.
20. Marcus Braybrooke, *Time to Meet*, p. 46, cited in Richard Rubenstein and John Roth (eds), *Approaches to Auschwitz* (London: John Knox Press and SCM Press, 1987), p. 309.
21. 'Kristallnacht Memorial Meeting', *Common Ground*, 1, (London: Council for Christians and Jews, 1989).
22. Alice L. Eckardt, 'Post-Holocaust Theology: A Journey out of the Kingdom of Night', *Holocaust and Genocide Studies*, 1, 2 (1986), p. 238.
23. Franklin Littell, *The Crucifixion of the Jews* (New York: Mercer University Press, 1986), p. 113.
24. See, John 8:44ff.
25. Marcus Braybrooke, *Time to Meet*, p. 105, from Marvin Wilson, *Our Father Abraham* (Grand Rapids: Eerdmans, 1989) pp. 87–101.
26. Jacques Maury, *Se Souvenir de la Rencontre de Stuttgart*, Cimade Information, No. 11–12 (1989), p. 3.
27. All the documents of the Roman Catholic Church mentioned here: 'Nostra Aetate', 'Guidelines and suggestions for implementing the Conciliar Declaration Nostra Aetate', 'Notes on the Correct Way to Present Jews and Judaism in Preaching and Catechesis in the Roman Catholic Church' are

cited in *Stepping Stones to Further Jewish–Christian Relations* (New York: Stimulus Books, 1977), and in Helga Croner (ed.), *More Stepping Stones to Further Jewish-Christian Relations* (New York: Paulist Press, 1985). The latter document is also available from the CMO Publications, Ashstead Lane, Godalming, Surrey GU7 1ST. See also *Notes on Preaching and Catechesis: A Handbook for Correct Presentation of Jews and Judaism in the Roman Catholic Church*. The journal, *Service International de Documentation Judéo-Chrétienne*, 19, 2 (1986), contains the Notes as well as theological considerations and practical help.

28. Leon Klenicki and Eugene J. Fisher (eds), *Roots and Branches: Biblical Judaism. Rabbinic Judaism, and Early Christianity* (Winona, MN: St Mary's Press, 1987), p. 18. I have relied heavily on this publication for an authentic Roman Catholic interpretation of the present position of the Church *vis à vis* the Jews and Judaism, and have quoted extensively from it; I have quoted similarly from an article by the Rev. Père Jean Dujardin, Secretary of the French Episcopate, in his article 'L'Eglise Catholique et le Judäsme', *Lumière et Vie*, 196 (1990), pp. 39ff.
29. Ibid., p. 22.
30. Marcus Braybrooke, *Time to Meet*, pp. 142 and 144.
31. Leon Klenicki and Eugene J. Fisher, *Roots and Branches*, p. 15.
32. See, Gospels of Matthew 4:23, 9:35: Luke 4:15–18; John 18:20.
33. Leon Klenicki and Eugene J. Fisher, *Roots and Branches*, p. 15. See in general, chapters on 'The Gospel of Jesus the Jew' in Geza Vermes, *Jesus and the World of Judaism* (London: SCM Press, 1983).
34. See, Mark 12; Luke 10; Matthew 22.
35. See, Matthew 6; Luke 11.
36. See, Proverbs 30:8–9.
37. Romans 9–11.
38. Leon Klenicki and Eugene J. Fisher, *Roots and Branches*, p. 19.
39. Leon Klenicki and Eugene J. Fisher, *Roots and Branches*, p. 18, and see, Matthew 23.
40. I have been greatly inspired by the work of Paul van Buren and by one of his latest papers published in *Lumière et Vie*, 196 (1990). He is, with Roy Eckardt, a foremost pioneer of the revised theology. Some people may disagree with some of their most extreme views but the fact remains that it is because of courageous people of their calibre that we may hope one day to emerge from the theological impasse into which false teaching has plunged us.
41. See Mordecai Paldiel, 'The Altruism of the Righteous Gentiles' in *Remembering for the Future* (Oxford: Pergamon Press, 1989), Vol. 1, pp. 517–25, and Pearl and Samuel Oliner, *The Altruistic Personality: Rescuers of Jews in Nazi Europe* (New York: The Free Press, 1988).
42. James Parkes, *Judaism and Christianity* (London: Victor Gollancz, 1948), p. 180.
43. James Parkes, 'The Way Forward', paper presented at the Colloquium of July 1977 (Southampton: Parkes Library), p. 5.
44. James Parkes, *Judaism and Christianity* p. 203.
45. The *Evening Standard*, 17 Sept. 1990.
46. Rabbi A. Bayfield, 'Still the Church Stays Silent (Editorial)', *Manna*, (Summer 1990).
47. James Parkes, *The Jew and his Neighbour*, p. 174.
48. James Parkes, *Judaism and Christianity*, p. 179.
49. Elisabeth Schüssler Fiorenza and David Tracy (eds), *The Holocaust as Interruption* (Edinburgh: T & T Clark, 1984), p. 28.

5

The Silent Retreat of the Fathers: Episodes in the Process of Re-appraisal of Jewish History and Culture in Eighteenth-Century England[1]

PAOLO BERNARDINI

ON THE EVE OF THE ENLIGHTENMENT: JEWS, CHRISTIANS AND THE BIBLE 1700–53

The very beginning of the eighteenth century can be regarded as a peculiar time in the history of Jewish settlement in England after the readmission in 1656. As David Katz has recently shown, at least two major events marked the life of the small Anglo-Jewish community on the eve of the new century: namely, the knighting of Salomon de Medina in 1700 and – an event more remarkable and influential – the appointment of the Venetian-born Leghorn Rabbi David Nieto (1652–1728) as Chief Rabbi of the Great Sephardi Synagogue of Bevis Marks.[2] Nieto's thoughts and personality have been re-evaluated recently in the context of Jewish–Christian relationships in the contemp-orary scholarly world; relationships which marked a new era in the evolution of Jewish dogma and religion on the one hand, and Jewish attitudes towards the outside world on the other.[3]

The beginning of the century, however, was also characterised in England by an apparent decline in the area of Oriental and Biblical studies. The greatest Hebraists of the late seventeenth century had died or were dying without leaving a great and immediate heritage in terms of disciples or 'schools'. Edward Pocock,[4] John Lightfoot,[5] John Marsham,[6] John Spencer,[7] Thomas Hyde,[8] to name just a few, were more learned, productive and influential than almost any of the major representatives of the following generation (excluding, for example, Jean Gagnier[9]), who lived in the troubled years between the Glorious Revolution and the ascension of George I to the throne of England.

The settlement of a Jewish community in England could hardly be expected to influence academic trends,[10] and the inclination towards conversion and production of propaganda seemed to disappear slowly among this new generation of Orientalists, probably owing to political events such as the Toleration Act of 1689, and the official readmission of the Jews to England in 1655/1656. The destinies of the growing Anglo-Jewish community and the declining learned community of biblical scholars seem to have run along parallel courses but without mutual awareness for some time. The Jew Bill controversy of 1753[11] and the publication, in that same year, of the first dissertation on the Bible by Benjamin Kennicot,[12] suddenly revealed a great interest in the quiet and elusive Anglo–Jewish community as well as in Jewish and biblical culture: an interest in which learned knowledge of the Jewish past as well as political, economic, and humanitarian–liberal arguments played an equal role. Finally, the first publication of the dissertation *De Sacra Poësi Hebraeorum* by Robert Lowth[13], in that same epoch-making year 1753, inaugurated a completely new age in the hermeneutics of the Old Testament, in its approach to the Psalms as a mere work of poetry.[14]

Both the Kennicot Bible dissertation and the Jew Bill controversy can be regarded as the effects of a long process and of slow changes undergone by English society and the learned world during the first half of the eighteenth century, a century after the readmission of the Jews to England. The early eighteenth century had been marked by the publication of a series of learned and sometimes less scholarly works in which Jews and Judaism were often dealt with in an unprecedented way. Taken individually, these works – both those in English, or Latin, and the translations from Oriental languages – often seem unremarkable. However, if one considers them as a whole, they represent signs of a new attitude towards particular traditional topics as well as the central themes of Jewish history: Bible and Judaism.

My essay is an attempt to single out and discuss some important episodes in this two-fold approach to the 'old and new' Jewish worlds as it unfolded in the first half of the eighteenth century, at a much slower pace and in a more fragmented way than in the years immediately surrounding the readmission of the Jews into England in 1655/1656.[15] In the process, I will examine the ways in which the persistence of prejudice influenced the historical and scholarly literature of this period.

HUMPHREY PRIDEAUX, THE OLD AND THE NEW TESTAMENT CONNECTED (1718)

The *Connection of the Old and the New Testament* – as it was generally called – by Humphrey Prideaux (1648–1724), Dean of Norwich, was first published in 1716–18 in two volumes.[16] A typically erudite work of ancient history, it was to become a kind of best-seller which ran into a great number of editions and translations until the end of the eighteenth century and was also reprinted in the nineteenth century.

Prideaux was a strenuous defender of the Anglican Church against all supposed enemies of Christianity who had haunted England in the last quarter of the seventeenth century (in particular, Deists, Quakers, Socinians, Infidels and Jews).[17] For instance, he wrote a biography of Mohammed, who was traditionally seen and despised as 'the Impostor', the great enemy of Christianity, and the perverter of the Gospel.[18] This work was as passionate (in depicting the Prophet's vices and frauds) as it was inaccurate and historically flawed, and its historical content was completely undermined by a later, more accurate, reconstruction of Mohammed's life (1736) written by Jean Gagnier, a French Hebraist who taught in England.[19] Furthermore, his attack on the Deists was philosophically much weaker than his opponents' arguments,[20] and later confutations of Deism owe little to it, including the much sharper critique by Charles Leslie in 1697.[21] Indeed, Prideaux's religious zeal went so far as to suggest that the East India Company should establish missions to India and all the other British colonies in order to convert the local populations.[22]

The *Connection*, however, went far beyond the limits of erudite apologetic. Its aim was to reconstruct, using an enormous variety of sources, the history of the Jews 'from the Declension of the Kingdoms of Israel and Judah to the time of Christ', which is to say the centuries not covered by both the Old and the New Testaments. The area to be covered was huge, and the task ambitious: to compile a third 'Testament' which might provide a bridge between the events treated in the first and those treated in the second Testament. The bridging of these Testaments was to be guided by the prophetic books in the Old Testament, especially Daniel, which represented a great matter of controversy among Millenarians and anti-Millenarians. Prideaux belonged to the former school of thought. His chronological reconstruction attracted, among others, Isaac

Newton[23] and Jean Le Clerc, and it was to became essential reading for all scholars in Europe throughout the century.

The large two-volume *folio* work, however, was aimed at a wider public than any work on a similar subject in the previous century. It was written with great clarity and was relatively accessible. Prideaux conceived of his work as an ecclesiastical history, here taking his inspiration from Michel Echard's *Ecclesiastical History*, which was published in Paris in 1700, but dealt exclusively with the time preceding the birth of the Christian Church.[24] On the whole, Prideaux showed great freedom in the choice of his sources, including, for the first time, travellers' accounts such as those collected by Melchisedec Thevenot in Paris at the end of the seventeenth century (1696).[25]

Prideaux's 'epilogue to the Old Testament and prologue to the New', as he referred to his work in the Preface to the first volume, was 'chiefly designed for the English reader'. The historical framework was quite new, for in the Preface Prideaux states:

> To make this history more clear, I have found it necessary to take in within its compass the affairs of all the other eastern nations, as well as those of the Jews, the latter not being thoroughly to be understood without the other.

Since the *Connection* encompasses Roman and Greek history, it can also be regarded as a comprehensive history of the western world for the period preceding the birth of Christ. Prideaux drew heavily on sources like the writings of John Marsham,[26] James Usher,[27] and, last but not least, Pierre Bayle, particularly when depicting the other major impostor, of supposed Jewish origin, who had appeared on the face of the earth, namely, Zoroaster.

The great philologist and theologian, Jean Le Clerc,[28] who was based in Amsterdam, was among the first to discuss the *Connection*, praising the way in which it dealt with other Oriental peoples, but without even mentioning its antisemitic views.[29] Le Clerc criticised some of the historical reconstructions put forward in the *Connection*, like the history of the Maccabees, as did other critics of Prideaux. Among these was Walter Moyle who, in 1728, singled out Prideaux's inaccuracies concerning the history of eastern trade through the Red Sea; the alleged influence of Pythagorism on Zoroaster; and his hypothesis on the arrival of Alexander the Great in Jerusalem.[30] However, in general, Prideaux's work was well accepted in its method, aims and conclusion, and criticism concerned minor points, especially relating to the exact meaning and ongoing fulfilment of the biblical prophecies.[31]

How then could such an erudite history of east and west, which did not even touch on the origins and development of the Jewish people, influence ideas about the Jewish people as a whole, including the present descendants of Moses? If one considers the success of the work, one may suppose that the learned public saw it as a kind of introduction both to Christian origins and Jewish religious tenets, as well as to political history. Prideaux clearly stated that the Jewish people had no reason to survive after the coming of Christ, unless they were to be converted as soon as possible. Relying on the Book of Daniel, he supported here the views of the Millenarian generation before his own. By concealing an antisemitic bias within a heavily erudite work, Prideaux stood in the same line of thought as the majority of the English Hebraists of the previous century. Prideaux, however, did not limit himself to concealing his antisemitism within his learning. History itself, according to the interpretation of Prideaux and others of the prophetic books of the Old Testament, amply showed that the survival of the Jews after the coming of Christ was justified by a particular purpose: namely that the Jews should convert or be forced to convert, so that Daniel's prophecy might be fulfilled.

DAVID LEVI'S REFUTATION OF PRIDEAUX (1782)

Prideaux's more or less concealed antisemitic message and implicit reference to contemporary Jews was pointed out and opposed at a much later date by David Levi, a Jewish intellectual and merchant of the middle-class, renowned for his disputes about the Jews and their conversion, in which he argued with, among others, Joseph Priestley.[32] In *A Succinct Account of the Rites, and Ceremonies of the Jews, as Observed by Them, in their Different Dispersions, throughout the World, at this Present Time. In Which, Their Religious Principles, and Tenets, are Clearly Explained: Particularly, their Doctrine of Resurrection, Predestination, and Free Will etc*, Levi addressed both Jewish and Christian readers, since the former were notoriously somewhat detached from religious life, particularly in England, while the latter still generally regarded the Jews negatively or with suspicion.[33] It is worth quoting a passage from the Preface:

> The work was undertaken for the benefit and instruction of two sorts of readers; viz. the Jew and the Christian: to the former, very little needs to be offered by way of preface to such a work; the nature of which is so obvious, and its utility so apparent: for although the rites and ceremonies of the Jews are all set forth in Hebrew, yet, as it has pleased the Divine Providence, to appoint our lot in a Country, where the Hebrew is not used as a common language, and therefore but imperfectly understood by many; it must certainly, then, be very acceptable to those, who are natives of England, to receive a clear, impartial, and Distinct account, of their Religious Tenets in English.[34]

In his effort to demonstrate the truth of the Christian religion and the necessity of its foreseen advent, Prideaux had offered the reader a partial and false image of some key tenets of the Jewish religion, which was neither original nor profound, but could, in such a learned context, be taken as correct by the reader. First of all, according to Prideaux, the Jews did not believe in the immortality of the soul.[35] Secondly, Prideaux identified a sect which had semi-mystical ideas about the resurrection – the Pharisees – with the bulk of the Jewish nation.[36] Thirdly, he considered free will and predestination as 'jumbled both together', which is to say that 'every man freely chuseth what he is unalterably predestinated to'.[37]

Levi attempted to refute this presentation, point by point using passages from Scripture and theological argument, and he concluded his defence of these tenets of the Jewish religion by demonstrating their similarity with Christian beliefs.[38] What he said with regard to Prideaux, however, can be extended to all those apparently objective historical works – especially those dealing with sacred and ancient history – which concealed and propagated Judeophobic views; views which silently influenced and strengthened the general attitudes of the English public towards real Jews by casting dark light on their ancestors:

> He [*i.e.*, Prideaux] has drawn both [Jews and Judaism] in such colours, as to make them appear in the most odious light: although, I must freely confess, that the Doctor does not stand single in this charge; having done no more, than what I have observed in the works of *all* that labour in Christ's vineyard, whether clergy or laity; their sole aim and business being to place *Jews* and *Judaism* in the most odious light, that they may thereby be enabled to establish their own doctrine upon the ruins of Judaism; to obtain which end, they have not scrupled to advance the grossest falsity; and therefore, the wire drawing, or wresting the different passages from Scripture, and vilifying of the Jews' principles and tenets, are not boggled at in the least; although by so doing they very often put a weapon in their adversary's hand.[39]

On the whole, however, Levi's refutation was but a

negligible attempt to restore the historiographical truth as regards past and present Jews, which could not alter the enduring influence of a best-seller such as Prideaux's *Connection* with all its potential consequences.

THE TRANSLATION OF BASNAGE'S HISTOIRE DES JUIFS (1708)

In 1708, the revised edition of Jacques Basnage's monumental work, *Histoire des Juifs*, was translated into English.[40] *The History of the Jews from Jesus Christ to the Present Time, Containing their Antiquities, their Religious Rites, the Dispersion of the Ten Tribes in the East and the Persecutions this Nation has Suffered in the West, being a Supplement and Continuation of the History of Josephus* has to be seen as providing a chronological extension to Prideaux's work, and not as a mere adjunct to Josephus, since it begins where the *Connection* ends. Yet even more than the *Connection*, it was intended both to stimulate the interest and curiosity of the learned, middle-class reader, and to secure the foundations of Christianity by showing the condemned destiny which the Jews had faced, and were still facing, scattered all over the world and subject to every kind of abuse.

This attitude was emphasised by the English translator, Thomas Taylor. In the dedicatory letter to Jonathan Lord, Bishop of Winchester, whom he praised for his 'apostolic zeal for the advancement of true religion and for the welfare of that Bulwark of it, the Church of England', Taylor stated that:

> ... the chiefest design of this book is to lay before the Scoffers and Despisers of our Religion, an Argument which if a Deist could consider in that amazing chain of Providence it is involved in, would effectually convince him, that not a tittle should fail of all the Promises and

Menaces of the Gospel. If he demands a present miracle of his Faith; Behold! Here the greatest of more than sixteen hundred years' continuance, the Jews wandring, and dispersed into all Corners of the Earth, by the Malediction of Heaven: often massacred and exiled ... despised, hated, persecuted by all Nations; and tho' mingled and confounded with them, still distinguished in their laws, customs and religion, remaining a standing evidence of divine Vengeance upon Unbelief, and an indelible Monument of the Truth of Christianity.

In his violent apologetic and judeophobic zeal the English translator went much beyond Basnage's intentions.[41] His *History* provided, among other things, updated accounts on the Jews wherever they could be traced in the world, including England. Moreover, explanations such as those of the *Kabbala* could appeal to a public increasingly attracted to curious, Oriental doctrines and events.

Basnage recalls, *inter alia*, an episode too often wrongly neglected in Anglo-Jewish history: the struggle led by an obscure Bishop of Bath and Wells, Richard Kidder, against the menacing heresies of that time, including the Jewish religion.[42] Richard Kidder (1633–1703) can be regarded as a provincial champion of Anglican orthodoxy in a time of widespread loss of faith and detachment from religious and moral life.[43] Strangely enough, in the second edition of *Demonstration of the Messiah, in which the Truth of the Christian Religion is proved especially against the Jews* (1699), he chose to demonstrate the truth of the Christian religion by confuting a no less obscure and probably unpublished Jewish disputation, *The Gate of Truth*, written by Jacob ben Amran in the 1630s. According to Basnage, Kidder decided to refute *The Gate of Truth*, because he 'was afraid it would stagger those that read it'. *The Gate* circulated as a manuscript; the only extant Latin manuscript copy in England,

Porta Veritatis, is at the British Library. It was unknown even to the great Italian Hebraist, Giulio Bartolocci, who wrote the most comprehensive bibliography of Hebrew works at that time.[44]

The arguments of Jacob ben Amran – who wrote at the same time as Herbert of Cherboury[45] – proved to be far more ingenious and clever than Kidder's dogmatic refutations. I shall quote but three examples from Basnage:

> 1. He (Jacob ben Amran) maintains that the purification of the Virgin contradicts the Immaculate Conception of the Mother and the Son. 2. That Christ did not eat the Paschal Lamb as the Law ordained and. 3. That the licence given the Devils to precipitate the Swine into sea, is contrary to charity, since private persons lost their Herds by it.[46]

OTHER HISTORICAL WORKS AND THE NEW ACQUAINTANCE WITH JEWS AND JEWISH HISTORY

Between the end of the seventeenth and the first half of the eighteenth centuries some other works which provided the English reader with new perspectives on the Jews, both ancient and contemporary, appeared. The Jews themselves, although for the most part cautiously and infrequently, wrote short accounts of their practices, customs and religious rites, which were intended, like David Levi's account referred to above, to offer abridged handbooks for the English and those Jews already in an advanced state of assimilation.

The first of these short books was Isaac Abendana's *Discourses of the Ecclesiastical and Civil Polity of the Jews, – viz. of their Court of Judicature, Laws Concerning Tithes, Institution of the Priesthood, their Liturgy, their Schools, their Feasts, their Fasts, Coins, Weights and Measures*, published in London in 1706.[47] His work had a very limited circulation, and it is likely that only a small number of copies were printed, one of which is now held in the Parkes Library at the University of Southampton.

The book offers the English reader a positive view of most elements of Jewish religion, by demonstrating the substantial role played in Jewish life by religion, education and, above all, the law and the judicial courts. The overwhelming emphasis placed on the law and on Jewish judicial authorities may have been intended as a plea for expansion in the legal autonomy granted to the Jews by the English government. Abendana echoes Hobbes in stating the necessity of firm laws for ruling over the potentially anarchic, violent state of nature after the expulsion from Eden:

> The necessity of administering Justice in all civil societies is sufficient to justifie this tradition; for, after the fall, Man lay under a fatal necessity of transgressing the Laws of his maker, and breaking all the measures of right and equity ... so that without the administration of Justice there could have been no government, but all must have lived in Anarchy and Confusion ... because of Government without Laws, Laws without their sanctions are in general mere cob-webs.[48]

Moreover, Abendana underlines the severity and the cruelty of the Jewish criminal laws, which appear to him even more implacable and bloody than those of the English, being in his opinion still inspired by Deut. 19:21. Like other works dealing with Jewish antiquities and with Oriental curiosities, the *Discourses* titillated the taste for violence by offering at the same time a crude vision of Jewish order and legality. In short, Abendana's *Discourses* was a work written in English for the English reader.

David Nieto, who took up office as the Chief Rabbi of Bevis Marks six years after the publication of Abendana's *Discourses*, and who seems not to have known Abendana, always wrote in Italian, Hebrew or Spanish, mainly for the

Sephardi Jews who clung to their original language, Spanish, and had a scant knowledge of English and Hebrew. Nieto's first work, published in London in 1702 (with the false place of publication of Cologne on the title page), was in Italian and had been completed in 1693 while the author still lived in Leghorn. It was, nonetheless, very relevant to the long-lasting dispute over the calendar and chronology in general, which was of great concern to those such as Prideaux, Marshall, and Newton (Newton's fundamental writings on chronology, prophecy and the calendar were published only after his death, in 1733). The booklet by Nieto, entitled *Pascalogia*, deals with the seemingly neutral subject of the difference between the festivals of the Christian Easter and the Jewish Passover. However, the official Church, both Anglican and Roman, sought the total invalidation of the Jewish calendar in all matters relating to the reassessment of the universal chronology, and therefore of history, from the Creation onwards. The Easter argument had given rise to fierce disputes among scholars beginning with Sebastian Münster, Azaria de' Rossi and Julius Caesar Scaliger in the sixteenth century. By writing in Italian, it is clear that Nieto was addressing a learned public, particularly the Oxford and Cambridge faculties, which at the time were well acquainted with Italian. Beneath its technical content, Nieto's *Pascalogia* appears to contain a cautious plea for toleration and mutual respect among the different faiths.

The works of Nieto and Abendana – the latter probably published in response to the former as a matter of rivalry between the two intellectual heads of contemporary Anglo-Jewry – had a much smaller audience than other works which dealt with the same matters but which had been written by Christian Hebraists or historians of religion. The first major works of this kind addressed to the English public, or at least to the elite who could afford to buy them, appeared in the 1730s.

The first to be published was the English translation, in 1732, of a major scholarly project, the *Dictionnaire Historique de la Bible* (1722), by the French Benedectine monk and outstanding biblical scholar Augustin Calmet. Translated by Samuel D'Oyly and John Colson, it was the result of the joint editorial venture of several major London publishers and was embellished by 160 beautiful copper plates.[49] The English reader could find in this three-volume *folio* work all that he or she wished to know about the Old and New Testaments: 'whether of Men, Women, Cities, Countries, Rivers, Mountains ... with accounts of all the natural productions, as animals, vegetables, minerals, stones, gems'.

The end of the Jacobite danger did not prevent the translators from explicitly warning the readers that, since the author was 'of a different and dangerous Communion', they should be very careful in approaching 'those articles which have a more immediate relation to the peculiar tenets of his [i.e., the author's] Church'. The translators, however, did not 'maim him by retrenching or disguising anything delivered by him'. Moreover, an engraving explicitly made for the English edition showed the triumph of Christianity – embodied by a virgin holding the Cross in one hand and the Grail in the other – over Judaism – dimly depicted in the background as a quasi-Egyptian, seated figure, with the statement: 'The Law was given by Moses but Grace and Truth came by Jesus Christ'. Although dealing mainly with 'the Antiquities of the *Hebrews*', Calmet's work also gives a rather detailed account of the 'Ceremonies of the (modern) *Jews*',[50] in which he is free of prejudice, and attempts at every opportunity to connect the old and the modern Jewish worlds.

The second major work of the 1730s, the English translation of the monumental work on *Ceremonies et Coutumes Religieuses de tous les Peuples du Monde*, was published in the following year (1733). Written by J. F.

Bernard in Amsterdam between 1723 and 1733, it aimed to provide a general view about all the religions of the world, including that of the Jews. It contains 600 plates, most of them engraved by the chief illustrator of his time, the Frenchman Bernard Picart. The English edition is considered to be one of the greatest publishing ventures in England up to that date. Thanks to Picart's plates the reader could form a vivid image of contemporary Jews, synagogues and ceremonies, particularly those of the Dutch Jews. Moreover, the increase in the number of engravings in the English edition, as well as their superior quality, made it particularly appealing in comparison to the original Amsterdam edition.

The *Ceremonies and Religious Customs of the Various Nations of the Known World* is also the first work in which the relationship between ancient and contemporary Jews was represented visually more than textually.[51] The novelty of the reader's ability to become visually acquainted with Jewish ceremonies and customs accounts not only for the fixation on many of the old prejudices which haunted the popular imagination, but also for an increased perception of the Jews as a peculiar people.[52] Although this work does not conceal a certain antisemitism, Picart criticised certain statements, considered in retrospect to be far too daring, in the *Addictions and Corrections* in the concluding volume:

> In representing the State of the Jews under the Christian Governments, we have mentioned several heinous Crimes, with which they have been charged; without entering into a strict Enquiry about the Truth or Falshood of such Accusations, we must mention two more of great Moment: 1.That they falsified the Scripture out of Hatred to Christianity 2. That they have destroyed the Books which explained the Mysteries of their Religion.[53]

By referring to Menasseh ben Israel's apology for the Jewish people, the *Vindiciae Judaeorum*,[54] the editor of this monumental work denies the validity of such accusations; and later on he refutes other 'typical' antisemitic motifs: the idea that the Jews 'commit Idolatry'; that they 'curse the Christians thrice every day'; and other misconceptions. The main source for this refutation is Menasseh ben Israel, together with what may be called common sense.[55]

THE BIBLE AND THE JEWS

The Bible was hardly regarded as a sacred source for moral and religious doctrines to be shared on the same level and to the same extent by Christian and Jews alike. From the Reformation onwards, Protestants, both in continental Europe and in England, had claimed to possess the sole, correct interpretation and reading of the Old Testament. The Jews – according to mainstream Protestant thought – not only diminished the Bible by not recognising the New Testament, but also misinterpreted it by relying on two major misleading sources: the Talmud and other rabbinic tradition.[56]

The debate surrounding this controversial issue dated back to the Renaissance and reached its peak in continental Europe in the second half of the seventeenth century. It seems that a direct Jewish concern with these charges only appeared at a later date.[57] However, vindication of the Hebrew Bible, and Jewish interpretation of it, against Isaac Vossius, Richard Simon and William Whiston, came from the pen of an English Jew, Moses Marcus, who, in 1729, issued an English translation of Carpzov's *Critica Sacra Veteris Testamenti*, published at Leipzig two years earlier. Marcus, a converted Jew, aimed to bring the whole issue to a wider public in his translation of, and commentary on, Carpzov's work, and also 'to vindicate the Jews, my own Brethen and Countreymen, from so heavy and heinous a Charge, as that of maliciously and sacrilegiously corrupting and depraving the *Sacred Text*'.[58] Whether Marcus succeeded in his goal it is hard for us to say. What is certain is that he contributed towards showing the Jews positively, as preservers of the values and tenets of the Sacred Text.

THE HISTORY OF THE JEWS IN ENGLAND BY TOVEY D'BLOSSIERS (1738)

The missing piece of the historiographic mosaic which I have attempted to reconstruct appeared some time in the course of the 1730s – a period of relative quiet for the English Jews[59] and for the non-Jewish scholarly world of the Hebraists – with the first comprehensive history of the Jews in England by Tovey D'Blossiers, a historian and principal at New-Inn-Hall, Oxford. In his *Anglia Judaica: or the History and Antiquities of the Jews in England, collected from all our Historians, both Printed and Manuscript, as also from the Records in the Tower, and other Publick Repositories*, D'Blossiers took a decisive step towards the propagation of a more positive view of the Jews in England.[60] This work has to be regarded as the very first use of Lockean arguments in favour of toleration in an historical context and in relation to the Jews. John Locke himself was extremely cautious when dealing with non-Christians. He referred to the Jews (and Muslims) only rarely in his works on toleration, including them in the category of individuals who should be granted the right to freedom of conscience. However, Locke's works should be considered as belonging to the political debate which followed the Toleration Act, in which the Jewish religion was not at stake.

Half a century later, the obscure D'Blossiers took up Locke's arguments[61] in order to provide a defence of the Jews and of their place in English history, the latter issue being no less innovative than the former. The preface is a cautious plea for toleration and mutual respect between the faiths:

> Christianity, indeed, has of late years met with many enemies amongst the licentious and profane; and it is high time for the Civil Magistrate to come in to its assistance. But then I would have such assistance to proceed no further than a resolute and uniform exclusion of all such from Publick Favours, who shall in any manner dissent from the religion of the publick. Nor can this, I hope, be stil'd persecution. For tho' all men have a natural right to worship God according to the dictates of their conscience, no man has a natural right to be rewarded for so doing. Temporal encouragements for religion are in the arbitrary Disposal of the Legislature, and may very justly be restrained to any set of men, according as their religious principles shall be found most advantageous to government ... I say restrain as well as encourage, because those religious tolerations I would plead for, are only such, as are consistent with the temporal welfare of the community. That the Jewish religion is of such a Nature, may very plainly appear from the accounts given us in the Holy Scripture.[62]

D'Blossiers redeems a substantial part of the Anglo–Jewish past, especially with regard to the Middle Ages, where Jews suffered from a series of assaults, injuries, bans and widespread harassment.[63] His use of Anglo–Jewish history up to the expulsion of 1290 is altogether different from any previous account. He is, however, very ambiguous in dealing with some crucial points of Anglo-Jewish history, and he accords credibility to the stories told by a virulent judeophobic chronicler, Matthew Paris,[64] regarding the alleged crucifixion, by the local Jews, of a boy at Lincoln.[65] Moreover, the two engravings on the back of the title-page show a couple of middle-aged Jews, with long noses and sad, afflicted expressions, poorly dressed and with traditional hats, so perpetuating some of the most typical Judeophobic stereotypes, though not the most hostile sort.

Historical legends, usually exaggerating the supposed vices and hatred of the Jews towards the Christian religion, clearly circulated in historical as well as in political tracts and pamphlets before the flood of philosemitic and antisemitic works originating from the Jew Bill controversy. For example, in 1715 an anonymous pamphlet attacked John Toland's plea for the naturalisation of the Jews of England[66] by referring to the tragic plight of mediaeval Anglo-Jewry as a sign of their destiny, and as evidence that they were *persona non grata* in terms of both English laws, mentalities and lifestyle, and divine providence. According to the anonymous author, the unbearable pain suffered by mediaeval Anglo-Jewry was merely what they had deserved, from God and mankind, for their 'crimes, frauds, insolencies'.[67] Twenty years later, D'Blossiers' work utterly reversed these tendentious interpretations, although it is important to note that these two contrasting uses of historical evidence were still common in many of the pamphlets which shaped the Jew Bill controversy in 1753.

I have focused here on a few single events amongst many. For instance, the first edition of the work of the Hebrew Renaissance geographer and historian Abraham Farissol, *Iggereth Oggereth Olam*, 'Letters from all over the world', appeared in Oxford in 1691 and included Latin text and scholarly footnotes with many references to Arabic geographical works. Among other things, the description of the inhabitants of the New World provided by so great a Jewish authority deeply undermined the political myth of the ten lost tribes as being scattered in America, a belief which suffered a period of temporary decline in the first half of the eighteenth century.[68] The Latin translation of the *Josippon* by Joseph ben Gorion should also be mentioned, along with the abridged and popular version of Josephus' *Jewish History*, already read widely before and after the readmission in 1655/1656, and then available in a far more accurate edition produced by Jean Gagnier and published in Latin in Oxford in 1706.[69]

Apart from the scholarly world other intellectual ventures attempted to cast new and positive light on the Jewish religion and its way of life, such as John Harrington's *Oceana*, which was edited by John Toland in 1700, or Toland's *Antiquitates Judaicae*. Many of these ventures drew on some peculiar philosophical and even scientific ideas from the rediscovered reservoir of the Old Testament and Jewish philosophy, including works of the Middle Ages and the Renaissance. For instance, this was the case with the great but neglected William Wollaston, a Deist and learned talmudic and rabbinic scholar, the author of a substantial investigation into – and a systematic construction of – natural religion, which ran into several editions in the 1720s, selling up to 10,000 copies.[70] It was also true of Edmund Dickinson, whose *Physica Vetus et Vera* of 1702 is a powerful reappraisal of Genesis, intended to provide a more solid basis, as well as counter-arguments, for contemporary physics and cosmology under the motto 'nihil philosophia mosaica vetustius, nihil verius'.[71] Likewise, in Newton's thought theology also played a substantial role, and God strongly resembled the biblical deity.

Thus, the period between the Glorious Revolution (1688) and the Jew Bill controversy (1753) was rich in terms of both intellectual and social Anglo-Jewish history and biblical scholarship. There was no single defining event, however, but rather a slow two-fold process of reappraisal. On the one hand, Englishmen expanded their knowledge of the biblical and Oriental worlds, and simultaneously began to get acquainted with the Jews as physical beings. On the other hand, the learned world began to approach biblical antiquities with new tools and fewer prejudices. To use Frank E. Manuel's metaphor in his *Broken Staff*,[72] the severed connections (Judaism–Christianity but also ancient

Jews–contemporary Jews) began to be reknitted. The ways in which this severed connection was restored were diverse and involved both antisemitic and philosemitic patterns of thought. As well as the rise of a more complex ambivalence towards the Jews, it is undeniable, however, that the discovery of the Jewish past affected, more positively than not, the perception of contemporary Jews, in England as well as in the rest of Europe.

ACKNOWLEDGEMENTS

This article is the first outcome of research undertaken whilst I was a Hartley Fellow at the Hartley Institute, University of Southampton between November 1994 and February 1995. I would like to thank Dr Chris Woolgar for his advice, warm welcome and constant help in practical as well as theoretical matters. Dr Tony Kushner was extremely helpful and caring, as were other members of the History and Literature Departments at the University of Southampton. Finally, I wish to thank Dr Miriam Silvera, University of Rome, with whom I have discussed several points related to this article.

NOTES

1. This chapter is based on a paper which was presented as part of the Parkes' seminar series at the University of Southampton in 1995.
2. D. Katz, *The Jews in the History of England 1485–1850* (Oxford: Clarendon Press, 1994), p. 190. For a comprehensive account of the years 1700–53 (according to Katz, 'nothing if not an era of adjustment', a judgement which this study somewhat confirms) see Katz, op. cit., pp. 190–239 and Todd Endelman, *The Jews of Georgian England 1714–1830* (Philadelphia: Congregation Emanuel, 1979), Chps. 1–3. On D. Nieto see J. Petuchowsky, *The Theology of Haham David Nieto* (New York: Jewish Publication Society of America, 1971); for a biography of Nieto, stressing his relationships with non-Jewish intellectuals, is I. Solomons, 'David Nieto and Some of His Contemporaries', *Transactions of the Jewish Historical Society of England* (from now on *TJHSE*), 12 (1931), 1–101 (also printed separately, London, 1931).
3. As argued by David B. Ruderman, *Jewish Thought and Scientific Discovery in Early Modern Europe* (New Haven–London: Yale University Press, 1995), pp. 310–31: Ruderman's conclusions are worth quoting: 'Seen as a whole, Nieto's major writings suggest a consistent and well-conceived educational strategy for presenting the Jewish faith in a social environment that was isolated from the mainstream of Jewish culture, highly secularized, and only tenuously attached to traditional Jewish norms. By choosing to construct his own public image of Judaism along lines similar to the Anglican social and intellectual elite, he hoped to make the most effective case for Jewish faith and to

ensure the civic welfare of the Jewish community. An examination of Nieto's theology thus offers a remarkable test case of adaptation and reformulation of Judaism in the light of the formidable challenge scientific advances had posed to traditional faith', D. Ruderman, op. cit., p. 331.

4. On Edward Pocock (1604–91), see the *Dictionary of National Biographies (DNB)*, 16, pp. 7–12. He was the author of several works, including the *Commentaries on the Prophecy of Micah and of Malachiah* (1677, 1692), the translation into Arabic for conversionist purposes of the *De veritate religionis christianae* by Grotius (1660), and that from Arabic into Latin of the *Porta Mosis* by Moses ben Maimun (1655). His *Theological Works* were collected and edited by L. Twells in 1740.

5. On John Lightfoot (1602–75) see *DNB*, Vol. 11, pp. 1108–10. He was probably the most learned and well-known English Orientalist of the seventeenth century. His collected works underwent several editions: 1648; 1686 (ed. by J. Texelius); 1825 (ed. by J.R. Pitman). His works include *A Few and New Observations upon the Book of Genesis* (1642); *The Harmony of the Foure Evangelists* (1644); *Horae Hebraicae et Talmudicae* (1663); *The Temple: especially as it stood in the days of our Saviour* (1650).

6. On John Marsham (1602–85) see *DNB*, Vol. 12, p. 1139. He was one of the very first authors to have connected the Egyptian history and chronology with the Hebrew and Greek ones in his *Chronicus Canon Aegypticus, Ebraicus, Graecus*, (1666, other editions include those of 1672, 1676 and 1696).

7. On John Spencer (1630–93) see *DNB*, Vol. 18, pp. 767–8. After John Selden (1584–1654), Spencer can be considered as the most thorough investigator in the area of Jewish biblical law and one of the first founders of the study of comparative religion in Europe. His *De legibus Hebraeorum ritualibus et earum rationibus libri III* was first published in 1685, re-edited in 1686, re-published in 1727, and finally in Tübingen in 1732 with an important introduction by Ch. Mattheus Pfaff. On Spencer see also Frank E. Manuel, *The Eighteenth Century Confronts the Gods* (Cambridge, MA: Harvard University Press, 1959), p. 197.

8. On Thomas Hyde (1636–1703) see *DNB*, Vol. 10. He was the author of, among other works, a translation into Malayan of the Gospels, which was published for conversionist purposes in 1677 at the expense of Robert Boyle. He also wrote an influential *Hystoria Religionis Veterum Persarum Eorumque Magorum* fully revising historiographical notions about Zoroaster. This was published in 1700 and reprinted in 1760. His unpublished works were partially published in 1767 with the title *Syntagma dissertationum et opuscula*. I shall refer later to his translation of Abraham Farissol's *Iggereth*.

9. On Jean Gagnier (1670?–1740) see *DNB*, Vol. 7. He was the translator of the *Josippon* in 1706, and a fierce opponent of the Roman Catholic Church (*L'Eglise Romaine Convaincue de dépravation, d'idolatrie, et d'antichrystianisme*, 1716). He was also the author of a documented and influential, though in some respects superficial, life of Mahomet, *La vie de Mahomet: traduite et compilée de l'Alcoran* (Amsterdam, 1732).

10. Although learned correspondence between newly arrived Jews and Hebraists continued for the late seventeenth century, see D. Katz, 'The Abendana Brothers and the Christian Hebraists of Seventeenth-Century England', *Journal of Ecclesiastical History*, 40 (1989), pp. 28–52. Examples of such correspondence include that of Isaac Abendana, published in 'Isaac Abendana's Cambridge Mishnah and Oxford Calenders', *TJHSE*, VIII (1915–17), pp. 98–121 and, later, David Nieto with John Covel, an eccentric

Orientalist and former diplomat based in Cambridge. The two letters (of 1706), published in the English translation by Solomons, 'David Nieto and Some of His Contemporaries', were written in Italian, since Nieto did not know English at that time.

11. On the Jew Bill controversy in its political and theoretical context see D. Katz, *The Jews*, pp. 240–83.

12. B. Kennicott, *The State of the Printed Hebrew Text Considered, in Two Dissertations* (Oxford, 1753, I dissertation; 1759, II dissertation). The Kennicott papers, held at the Bodleian Library, are a testimony of his long-lasting relationships with, among others, Jewish intellectuals and rabbis, including Italian writers such as Jacob Saraval. On B. Kennicott see Isabelle Major, *The History of Benjamin Kennicott* (London: Rider & Co., 1932).

13. An enormously influential work, published for the first time as *De Sacra Poësi Hebraeorum Praelectiones Academicae Oxonii Habitae* (Oxford, 1753) and re-edited or re-published several times (e.g. 1763; 1766; 1770; 1775; 1810; 1815; 1821). An important English edition was that of 1787 (*Lectures on the Sacred Poetry of the Hebrews*, 2 Vols, London, 1787), with explanatory notes by the Göttingen Professor Johann David Michaelis. On Lowth see B. Hepworth, *Robert Lowth* (Boston: Twayne, 1978).

14. This new attitude also influenced Herder's revolutionary approach to the Old Testament: see B. Stemmrich-Köhler, *Zur Funktion der orientalischen Poesie bei Goethe, Herder, Hegel* (Frankfurt–New York: P. Lang, 1992).

15. The best historiographical assessment of these years is still D. Katz, *Philosemitism and the Readmission of the Jews to England 1603–1655* (Oxford: Clarendon Press, 1982).

16. *The Old and The New Testament Connected* ran into several editions even before the second volume came out in 1718.

17. On his biography see *DNB*, Vol. 16, pp. 352–4. See also *The Life of H. P. Dean of Norwich, with Several Tracts and Letters of his Upon Various Subjects, Never Before Published* (London, 1748), and E. M. Thompson, (ed.), *H. Prideaux's Letters to John Ellis 1674–1722*, (London: J. & P. Knapton; Publications of the Camden Society, 1875).

18. H. Prideaux, *The True Nature of Imposture Fully Displayed in the Life of Mahomet* (London, 1697).

19. See note 9.

20. H. Prideaux, *A Letter to the Deists, Shewing that the Gospel of Jesus Christ is no Imposture but the Sacret Truth of God* (London, 1697).

21. C. Leslie, *A Short and Easy Method with the Deists* (London, 1697). Leslie also applied his method to the Jews in a strongly antisemitic tract, *A Short and Easy Method with the Jews*, which he added to the second edition of the first pamphlet against the Deists (1699).

22. See H. Prideaux, *The Validity of the Church of England* (London, 1688).

23. See James E. Force, 'Jewish Monotheism, Christian Heresy, and Sir Isaac Newton', in R.B. Waddington and A.H. Williamson (eds), *The Expulsion of the Jews. 1492 and After*, (New York–London: Garland, 1994), pp. 259–80. Newton's theology and his related interest in chronology, emphasised as his foremost concerns by Frank E. Manuel, *The Theology of Isaac Newton* (Oxford: Clarendon Press, 1974), have been the object of several historiographical reappraisals. See, for instance, Scott Mandelbrote, 'Isaac Newton and Thomas Burnet: Biblical Criticism and the Crisis of Late Seventeenth-Century England', in James E. Force and Richard H. Popkin, (eds), *The Books of Nature and Scripture* (Leiden: Brill, 1994), pp. 149–78.

24. M. Echard, *Ecclesiastical History*, ET (London, 1700).
25. Melchidesec Thevenot (ed.), *Relations de Divers Voyages Curieux, Qui n'ont Point ésté Publiées, et qu'on a Traduites ou Tirées des Originaux des Voyageurs François etc.* (Paris, 1696).
26. See note 6.
27. Even more accurate than Prideaux's work, Archbishop James Usher's great work, *Annales Veteris Testamenti*, which first appeared in 1650, can be regarded, together with Echard's work, as the model and the background for Prideaux as well as for other chronological treatises. As Prideaux states at the beginning of his work, Usher's work is 'the greatest and most perfect work of chronology that hath been published'. It conflicted strongly, however, with Newton's chronology: see further Frank E. Manuel, *The Eighteenth Century*, pp. 93ff.
28. On Le Clerc's theological thought and its liberal inclination see Maria Cristina Pitassi, *Entre Croire et Savoir, le Problème de la Méthode Critique Chez Jean Le Clerc* (Leiden: Brill, 1987). On his historiographical method, see Mario Sina, *Vico e Le Clerc. Tra Filosofia e Filologia* (Naples: Guida, 1978).
29. Jean Le Clerc, *A Critical Examination of the Rev. Dean Prideaux's Connection of the Old and New Testament* (London, 1722), translated from the French.
30. Walter Moyle, *Remarks Upon Dr. Prideaux's Connection of the Old and the New Testament* (Dublin, 1728).
31. See Benjamin Marshall, *A Chronological Treatise upon the Seventy Weeks of Daniel; wherein is evidently shewn the accomplishment of the predicted events* (London, 1725), and Anonymous [Aristea], *A Vindication of the History of the Septuagint from the misrepresentations of Scaliger, Dupin, Hody, Prideaux, and others* (London, 1736).
32. See D. Katz, *The Jews*, pp. 295–300 and S. Singer, 'Early Translations and Translators of the Jewish Liturgy in England', *TJHSE*, Vol. 3 (1896–98), pp. 36–71.
33. An anonymous reviewer in *The Critical Review* (February 1784) welcomed this work as follows: 'The use of such a work as this, with regard to Christian readers, is equally manifest. Theological and historical writers have frequent occasion to mention the notions of modern Jews: it is therefore very proper that they should know how the Jews themselves explain their own rituals, and exhibit their credenda; for we make no doubt, but that some of our learned writers have mistaken their principles, or their practices, and charged with absurdities, which are susceptible of a more favourable construction. The writer, whose work is now before us, on the contrary, always cites the Talmud, and other Jewish books; and consequently gives the inquisitive reader as much satisfaction as the nature of the subject will admit.'
34. D. Levi, *A Succinct Account* (London, 1782), 'Preface', p. i.
35. Ibid., pp. 252f.
36. Ibid., pp. 256–61.
37. Ibid., p. 267: '... for as to predestination, they [i.e., the Jews] held that, before man is born, it is predestinated, whether he shall be wise, or foolish, weak, or strong, rich, or poor. But, whether he is to be wicked, or righteous, vicious, or virtuous, is entirely in his own freewill; for otherwise, why should the righteous man have a reward, or the wicked have a punishment?'
38. Ibid., pp. 268–74.
39. Ibid., p. 275. Levi used the Edinburgh edition (1779) of Prideaux's work.
40. For a general introduction to Basnage's life and work, see G. Cerny, *Theology, Politics and Letters at the Crossroads of European Civilization: Jacques Basnage and the Baylean Huguenot Refugees in the Dutch Republic* (La Haye: Martinus Nÿhoff, 1987).

41. The introduction by Basnage has fewer antisemitic remarks than Taylor's Preface. Basnage refers only to rabbis in a polemical tone, stigmatising their 'Ignorance and Imposture' and the 'Romances they have invented concerning Christ' (p. vii). Regarding the prophecy about the coming of Christ among the Jews, Basnage inclines to defend them: 'yet we cou'd not be induc'd to father upon the *Jews* a Tenet, which they never received, and thereby make their Incredulity, which is but too deplorable, more criminal than really is' (vii). At the end, Basnage displays his tolerant and open-minded spirit when summarising the destiny of the Jews in the west: 'The *West* is much more fruitful in Events in these last Centuries; but most of them are Tragical and Calamitous. In the Declension and Dregs of Ages, People have been inflam'd with a Spirit of Cruelty and Barbarity against them. They were accused of being the Cause of all the Calamities that happen'd; and charg'd with a World of Crimes, which they never thought of. A vast number of Miracles were invented, in order to convict them, or rather upon a Pretence of Religion, to trample upon and oppress them. We have made a collection of the Laws, which the Councils and Princes have published against them, whereby a Judgement may be made of the Iniquity of the Ones, and of the Oppression of the Others. People did not keep within the Bounds of the Decrees against them. For they were frequently expos'd every where to Military Execution, popular Commotions and Massacres: Yet by a Miracle of Providence, which ought to astonish all Christians, this Nation, hated and persecuted in all Places for so many Ages, still subsists in all Parts of the World'(x). See also pp. 638–45. On the co-existence, in Basnage's work, of Christian apologetic and plea for Jewish toleration see M. Silvera, 'L'Ebreo in Jacques Basnage. Apologia del Cristianesimo e difesa della tolleranza', *Nouvelles de la Republique des Lettres*, Vol. 1 (1987), pp. 103–15.

42. See J. Basnage, *History*, p. 681.

43. A clear example of his zeal, which damaged his reputation even among the Anglican clergy of the lower and upper hierarchy, is given by his *Twelve Sermons* (London, 1697).

44. *Biblioteca Magna Rabbinica* (Rome, 1675–83).

45. The (possible) use of Herbert of Cherboury's Deist arguments in Jacob ben Amran's work is worth further investigation.

46. J. Basnage, *History*, p. 677.

47. Second edition, 1709.

48. I. Abendana, *Discourses of the Ecclesiastical and Civil Polity of the Jews* (London, 1706), p. 15. On Abendana and the Abendana family (of Sephardic origin) see *Encyclopedia Judaica*, Vol. I, (1971), Cols. 65–8.

49. A. Calmet, *An Historical, Critical, Geographical, and Etymological Dictionary of the Holy Bible etc*, 3 Vols (London, 1732).

50. Ibid., 'The Author's Preface to This Edition', p. ix.

51. See Alfred Rubens, *A Jewish Iconography* (London: Jewish Museum, 1954), and idem., *A History of Jewish Costume* (London: Weidenfeld and Nicolson, 1973).

52. Especially in popular and satirical prints, see F. Felsenstein, *Anti-Semitic Stereotypes: A Paradigm of Otherness in English Popular Culture* (Baltimore: Johns Hopkins University Press, 1995).

53. *The Ceremonies and Religious Customs of the Various Nations of the Known World*, (London, 1739), 7 Vols, Vol. VII, p.158. Such editorial enterprise completely replaced the old Alexander Ross, *A View of All Religion in the World*, (London, 1653). See Frank E. Manuel, *The Eighteenth Century*, p. 7.

54. On which see D. Katz, *Philosemitism, passim*.

55. *The Ceremonies and Religious Customs of the Various Nations of the Known World,* Vol. 7, (London, 1739), p. 159: 'The learned Buxtorfius taxes the Synagogue with Blasphemy, upon account of a Prayer, in which it is said, *that the Nations bow down before Things of no value, and offer their Prayers to Gods who cannot save them, &c.* To this it is answered, that this was true at the Time of *Esdras,* when that Prayer was composed, which being long before Christ, it did not regard Christians; but that however it is now left out of their Rituals. Neither is it probable that in their Synagogues they spit whenever the Name of Christ is pronounced; since so publick an Injury could not be concealed from Christians, who often see their publick Service performed, and would severely punish them for it.

   The fifth Accusation objected to the *Jews* is that they do their utmost to pervert Christians, and bring them over to *Judaism.* This is easily confuted; for though it must be owned that Christians now and then embrace their Religion, yet in *Holland* where Toleration puts them almost on the Level with Christians, they avoid, out of Fear and Policy, using any Persuasions to induce those Christians to do it . . . .

   As to their Cheats and exhorbitant Usuries, the same Apologist says, they are obliged to this by the Persecutions raised against them, and Taxes laid upon them; and that their Law does not enforce the Practice of them against Christians, only some Passages have been interpreted wrongfully by some of more corrupt Principles; or who, as most Men are apt to do, by false Reasons persuade themselves they may hate any Religion but their own.'

56. See the last chapter of Henning Reventlow, *The Authority of the Bible and the Modern World* ET, (London: SCM, 1984).

57. In 1762, for example, the defence of the Jews against the accusation of perverting the Old Testament was taken over by Robert Findlay: see Philaletes [R. Findlay], *Two Letters to Dr. Kennicott, Vindicating the Jews from the Charge of Corrupting Deut. XXVII:4* (London, 1762).

58. See D. Katz, *The Jews,* pp. 213f.

59. On the problems faced by the Sephardi Community, see M.S. Diamond, 'Problems of the London Sephardi Community 1720–1733. Philip Carteret Webb's Notebook', *TJHSE,* Vol. 21 (1962–67), pp. 39–63.

60. London, 1738. See the recent retelling by E. Pearl, *Anglia Judaica or A History of the Jews in England by D'Blossiers Tovey LL.D* (London: Weidenfeld and Nicolson, 1990), which is extremely useful since Pearl adds a list of short biographies of those historians and writers – the majority of whom share antisemitic attitudes – used and commented on by Tovey (pp. 181–90). It is possible that the title recalled John Toland's *Anglia Libera.* In the British Library copy (457.b.18.) there is a manuscript insertion – in an eighteenth-century hand – which tells in Latin a judeophobic short episode.

61. See T. D'Blossiers, *Anglia Judaica,* 'Preface': 'All Men have a natural Right to worship God according to the Dictates of their Conscience provided their religion does not clash with the state'. For Tovey, the Jewish religion seems '*consistent* with the temporal Welfare of the Community'. In his Preface there is also a mild interpretation of the New Testament's precept of the *Compelle intrare:* 'Compell them to come in, it is true, is a Precept of the Same Divine Authority . . . . But, alas! What kind of Compulsion was intended by our Saviour in the Parable? Not, surely, Bonds or Imprisonment! Not cruel Mockings or Scourging! Not pecuniary Mulcts or Banishment! No: that insistable Force only of a *Godly Conversation*'. Finally, Tovey's account is the first to refer to the Jews as the 'Jewish race' (p. 1).

62. T. D'Blossiers, *Anglia Judaica*, 'Preface'.
63. Ibid., pp. 12f; 129ff; 20ff (massacre of Stanford). Among other references to the present time, Tovey asserts that Jews 'do not stink more than Christians' (p. 95), so confuting a popular judeophobic belief.
64. On Paris see E. Pearl, 'Appendix', pp. 185f.
65. T. D'Blossiers, *Anglia Judaica*, pp. 136ff. See also pp. 168f, for an alleged 'insult to the Holy Cross at Oxford', which supposedly took place in 1268: '... during a solemn Procession, a certain *Jew*, of consummate Impudence, violently snatch'd it from the Bearer, and trodd it under his Feet, in Token of his Contempt of *Christ*'.
66. Anonymous [John Toland], *Reasons for Naturalizing the Jews in Great Britain and Ireland, on the same foot with all other Nations* (London, 1714) reprinted in P. Radin, (ed.), *Pamphlets relating to the Jews in England in the 17th and 18th Century*, (Sutro Branch Library, CA, Occasional Series, No. 3, 1930); German translation by H. Mainusch, (Stuttgart–Berlin–Köln–Mainz, 1965); Italian translation by P. Bernardini (Florence, 1996, in press).
67. Anonymous, *A Confutation of the Reasons for Naturalizing the Jews; containing their crimes, frauds, insolencies, etc.* (London, 1715).
68. See A. Farissol, *Itinera mundi* Chp. 29, 'On the Discovery of a New World', pp. 182–85. On Farissol, see David B. Ruderman, *Kabbalah, Magic and Science. The Cultural Universe of a Sixteenth-Century Jewish Physician* (Cambridge, MA: Harvard University Press, 1988).
69. As Lucien Wolf wrote, '*Josippon* was essentially a *Volksbuch*. If we consider how important a factor in the dissipation of anti-Jewish prejudice was the popular apprehension of the identity of the Jews with the people of the Bible, we shall see what was the particular service rendered by the *Sepher Josippon*. It supplied the first connecting link in the gentile mind between the Bible and the Ghetto': see L. Wolf, '"Josippon" in England', *TJHSE*, Vol. 6 (1908–10), pp. 277–88. On this edition, see p. 288.
70. William Wollaston, *The Religion of Nature Delineated* (London, 1722, definitive edition, 1724). On Wollaston see C.G. Thompson, *The Ethics of William Wollaston* (Boston, 1922). On his massive use (in the original) of biblical, talmudic and rabbinic sources, see Alexander Altmann, 'William Wollaston. English Deist and Rabbinic Scholar', *TJHSE*, Vol. 16 (1945–51), pp. 185–211.
71. E. Dickinson, *Physica vetus et vera, sive Tractatus de naturali veritate hexaemeri mosaici, per quem probatur in historia Creationis, tum Generationis universe methodo atque modum, tum verae Philosophiae principia, strictim atque breviter a Mose tradita* (London, 1702). Among other peculiar statements in this curious treatise, there is the idea that Aristotle derived his theology from the Jews, to whom he taught his physics, and that the Jews are all philosophers, derived from Theophrastus (p. 283).
72. Frank E. Manuel, *The Broken Staff. Judaism through Christian Eyes* (Cambridge, MA: Harvard University Press, 1992).

JEWISHNESS AND THE CONSTRUCTION OF 'RACIAL' AND NATIONAL IDENTITIES

6

Shakespeare and the Jews[1]

JAMES SHAPIRO

SHAKESPEARE AND THE JEWS

Roughly a hundred years have passed now, since the Anglo-Jewish Historical Exhibition of 1887, and the founding of the Jewish Historical Society of England in 1893, landmark events in the history of scholarship about Shakespeare and the Jews. From the archival work of Lucien Wolf, Cecil Roth, Edgar Samuel, and many others, a picture of the small Jewish community of early modern England has gradually come into focus, a community that existed, for the most part in London, between the expulsion of the Jews in 1290 and the so-called 'readmission' under Oliver Cromwell in 1656. No longer can scholars insist – though, surprisingly, many on both sides of the Atlantic still do – that there were no Jews in Shakespeare's England. Perhaps a hundred or more Jews might have jostled Shakespeare in the crowded streets of London, and we know from Spanish Inquisition records and the complaints of various Catholic ambassadors, that Jewish holidays like Passover and Yom Kippur were celebrated in England in the late sixteenth century.

Virtually all those Jews practised their faith in secret – since most were of Spanish or Portuguese descent, *marranos*, they surely had had enough experience with disguising their beliefs because of their experience of the Inquisition, far harsher than any repression they might face in England. A Londoner in early Stuart England, curious about what the word '*marrano*' meant, might have turned for help to John Florio's dictionary, *Queen Anne's New World of Words* (London, 1611), where the term is described as 'a nick-name for Spaniards, that is, one descended of Jewes or Infidels and whose Parents were never christened, but for to save their goods will say they are Christians'. But Florio's definition seems to raise more questions than it resolves: is this a nickname for all Spaniards? Were the *marranos* simply dissimulators or did they hold any religious beliefs at all? Were they Jews, infidels, or Christians? Lapsed Jews? Fake Christians? How could one know for sure, after all, since to save their goods they 'will say they are Christians' anyway? We have here some glimpses of the problems that Jews caused for the emerging categories of social, national, racial, and religious differences in early modern England.

Had Shakespeare wished to speak with someone who had converted from Judaism to Christianity he could have done so easily enough: there was a converts' house in London, the *Domus Conversorum*, which was in existence in Chancery Lane from 1232, when it was founded by King Henry III as a home for poor Jewish converts to Christianity. Throughout the sixteenth century, with the exception of the years 1551–78, there were always a tiny handful of residents there. One of the residents, Nathaniel Menda, had been publicly converted at All Hallows Church, Lombard Street, London, in 1577 by John Foxe, more famous for his *Book of Martyrs*. We learn from Foxe's *Serman Preached at the Christening of a Certain Jew, at London* (London, 1578) that Menda had lived in London as a Jew before his conversion, having been 'transported from our uttermost parts of Barberie into England, and conversant amongst us, by the space of five whole yeeres', before his baptism. The sermon is a remarkable document for what it says about Christian beliefs about Jews in Elizabethan London. In his long discourse Foxe addresses the 'circumcised Race' directly, decrying their 'intolerable Scorpionlike savagenes, so furiously boyling against the innocent infants of the Christian Gentiles: and the rest of your haynous abominations, insatiable butcheries, treasons, frensies, and madnes'.

For his part, Menda dutifully added his *Confession of Faith, which Nathaneal a Jewe borne, made before the Congregation in the Parish Church of Alhallowes in Lombard Street at London* (London, 1578), which was 'written first by him selfe in the Spanish tongue and now translated into English for the most benefite of the godlie Reader'. In his *Confession* Menda promises:

> [I will] utterly foresake my former wayes and the steps that my nation walketh in, leaving with them not only that false looking for another Christ, but my name also which was given me at my circumcision (being Iehuda) though in it selfe it be honourable: desiring that as I have received a new gift from the Lord, so in token thereof I may be called Nathaneal.

The sermon and confession, bound together, were popular enough to be cited a half-century later.

There were other Jews as well in London, including Dr Roderigo Lopez, Elizabeth's personal physician, put to death in 1594 for allegedly conspiring to poison the Queen. And Roger Prior has recently described how a smaller Jewish group of Italian descent, the Lupos, Comys, and Bassanos, brought over by Henry VIII around 1540, were court musicians. Predictably, Jews, usually converted ones, could also be found teaching Hebrew at Oxford and

Cambridge, or helping Bodley with the Hebrew catalogue at the University Library. One of the more interesting Jews – in part because he was unwilling to deny his Judaism – was Joachim Gaunse, a mining expert from Prague who lived openly as a Jew until his run-in with a Protestant minister in Bristol in 1589. Outraged with Gaunse's evasive response to Christ's authority – 'What needed the almightie God to have a sonne, if he is not almightie?' – the Reverend Curtys and the mayor and alderman of Bristol referred the dangerous matter to the Privy Council, and Gaunse, despite his earlier service to the state and his participation in Raleigh's Roanoke expedition, was probably hustled out of the country – for that is the last we hear of him.

The lives of many other, anonymous, Jews in England will necessarily remain unrecorded – we have just glimpses of a few, like the Jew that Sir John Lancaster took with him from London to serve as his translator on his East Indies expedition; or the unnamed Jew asked to assist in translating a letter sent to Queen Elizabeth from Constantinople, concerning Hugh Broughton's efforts to convert the Jews. By the end of the sixteenth century, years before the full-fledged philosemitism of the early seventeenth century, so ably described by David Katz, Richard Popkin and Jonathan Israel, interactions between Jews and the English were more and more frequent, not simply in London, but in the foreign ports in Morocco and Turkey where English merchants were trading, and on the continent as well, especially Antwerp and Amsterdam, where Jewish communities were flourishing.

Frustratingly, the findings of these Anglo-Jewish historians have yet to find their way into mainstream histories of England. Gavin Langmuir, a Scot and something of an outsider in the matter, has surveyed what he calls 'Majority History', and has concluded that having inherited a historiographic tradition hostile or ignorant of Jews, or both, and writing for a society little interested in Jewish history or more or less hostile to Jews, historians of the majority have been little attracted to Jewish history.

One would have hoped that the 'new historicism' (popularised in the United States for the past decade or so by Stephen Greenblatt and his followers), an historical approach dedicated in large measure to writing the history of the Other in the Renaissance, would have compensated for the relative silence of the mainstream historians of early modern English culture when they came to the matter of the Jews. Disappointingly, this has not occurred. Though the new historicists have rediscovered virtually every marginalised Other imaginable in early modern England – including witches, hermaphrodites, Moors, cross-dressers, Turks, sodomites, criminals, prophets, and vagabonds – they have steered carefully around the Other of Others in the Renaissance, the Jews (all the more strange, perhaps, because so many of these scholars are themselves of Jewish descent). Greenblatt himself has written that 'there is no "Jewish Question" in Marlowe's England', and that the Jews in their real historical situation are finally incidental in works like Marlowe's *The Jew of Malta*.

I have not come here today with any new discovery that Shakespeare might have known Jews personally, nor have I any new Jews to add to the lists compiled – and still being enlarged – by Anglo-Jewish scholars. I am a literary and cultural historian, and the kinds of questions I'm interested in exploring have largely been ignored by both Anglo-Jewish and mainstream British historians. Simply put, *how* and *why* were the English so obsessed with Jews in the sixteenth and seventeenth centuries? The Elizabethan obsession with Jews is far out of proportion with their actual presence and role in late sixteenth-century English social and political life. Yet when we turn to Tudor and

Stuart drama, the chronicles of English history, travel literature, and sermons, let alone the various discourses of
trade, millenarianism, usury, magic, race, gender, and
nationalism we find an unusual and persistent interest in
the Jews. What, ultimately, defines the difference of the
Jews? Were they a nation or still a nation in their diaspora
(John Donne calls them 'a whole nation of Cains, fugitives,
and vagabonds')? Some Englishmen even believed that
after the expulsion from England the Jews had gone to
Scotland (why else, they argued, were the Scots so frugal
and hated blood pudding). The international–nation of
Jews clearly complicated the emerging notion of the
'nation' in early modern England.

Alternatively, were the Jews, as the Spanish believed, a
separate race, one that could contaminate the blood lines of
Christians? Or were the Jews defined simply by their
religious practices? If this were so, what happened when
radical Puritans, seeking to emulate Old Testament rituals,
began to resemble Jews? Anne Curtyn, for example, was
committed to New Prison at Clerkenwell in 1649 'for being
a professed Jew and causing children to be circumcised',
though she was clearly a Christian and a follower of John
Traske. While Curtyn was released from prison, Traske
himself was not so fortunate: we learn from John
Chamberlain's letter of 14 February 1618 that Traske had
been stamped with the letter J on his forehead 'in token
that hee broached Jewish opinions'. In Traske's case insult
was added to injury:

> William Hudson, a treatist of the Court, adds that [Traske]
> was also ordered to eat swine's flesh whilst in prison, an
> admirable example from Hudson's point of view of the Star
> Chamber's habit of making the punishment fit the crime
> where possible.

Who or *what* then, for the confused Elizabethans, was a
Jew?

Clearly, even as the Elizabethans have something to tell us about the Jews, their obsession with Jews tells us even more about the Elizabethans. The kind of Anglo-Jewish history that remains to be written is one that explains why such powerful myths as those of ritual murder and the wandering Jew originated in mediaeval England, with bloody historical consequences throughout Europe in ensuing centuries. Ultimately, it is not the raw number of Jews in early modern England that is of interest as much as the kind of cultural preoccupation they became, the way that Jews complicated a great range of social, economic, legal, political, and religious discourses, and turned other questions into Jewish questions as well.

In trying to redress these omissions, and in trying at the same time to explain how the problems posed by 'Jews' were central to English conceptions of both difference and of national identity, I focus upon how these cultural negotiations are worked out in Shakespeare's *The Merchant of Venice*. In its restitution of the Jew in terms of various cultural myths, as well as within the nascent discourses of nation, gender, and race, Shakespeare's play explores what may be described as a cultural identity crisis, an insistence on difference that ends by undermining the very terms of identity by which the difference is affirmed: male, Christian, English.

• • • • •

In exploring the Jews as source and site of cultural anxiety in *The Merchant of Venice* I focus today even more specifically on 'the pound of flesh' narrative and its relationship to the myth – still current in Shakespeare's day (and indeed, still promulgated in England as late as the 1930s by Arnold Spenser Leese) – that Jews committed ritual murder. How this myth passed into history, and from history into literature and back into history (with terrible consequences for the Jews persecuted for this alleged crime in Europe) is part of the larger context of my talk. The basic narrative of this myth is familiar enough and can be dated back to its English origins in 1144, in Thomas of Monmouth's account of William of Norwich. By the late fifteenth century, with the invention of the printing press, the myth spread rapidly through Europe, disseminated in works like Hartmann Schedel's *Nuremberg Chronicle*, which recounts and gruesomely illustrates the ritual slaughter of Simon of Trent, until a master narrative emerged: the accusations generally included the abduction of a Christian boy by the Jews around Easter time, followed by his circumcision, then execution, the blood being used, often cannibalistically, for a range of mysterious purposes, ranging from the preparation of *matzot*, to anointing rabbis, as part of the circumcision rite, stopping menstrual bleeding, and painting the bodies of the dead.

The various connections between *The Merchant of Venice* and the discourse of ritual murder extend beyond the physical act of taking the knife to Christian flesh to encompass its setting at Easter time, cannibalism and abduction. Given the recurrent emphasis on Christ's crucifixion and the cannibalistic use of Christian blood, it is no accident that accusations of blood-libel repeatedly occurred during Easter week. Notably, the only specific mention of the time of year in *The Merchant of Venice* is to this holiday: Launcelot, Shylock's servant, says that it 'was not for nothing that my nose fell a-bleeding on Black Monday last at six a'clock i' the' morning'. Black Monday was Easter Monday, so called in commemoration of the freezing cold Easter of 1360. While Launcelot's superstitious remark offers only the slightest connection to the popular myth of ritual murder, it may have called to mind the set of popular beliefs associated with Easter. The most prominent was the annual abduction of a Christian boy. Another, stemming from the period before the expulsion of the Jews from England, had to do with Christians like Launcelot who were servants to Jews. D'Blossiers Tovey records in *Anglia Judaica* (Oxford, 1738) an unusual royal proclamation 'against Christian Women's entering into Service with Jews', in response to alleged Jewish mistreatment of Christian wet-nurses at Easter. He explains that

> The Reason of which Prohibition (particularly with Relation to their being Nurses) is mention'd by none of our Historians. But I suspect it to have been foolish Custom, which at this time prevail'd amongst the Jews, of obliging them to milk themselves into a Privie, for three Days after Easter-Day; for fear that the Body and Blood of Jesus Christ, which all Christians were oblig'd to receive upon that Holy Festival, shou'd, by Incorporation, be transfus'd into their Children.

Christ's sacrifice, physically embodied in the Eucharist, was central in Easter's celebration. And the celebration, which involved the taking and eating of the blood and body of Christ, finds its inversion in the Jewish devouring of the blood of Christian children. Trace elements of Jewish cannibalism are to be found in Shakespeare's play, where Shylock is repeatedly described as feasting upon his Christian enemies' bodies. We learn in his first appearance that he 'will fat the ancient grudge' he bears Antonio, and he later adds that he'll 'go in hate, to feed upon/The prodigal Christians'. When asked by Salerio what possible use he could have for Antonio's flesh Shylock replies, 'To bait fish withal; if it will feed nothing else, it will feed my revenge.' And Gratiano, calling Shylock 'wolfish, bloody, starved, and revenous', compares him to a predatory wolf who has fed on human flesh and is 'hanged for slaughter'.

Yet another example whereby features of the myth of ritual murder recur in inverted form in Shakespeare's play concerns the abduction of the innocent male child. Where in the traditional accusations of ritual murder it is the Jew

who steals away the Christian child, in *The Merchant of
Venice* it is the Christian Lorenzo who, in Antonio's words
'lately stole [Shylock's] daughter'. In this reversal the
abducted Jewish child '[b]ecome[s] a Christian'. The connection to the blood ritual plot is strengthened when
Jessica acknowledges that she is 'transformed to a boy'
when leaving her father's house, giving her cross-dressing
a significance that has to do with multiple discourses, gen-
dered and religious. Launcelot underscores the dark
undercurrent of ritual murder accusations and the ensuing
retaliations against Jews when he punningly warns Jessica
in the proverbial jingle: 'There will come a Christian
by/Will be worth a Jewes eye.' Lorenzo is indeed the
Christian for whom Jessica waits; but the 'worth' of the
proverb has less to do with the value of a lover than the
revenge exacted upon the Jewish community.

Tovey offers an anecdote that draws together the various strands of such revenge and threatened circumcision,
set in motion by the abduction of a Jewish daughter in the
year 1260, when

> all the Jews in England were commanded by this King
> [Henry III], to change their Religion; having their Children,
> under six years of Age, taken from them, and brought up
> Christians: which he says was occasion'd by the Marriage of
> a Christian Priest with a Jewish Woman, whom he was
> desparately in Love with, but cou'd obtain from her Parents
> on no other Condition than Circumcision; which so enrag'd
> the Populace, that they wou'd have burnt all the Jews alive,
> if the King, to pacify them, had not given the aforemen-
> tioned Orders.

And Act Four of *The Merchant of Venice* reproduces a
number of key features of ritual murder accusations and
trials, the most striking of which is its visual representation
of the secret and unobserved (except in pictures or plays)
bloody rituals of the Jews. We actually watch Shylock

sharpen his knife, as Antonio stands with his bosom bared, prepared to meet his fate at the hands of the murderous Jew. The trial in this scene also moves the conflict to a courtroom, the site of legitimate (though contested) legal jurisdiction so crucial to the blood-libel cases. At the same time it reproduces the Jewish strategy of insistently refusing to provide motives for the murderous intent. Finally, it offers the retribution brought upon the Jew for threatening the life of a Christian. In covering this ground Act Four of *The Merchant of Venice* offers a fantasy solution to some of the pressing social, political, and economic contradictions of early modern European society: a world in which usury was balanced against the need for venture capital; where emerging nationalism was threatened by the internationalism of groups like the Jews who were a 'nation' and yet scattered over the world, especially in the economic sphere; where local authority was pitted against central control; where social anxieties about religious faith could be exorcised by the conversion of the Jew.

· · · · ·

My particular interest today, is on that unusual aspect of the myth of ritual murder: that Jews took the knife to Christians, circumcising and in some cases, castrating, their Christian foes. When my undergraduates, reading *The Merchant of Venice* for the first time, learn of Shylock's desire to exact 'an equal pound' of Antonio's 'fair flesh, to be *cut off* and taken/In what part of your body pleaseth me', they often wonder just what part of Antonio's body Shylock has in mind. Those of you all too familiar with the play may easily forget that it is not until the trial scene in Act Four that this riddle is solved and we learn that Shylock intends to cut Antonio's 'breast' near his heart. But why, my students then ask, is Antonio's breast the spot most pleasing to Shylock? And why, the more literal wonder, would one cut 'off' and not 'out' a pound of flesh from 'nearest his heart'? Often, one of my students who has not read through to the trial scene will wonder whether Shylock, in exacting that pound of flesh, intends to castrate Antonio, and his or her classmates laugh nervously.

I want to follow up on that line of thought, since for Elizabethans, no less than for modern audiences familiar with theories of castration anxiety, the phrase 'cut off' could easily suggest taking the knife to a male victim's genitals. In fact, the judgement read to convicted male traitors and felons in Shakespeare's day includes the decree that 'at the place of execution . . . you will be hanged by the neck, and being alive cut down, *and your privy-members to be cut off'*. Moreover, the word 'flesh' was the standard euphemism for penis, not only in the various Elizabethan Bibles, but in popular writing as well: the extended play on male erection and tumescence in Sonnet 151, culminating in the lines 'flesh stays no farther reason, But rising at thy name doth point out thee', is typical. Castration is never far from the centre of the sexual anxieties that pervade *The Merchant of Venice*; allusions to it occur not only in Antonio's description of himself as 'a tainted wether', that is, a castrated ram, but also in Salerio's joke about Jessica having Shylock's 'stones [or testicles] upon her', and Gratiano's comment about 'mar[ring] the young clerk's pen[or penis]'.

I want to distinguish my argument (which is an historical one) from earlier psychoanalytic, feminist, and philosophical ones that point at similar conclusions. It was Freud who first argued that '[c]ircumcision is unconsciously equated with castration', and it was Freud's most Jewish disciple, Theodore Reik, who applied this insight to *The Merchant of Venice*, and proposed that Shylock threatened Antonio with such a cut. That similar readings have been proposed by the feminist scholar Margorie Garber and the philosopher Stanley Cavell in the context of broader arguments about gender and identity in Shakespeare suggests that Shylock's threat is a site of multiple significa-tion – and is situated at the heart of the cultural anxiety explored – and produced – in the play.

These psychoanalytic insights dovetail with my histori-cal arguments about ritual murder. Thus, Samuel Purchas, drawing upon the notes of John Selden, can write in 1626 of:

> One cruell and (to speake the properest phrase) *Jewish crime* was usuall amongst them, every yeere towards Easter, though it were not always knowne ... to steale a young boy, *circumcise him*, and after a solemn judgement, making one of their owne Nation a Pilate, to crucifie him out of their divellish malice to Christ and Christians.

So pervasive was the belief that Jews circumcised their victims – retailed by enormously influential writers like John Foxe the martyrologist in his account of Hugh of Lincoln, whom the Jews 'first had circumcised, & then deteined a whole yeere in custodie, intending to crucifie him' – that Menasseh ben Israel, the Dutch rabbi who sought from Cromwell the readmission of the Jews in 1656, had at considerable length in his *Vindiciae Judaeorum* refut-ed this claim; after all, Menasseh argued, since circumcision signified conversion to Judaism, it doesn't make any sense for Jews first to turn a boy into a Jew and then kill him. Nonetheless, William Prynne, Menasseh's most stalwart adversary, continued to insist in the 'Second Part' of his *Demurrer of the Jews* (London, 1656) that the Jews of England had engaged in 'circumcising and crucifying Christian children'.

The English chronicles that Prynne drew upon for his information – chronicles that circulated widely in late sixteenth century England – were full of such accounts. One of the more remarkable concerns a circumcision that turned into a total castration: D'Blossiers Tovey, who also drew upon these sources, describes how, during the reign of King John, the Jews

> began soon, again, to be calumniated, as Crucifyers of Children, false coiners, and Emasculators; so far that, in the fourth year of this King, one Bonefand, a Jew of Bedford was indicted, not for Circumcising, but tota[l]ly cutting off the Privy Member of one Richard, the Nephew of Robert de Sutton.

For the record, Bonefand, we learn, 'pleaded not guilty, and was honourably acquitted', raising the interesting question of how, given the medical evidence, the case could ever have been successfully prosecuted.

When we turn to one of Shakespeare's main sources for the 'pound of flesh' narrative we find a clear precedent for the argument that a Jew considers the possibility of castrating the Christian. In Alexander Silvayn's *The Orator*, translated into English in 1596, we read of 'a Jew, who would for his debt have a pound of flesh of a Christian': asking *'what a matter were it then, if I should cut off his privie members, supposing that the same would altogether weigh a just pound?'*

The threat embodied in these lines proved far too disturbing for the Victorian editor H.H. Furness to reproduce in his important Variorum edition of *The Merchant of Venice*. In a deliberate act of textual castration, Furness changes the line from 'cut off his privie members' to 'cut off his [head], supposing that the same would weigh a just pound'. This makes little sense, no matter how light-headed his victim might be, since in the very next sentence the Jew continues, 'Or else his head'. Furness's textual intervention immediately influenced subsequent editions of the play and its sources; a year after his Variorum was published, for example, Homer Sprague would write 'head' (without Furness's brackets) in his popular school edition of the play. Disturbingly, the bowdlerisation of this source had deflected critical attention away from that part of the play that touches upon alleged ritual Jewish practices.

For Shylock to take the knife to Antonio's privy members would be to threaten circumcision (and symbolically conversion) since it is a ritual whose complex function is to separate Jew from non-Jew, and Jewish men from Jewish women. Only through the male could this covenant be transmitted, which helps explain why Jewish daughters like Jessica and Abigail can so easily cross the religious lines that divide their fathers from the dominant Christian community; their difference is not physically inscribed in their flesh. Given Antonio's anxious assertion of difference in terms of both gender and faith a potential circumcision is understandably threatening.

Before turning to what Elizabethans thought about circumcision, it is worth indicating what their actual experience of it was. With the exception of a handful of infants circumcised by the radical Puritan group led by John Traske around 1620, there is no evidence that circumcisions took place in early modern England. Nor would there have been many opportunities at home or abroad, for Elizabethans to see a circumcised penis. This did not mean that they were not curious. Contemporaries of Shakespeare, in particular some of the intrepid Elizabethan travellers, expressed considerable interest in observing this ritual, and several of their detailed accounts survive. It is unlikely that Shakespeare ever witnessed this rite, though he could have been familiar with all aspects of this practice not only through biblical injunctions, but also from reactions in contemporary sources, such as *Purchas His Pilgrimage* (London, 1613), or the stories in circulation that led to the publication of such accounts.

Those Elizabethans who did witness circumcisions have left accounts that emphasise the child's transition from his mother to the community of men. Fynes Morison thus observes that at 'the dore, the wemen [were] not permited to enter, [and] delivered the Childe to the Father'. And Thomas Coryate observes that the final act of the ritual is a presentation of the foreskin to the mother, symbolising the cut between her and her son as he enters the community of men: the 'prepuce that was cut off was carried to the Mother, who keepeth it very preciously as a thing of worth'. Both Morison and Thomas Coryate are struck by the practice of *mezizah*, in which the circumciser sucks the blood from the penis of the circumcised infant. Morison writes that 'the Rabby cutt off his prepuce, and (with leave be it related for clearing of the Ceremony) did with his mouth sucke the blood of his privy part, and after drawing and spitting out of much blood, sprinckled a red powder upon the wounde'. In a comment that reveals just how complex the gendering of Jewish circumcision was, Morison is clearly uncomfortable with describing *mezizah* – 'with leave be it related' – a practice for which he can find no Biblical authority.

Thomas Coryate, who had long sought to observe a circumcision, finally had his wish granted in Constantinople, at the 'house of a certaine English Jew, called Amis, borne in the Crootched Friers in London, who hath two sisters more of his owne Jewish Religion, Commorant in Galata, who were likewise borne in the same place'. He expresses no surprise, it might be noted, that Amis was a Jew who had spent 30 years in a London district that many scholars assume was free of Jews. Coryate's description is worth quoting at length:

> [D]ivers Jewes came into the room, and sung certain Hebrew Songs; after which the child was brought to his Father, who sate downe in a chaire, and placed the child being now eight days old in his lap. The whole company being desirous that we Christians should observe the ceremonie, called us to approach neere to the child. And

when we came, a certaine other Jew drawing forth a little instrument made not unlike those smal [sic] Cissers that our Ladies and Gentlewomen doe much use, did with the same cut off the Prepuce or fore-skinne of the child, and after a very strange manner, unused (I believe) of the ancient Hebrewes, did put his mouth to the child's yard, and sucked up the bloud. All his Privities (before he came into the roome) were besprinkled with a kind of powder, which after the Circumciser had done his businesse, was blowed away by him, and another powder cast on immediately. After he had dispatched his worke, the same also after his worke was done, he tooke a little strong wine that was held in a goblet by a fellow that stood neere him, and powred it into the child's mouth to comfort him in the middest of his paines, who cried out very bitterly; the paine being for the time very bitter indeed, though it will be (as they told me) cured in the space of foure and twentie houres. Those of any riper yeeres that are circumcised (as it too often commeth to passe, that Christians that turne Turkes) as at fortie or fiftie yeeres of age, doe suffer great paine for the space of a moneth.

Circumcision was usually identified as a Jewish (or Turkish) custom, though Elizabethans who travelled to Africa were also aware that other cultures practised this rite; Samuel Purchas, for example, argued strenuously that the practice of circumcision by the Egyptians pre-dated the Jews. While the anthropological interest of explorers like Purchas and Jobson helped demystify the practice as an exclusively Jewish one, for many, if not most, Christian men the act was still seen as one that marked men as Jewish. Thomas Thorowgood's *Jews in America* (London, 1660) is representative. In arguing that Native Americans were Jewish, having descended from the Ten Lost Tribes, Thorowgood's first evidence is that they practise circumcision:

> I begin with Circumcision, and justly, for it is the mainest point of Jewish Religion, saith Bishop Montague ... [after citing many testimonies to this effect he concludes that] it will doubtless seem probable also, that many Indian Nations are of Judaicall race, seeing this frequent and constant Character of Circumcision, so singularlie fixed to the Jews, is to be found among them.

It comes as no surprise that Jews would be prosecuted for this act alone, not simply as part of a more complex ritual murder. Tovey recounts in *Anglis Judaica* 'the famous Trial of Jacob of Norwich, and Accomplices, for Stealing away, and Circumcising, a Christian childe':

> The Case was this. As a Boy, of the five Years old, was playing in the Street, several Jews seiz'd and convey'd him to the House of the aforesaid Jacob; where they kept him a Day and a Night; and then binding his Eyes with a Napkin, cut off his Foreskin, which they put into a Bason, and covered with Sand; after which, blowing the Sand with their Mouths, till they found it again, (the Person, who first discover'd it being call'd Jurnepin,) the Boy, from him, was order'd to be call'd Jurnepin, and declar'd a Jew.

Of particular interest in this story is the question of the reversibility of the act, since circumcision is seen as determining the male child's religious identity. At the trial 'one Maud ... depos'd, that, after the Boy was taken Home again, several Jews came to her, and bade her have a care how she gave him any Swines Flesh to eat, for he was a Jew'. Popular interest in the same stemmed from the denouement: the boy's foreskin 'by some Art or other, had been made to grow again'. So complex were the religious and political implications of this action that the authorities were at loss to determine proper jurisdiction:

> The Matter therefore appearing doubtful; and the Bishops protesting, that, as Baptism and Circumcision were Matters

of Faith, the Cause ought to be tried in their Courts, the Parliament consented to part with it.

For Elizabethans, circumcising fell into the same category of baptism (which replaced it) in determining one's religious identity. As Samuel Purchas put it, through circumcision one 'is thus made a Jew'.

One of the most widely circulated and humorous identifications of circumcision with castration can be found in the dedicatory poems prefaced to Thomas Coryate's *Coryates Crudities*, published in 1611. These poems were apparently inspired both by Coryate's narrative and by one of the several scenes depicted on the title page which shows a Jew, knife in hand, in hot pursuit of the fleeing Coryate. While this woodcut no doubt relates to Coryate's celebrated escape from a crowd of hostile Jews of Venice whom he had sought to convert, there is no evidence anywhere in the text that these Jews bore weapons against him. Evidently, the woodcut is based either on the artist's imagination or on Coryate's no doubt embellished personal account; in either case the prefatory poems return to this image repeatedly. The knife-wielding Jew, however, threatens not death but circumcision, for Laurence Whitaker:

> Thy Cortizen clipt thee, ware Tom, I advise thee,
> And flie from the Jewes, lest they circumcise thee.

Hugh Holland writes in a similar vein (comparing Coryate to Hugh Broughton, the great Elizabethan Hebraist and converter of Jews):

> He more prevaild against the'excoriate Jewes
> Than Broughton could, or twenty more such Hughs.
> And yet but for one pettie poore misprision,
> He was nigh made one of the Circumcision.

And in another couplet Holland again draws attention to the danger to Coryate's foreskin:

> Ulysses hear no Syren sing: nor Coryate
> The Jew, least his praepuce might prove excoriate.

Given the absence of textual evidence for a Jew wielding a knife threatening to attack Coryate, let alone circumcise him, it is at least worth considering whether the memory of Shylock, knife in hand, threatening Antonio, coloured either the artist's rendition or these poets' commendatory descriptions of the woodcut.

• • • • •

Two other and interconnected aspects of circumcision found in early modern English texts cast additional light on Shylock's threatened cut of Antonio's flesh. The first concerns why, if this is indeed threatened circumcision, Shylock ultimately chooses to cut the pound of flesh from near Antonio's heart. An explanation for this shift can be found in a series of Old and New Testament discussions of circumcision and the commentary and sermon literature that grew out of them.

John Donne's sermon on the 'Feast of the Circumcision' clarifies how the circumcised *heart* of the Christian has replaced the circumcised *penis* of the Jew. For Donne, quite simply, 'the principall dignity of this Circumcision, was, that it ... prefigured ... that Circumcision of the heart'; the 'Jewish Circumcision was an absurd and unreasonable thing, if it did not intimate and figure the Circumcision of the heart'. To circumcise a penis was, frankly, too 'obscene a thing, to be brought into the fancy of so many Women, so many young Men, so many Strangers to other Nations, as might bring the Promise and Covenant it selfe into scorne'. So strong was the Christian revulsion against circumcision (which some radical Protestants on the continent and in England began to practise) that Martin Luther would angrily observe 'I hope I shall never be so stupid as to be circumcised. I would rather cut off the left breast of my Catherine and of all women'.

John Donne, who apparently believed in a version of the myth of ritual murder, writes elsewhere of his belief that Jews observed a 'barbarous and inhumane custome' of

> always keep[ing] in readiness the blood of some Christian, with which they anoint the body of any that dyes amongst them, with these words, 'if Jesus Christ were the Messias, then may the blood of this Christian availe thee to salvation'.

For Donne, with the coming of Christ the thing signified – 'the spiritual Circumcision of our hearts' – happily replaced the 'mutilation' of the Jews' crude signifier. Viewed in light of this familiar exegetical tradition, Shylock's decision to cut a pound of flesh from near Antonio's heart could be seen as the height of literalism that informs all of his actions in the play, a literalism that when imitated by Portia leads to his demise. Shylock will literally circumcise his Christian adversary in that part of his body where Christians are figuratively circumcised: their hearts.

Donne's sermon also provides insight into a related issue: 'uncircumcision'. At the conclusion of his sermon Donne demands of his congregation that they ask of themselves 'whether those things which you heard now, have brought you to this Circumcision, and made you better this yeare than you were the last, and find you not under the same uncircumcision still'. This concept of 'uncircumcision' is also grounded in the notion that in a post-Judaic world, circumcision is to be understood metaphorically, an act of self-renewal. After Shylock's circumcising threat against Antonio fails, the punishment Antonio begs of the court for his enemy – baptism – becomes, ironically, an act of uncircumcision performed upon the Jew.

The threat to cut Antonio's 'flesh' also suggests that Shylock, like Bonefand (mentioned above, p. 142), is a

Jewish 'emasculator', one who somehow threatens to transform Antonio from a man to something other and less than a man. The principle of inversion or substitution that operates throughout the play obtains here as well. The threatened feminisation occurs within a larger context in which the dominant early modern Christian culture projected its fear of feminisation by investing the Jewish male with female qualities. A good example occurs in Edwin Sandy's *A Relation of the State of Religion* (1605) where, writing about religion in Italy, Sandy draws an analogy between Jews and female prostitutes, who 'sucke' on those of lesser social station, only to be 'sucked' by those more powerful.

Still others advanced the peculiar argument that Jewish men menstruated (a belief that seems to have derived from assertions about *foder Judaicus*, the awful smell of the Jew, addressed most directly in Sir Thomas Browne's essay on whether Jews stink). While there are a number of such accounts in sixteenth-century Spanish writers, there are fewer in English texts. One example appears in Thomas Calvert's *Diatriba of the Jews' Estate*, where Calvert causally relates Jewish male menstruation to the practice of 'Child-Crucifying among the Jews'. Calvert reports third-hand that the Jews

> can never bee healed of this shamefull punishment where-with [they] are so vexed, but onely by Christian blood. This punishment so shameful they say is, that Jews, *men*, as well as females, are punished *curso menstruo sanguinis*, with a very frequent Bloud-fluxe.

Not entirely convinced, Calvert chooses to 'leave it to the learned to judge and determine by writers or Travellers, whether this be true or no, either that they have a month-ly Flux of Blood, or a continuall mal-odoriferous breath'.

The Jewish male body was, then, a leaky body, and as such a suspect one. Again and again the Jewish man was constructed as a creature of bodily fluids: spitting, stinking, menstruating, smearing faeces on Christian symbols, constantly falling into privies. In their androgyny, monstrosity, implication in local and unsolvable crimes, apostasy, secret rituals, 'Sabbath', and interest in sorcery and magic, the Jews resembled the other great marginal and threatening social group of the early modern period: witches. Indeed, some of the earliest individuals prosecuted for sorcery in England were Jews. There may well be a relationship between the banishment of the Jews from England at the close of the thirteenth century and the emergence of witch prosecutions shortly thereafter; certainly, there is a common thread in monstrous allegations, torture, and executions to which both groups were subjected in early modern Europe.

• • • • •

The social anxieties that circulated through Shakespeare's play have had an afterlife over the course of the next four centuries, in large measure because the play continues to give voice to recurrent cultural problems of nation, race, and gender. The anxieties I am describing are not merely English ones, and as Shakespeare's popularity spread over the next two centuries we find *The Merchant of Venice* intervening in other cultural and national crises. I described in my lecture earlier this week – 'Shakespeare and the "Jew Bill" of 1753' – how *The Merchant of Venice* entered into English political discourse during the heady days of the Jewish Nationalisation Act. In this century there have been many more examples, for example, when, shortly after Kristallnacht in 1938, *The Merchant of Venice* was broadcast for propagandistic ends over the German airwaves; productions of the play followed in Lubeck (1938), Berlin (1940), Vienna (1943), and elsewhere in Nazi territory. Of course, while the sinister aspects of a usurious Shylock were appealing to the Nazis, the successful intermarriage of Jessica and Lorenzo was not. The play was frequently altered to accommodate different kinds of national and religious beliefs in this century. Barry Kyle's 1980 production of *The Merchant of Venice* in Israel, for example, completely omitted Shylock's conversion to Christianity. And in the United States, the play has long been banned from many high school curricula, and is the source of controversy virtually every time it is staged.

The cultural anxieties, the deep, disturbing myths about Jews, about otherness, that Shakespeare raises in the play, continue to trouble us. As long as cultural 'difference' – of race, of gender, of religion, of nationality – continue to be the basis of social antagonism and prejudice, *The Merchant of Venice* will ironically fulfil that dictum, that Shakespeare's plays 'were not of any age, but for all time'.

NOTES

1. This paper was delivered as the annual Parkes Lecture in 1992 and published as a pamphlet by the University of Southampton.

7

Radical Identities? Native Americans, Jews and the English Commonwealth[1]

CLAIRE JOWITT

Why were the native Americans represented as Jews by Thomas Thorowgood in the 1650s and 1660s? What special status did a Jewish history and culture give to Amerindian peoples? And what motives would an English Puritan theologian have had for such an extraordinary identification? These are the questions that this chapter addresses. The texts discussed here are the two editions of Thomas Thorowgood's *Jewes in America, Or, Probabilities that the Americans are of that Race* whose publication straddled both the crucial date of 1656 in the apocalyptic calendar and the years of Oliver Cromwell's 'reign'.[2] First printed in 1650, and republished in 1660, almost at the moment of Charles II's triumphant return to England, both editions of *Jewes in America* are concerned with the question of the identity of the Native Americans. Thorowgood argues that Native Americans were descended from the Lost Tribes of Israel who had wandered into America many centuries before and had since lived in isolation from other Jewish communities with the result that much of their original religion and culture had been lost. In both texts Thorowgood uses his analysis of the ancestry of Amerindian peoples to support the territorial interests of the Protestant English state. There are, however, major differences between these two editions. These differences will be read here as a reflection of the changing political circumstances in England throughout this decade. More specifically, this paper argues that Thorowgood's representations of Native Americans as 'primitive' in 1650 and 'degenerate' by 1660 were motivated by the disappointment he felt at the failure of the English Commonwealth. By 1660 the territory and peoples of America have become implicated in this failure as Thorowgood creates a history for the Old Testament figure of Nimrod – who he argues was the original coloniser of America – who can be seen as an analogy of the Protector. He also reads Amerindian conversion to Spanish Catholicism as further provocation for the Puritan missionary to arrest what he saw as the degenerate influence of Romanish practices. I argue that, in 1660, anti-Spanish foreign policies and the identification of militant Jesuits as the perpetrators of the English revolution were strategies used by an apprehensive and disillusioned Republican sympathiser as he attempted to both come to terms with the failure of the Republic and protect himself from a newly restored and potentially avenging monarchical gaze.

APOCALYPSE AND CONVERSION: INTERPRETATIONS OF JEWISH IDENTITY

Thorowgood's identification of a Jewish origin for Native American peoples was by no means a new idea. Spanish commentators, ever since Columbus' first footfall on the islands off the coast of America in 1492, had perceived similarities between the culture of the peoples they encountered and the Jews. The significance of these resemblances was repeatedly debated from the fifteenth to the seventeenth centuries. Spanish ecclesiastical historians who discussed the alleged 'Israelitish' origin of the Amerindians were divided into two schools of thought. One hailed the new subjects of Spain as the progeny of Israel, while the other conceived of apparent Hebrew practices and customs among the inhabitants of the New World as having a satanic origin.[3] As Barbara Anne Simon details in her 1836 digest of Viscount Kingsborough's nine-volume *Antiquities of Mexico*, 'Satan had counterfeited in this People (whom he had chosen for himself), the history, manners, customs, traditions, and expectations of the Hebrews, in order that their minds might thus be rendered inaccessible to the faith, which he foresaw the church would in due time introduce among them'.[4] In his 1607 text *Origen de los Indios* the Spanish ecclesiastic Gregorio Garcia strongly supported a Hebrew ancestry for the Amerindians. He also argued for the influence of Satan on Native American culture. In reply to an enquiry about what had become of the Hebrew tongue which the descendants of the Ten Tribes were supposed to possess, he asserted that in the first place the language had gradually changed in keeping with the universal experience among other races; secondly, there were many traces of Hebrew still remaining in the American languages; and thirdly, Satan had prompted Amerindians to learn new tongues in order to prevent them from receiving Catholic instruction. Fortunately, according to Garcia, missionaries had become acquainted with these new and strange dialects and thus had outwitted Satan.[5]

In Garcia's text we can see an amalgam of what seem to be mutually exclusive arguments. American natives were represented both as 'Israelitish' – awarding them a 'civilised' status – and simultaneously seen as contaminated by Satan. Garcia's text did not attempt to reconcile these contradictions within his representation of Amerindian peoples, rather he used both arguments to substantiate his belief in the moral mission and legitimacy of the Spanish conversion impulse. As we shall see, Thomas Thorowgood's *Jewes in America* also conflated similarly contradictory arguments. He combined the belief in a shared ancestry between Amerindians and English Puritans with an argument for the 'racial' superiority of English over American peoples.

Thorowgood's texts were also influenced by later Spanish writers. By the mid-seventeenth century some ecclesiastics had begun to question the moral and divine sanction for the Spanish presence in the New World. Bartoleme de las Casas, a Spanish missionary and Antonio de Montesinos, alias Aaron Levy – a Jew – both argued for a Jewish genealogy for Amerindians and used this theory as part of their denunciation of Spanish treatment of native peoples.[6] If Amerindians were of Hebrew descent and their migration took place before the advent of Christianity then the Spanish system of encomienda and the atrocities perpetrated under it were doubly iniquitous. The Spanish had based their conquest policies on the papal bulls and briefs of 1452 which had granted them a broad combination of privileges and rights in the New World in exchange for promoting missionary activity. But these bulls had assumed that the conquered people would have had some previous contact with Catholicism and were either ignoring the true faith or actively opposing missionary activity. A Hebrew ancestry that was traced back to a time before Christ revealed the inaccuracy of the conquistadors' arguments. It meant, of course, that the Amerindians could not possibly have had any association with Christianity and therefore could not be deliberately neglecting Catholicism. Moreover, it was also argued that a Hebrew origin, in spite of the regression that centuries of Amerindian isolation had engendered, must modify Spanish Thomist's arguments for Amerindians status as either 'natural children' or 'natural slaves'.[7] An original

Hebrew culture, however debased by the time of the Spanish conquest, revealed the application of such terminology to be misguided. Amerindians were not 'naturally' inferior; rather, according to las Casas, they had endured an unfortunate isolation which in no way precluded their status as free subjects of the Castilian crown.

Thomas Thorowgood's successive editions of *Jewes in America* were undoubtedly indebted to this specifically Catholic and Spanish missionary debate. But Thorowgood's texts were similarly served by a Puritan polemic concerning the imminent end of the world. In the writings of the Puritan divines from the reign of Elizabeth I until the days of Cromwell there was a growing conviction – derived from Paul in Romans II, John in Revelations 16:12, and the great Prophets of Israel, Isaiah and Ezekiel – that the whole nation of the Jews would be converted to Christ and become a Protestant Christian people in the Last Days. Throughout the late sixteenth and early seventeenth centuries European Protestant theologians had suggested timetables for this approaching apocalypse. These calculations pointed to the years 1650–56 for the destruction of the anti-Christ, the gathering of the Gentiles, the conversion of the Jews and the return to Palestine.[8] In the wake of these apocalyptic timetables, in the generations leading up to the critical dates between 1650–56 the leitmotif of Jewish identity was awarded a special significance. As 'the Jew' was believed to be about to convert, Puritan discourses concentrated upon this imminently expected change in religious status; they then translated it into a metaphor for a wider theological, political and social context.[9] Jewish conversion was a motif that possessed considerable power as it was seen by both radicals and more traditional commentators as a harbinger of the reign of the Saints on earth which was to precede the Second Coming. Scores of pamphlets were produced on the subject by such diverse writers as Mary Carey, Comenius, Archbishop

Ussher and Benjamin Worsley.[10] Some of these texts were addressed to particular groups of practising Jews, for example the comparatively large Jewish community in Amsterdam, and attempted to persuade them to convert.[11] The shared currency between all these writers was that they constructed Jews as proto–Christians.[12]

However, in the historical matrix of 1649, in the work of the Orientalist and lawyer John Sadler, and more conspicuously in the texts of the Leveller Gerrard Winstanley, new and radical appropriations of Jewish identity emerged. In his 1649 text *Rights of the Kingdom*, though nominally concerned with the English constitution, Sadler hinted at an 'Israelitish' ancestry for the English. Sadler catalogued numerous agreements between English and Jewish laws and customs, but in the end did not commit himself to any definite theory concerning the first settlement of England.[13] Winstanley's texts were much less equivocal in their conclusions. He constructed England as the site of New Israel, and represented both the people and country of England as God's chosen people and place for the coming millennia.

In 1649 Gerrard Winstanley appropriated the motif of Jewish identity to support his radical political beliefs. Winstanley in *The True Levellers Standard Advanced* used allusions to Old Testament Israel as metaphors of contemporary England.[14] He provided a universal history lesson from the time of the Creation to the English Civil War in which the emergence of the twin evils of monarchism and the law served to oppress and enslave the 'Spirit Reason' (which was the term used to describe the essence of humankind's connection with God, the 'great Creator Reason').[15] Winstanley argued that the presence of the Spirit Reason within humanity made any person self-sufficient, 'a perfect Creature of himself'.[16] In Winstanley's history lesson the Spirit Reason, also called Jacob, had been overcome and oppressed by the flesh, or Esau, 'which is

Covetousness and Pride'.[17] The results of this enslavement were monarchy and law.

Winstanley made a direct parallel between the history of oppression of the Israelites and that of the English:

> This outward Teaching and Ruling power, is the Babylonish yoke laid upon Israel of old, under Nebuchadnezzar; and so Successively from that time, the Conquering Enemy, have still laid these yokes upon Israel to keep Jacob down; And the last enslaving Conquest which the enemy got over Israel, was the Norman over England; and from that time, Kings, Lords, Justices, Bayliffs, and the violent bitter people that are Free-holders are and have been Successively. The Norman Bastard William himself, his Colonels, Captains, inferior Officers, and Common Soldiers, who still are from that time to this day in pursuite of that victory, Imprisoning, Robbing, and killing the poor enslaved English Israelites.[18]

Significantly, this quotation reveals that it was not merely that the oppression of the English under the Normans mirrored the suffering of the Jews under their Babylonian captors, but Winstanley asserted a direct line of descent for the English from the Israelites.[19] William the Conqueror's occupation of England and his introduction of Norman laws and culture were not only analogous to the imposition of Babylonian laws and culture upon the Hebrews, they were also the last in the series of oppressions inflicted upon the race of Jacob, the younger brother, to which the English and the Israelites both belonged.

This identification of the English nation with the Hebrews pivoted on the notion of a shared history of oppression. Winstanley imagined the oppressed Israelites to have been matched in the landless, disenfranchised English nation which had been overrun by a foreign conqueror. Moreover, he argued for a process of decline from an original state of Arcadia where Man and Reason had been united. He sought to embrace a world before the introduction of the tyrannous concepts of property and law and he identified this arcadian world as Ancient Israel. What was so radical about Winstanley's text was that it described Jewish identity as having more in common with Leveller principles than Protestantism. The recognition of the English nation in terms of a Hebraic identity had become for him a crucial factor for substantiating and legitimising arguments for the common ownership of property.

SHARED ANCESTORS? PROTESTANT TERRITORIAL INTERESTS IN AMERICA

What were the cultural and political resonances of the appropriation and imposition of a Jewish identity onto Amerindian peoples by English early modern writers? Thomas Thorowgood's text *Jewes in America* was first published in 1650 and then republished in a substantially modified new edition in 1660. Rather than constructing his own English history as Jewish, Thorowgood, as the title of his text suggests, imposed this identity upon the Native Americans. Like Winstanley, Thorowgood also imagined a non-Jewish people as 'Israelitish'. However, as a host of other millenarians had already done and the early Quakers would do in the 1650s, this Puritan writer also intended to convert these 'Jewish' peoples to Christianity.[20] Thorowgood's texts can be seen as a conflation of these two motifs as he both appropriated and imposed a Jewish identity upon a non-Jewish culture whilst combining this with a conversion impulse.

Thorowgood argued that the Amerindians were some of the descendants of the Ten Lost Tribes of Israel. The 1650 edition included a substantial introduction by John Dury, the ecumenical churchman who was involved in many philo-semite projects during the 1630s and 1640s. It also included a post-script by Menasseh ben Israel, the Dutch rabbi who tirelessly campaigned for the readmission of the Jews into England through the 1640s and 1650s.[21] Dury's Prefaces accounted for the textual production of Thorowgood's *Jewes in America*. After reading a manuscript copy of Thorowgood's text, John Dury wrote to Menasseh ben Israel to ask him for a transcript of the story Dury had heard in the Hague which concerned a Jew, Antonio de Montezinos. Whilst travelling in South America, Montezinos claimed to have come across a tribe of Indians in the Cordilleros (Andes) who recited the *Shema*, practised Jewish ceremonies, and were members of the lost tribe of Reuben. This transcript was duly dispatched and appeared as an Appendix to Thorowgood's text.

The main body of the text comprised the following sections. After the several Prefaces, Thorowgood's text was sub-divided into three parts: 'Six several conjectures', which outlined the arguments which Thorowgood believed demonstrated his theory that the Americans were Jewish; then 'Some contrary reasonings removed' which aimed to pre-empt objections to his thesis; and finally 'Earnest desires for hearty endeavours to make them Christian', in which Thorowgood expressed the standard argument of the Christian's moral imperative to convert heathen peoples.

Thorowgood, in his 1650 edition of *Jewes in America*, uses the motif of Jewish identity as an intermediate term between Protestantism and Native American culture. This is most clearly revealed by an hierarchy of terms which Thorowgood established in his text to describe different cultures. Chapter III and Chapter IV of Thorowgood's text discussed what he called the 'customs' of the Americans. 'Customs' could be separated, it seemed, into two distinct categories:

> The rites, fashions, ceremonies, and opinions of the
> Americans are in many things agreeable to the custome of
> the Jewes, not only prophane and common usages, but
> such as be called solemn and sacred.[22]

The word 'custom' functioned therefore as a generic term
for 'rites, fashions, ceremonies and opinions', and these
could be either 'prophane and common' or 'solemn and
sacred'. Significantly, Thorowgood did not state that the
'customs' of the two peoples were exactly the same; rather
the 'customs' were 'agreeable', which implied resemblance
rather than duplication. In contrast, when Thorowgood
described the Christian duty of colonial settlers, he used a
noticeably different term to describe their English culture.
In the third section of *Jewes in America* Thorowgood offered
motivation to Christian settlers in an attempt to speed up
the process of conversion. He attempted:

> to stirre up and awaken more able inquisitors, to looke after
> the beginning, nature, civilizing, and Gospellizing those
> people, and to cast in my poore mite towards the
> encouragement of our Countrymen in such their pious
> undertaking.[23]

This statement made explicit the aim of Thorowgood's text;
but it is the juxtaposition of the terms 'civilizing' and
'gospellizing' that reveals the hierarchical nature of the
relationship between the English and the Americans which
is embedded in *Jewes in America.*

Early modern usage of the term 'culture' was complex.
From the end of the sixteenth century until the nineteenth
century the main sense of 'culture' was to mean 'human
development' especially in relation to an earlier connota-
tion of husbandry, for example in 1605 Bacon describes 'the
culture and manurance of minds' and in 1651 Hobbes
wrote of 'a culture of their minds'. Over this period of time
there were two important changes.[24] Firstly, 'culture'

became a standard metaphor for human growth and secondly, the term widened from a particular process to cover an abstract and general process. These instances all located 'culture' within the mind of individuals or groups; none of them considered that 'culture' could be demonstrated in material terms. By the nineteenth century 'culture' had evolved to mean 'the intellectual side of civilisation', further emphasising the abstract and spiritual predilection. The description of the missionaries' role, as 'civilizing, and Gospellizing', thus accommodated this spiritual and conceptual emphasis in a way that the blanket term 'custom', covering both material and spiritual aspects of people's ways of life, did not. Clearly then, there was an hierarchy of terms with which to describe a way of life of a group of people progressing from 'custom', through 'civilisation', and ultimately to 'culture'. In terms of this index of value, Thorowgood's text denigrated the 'customs' of the Amerindians, and privileged the 'civilizing, and Gospellizing' impetus of the Puritan missionaries. Moreover, when Thorowgood described the correspondence between Native American beliefs and Jewish beliefs, the 'customs' of the Indians were presented as primitive reflections of Judaeo-Christian doctrine. For example:

> they knew of that floud which drowned the world, and that it was sent for the sin of man, especially for unlawfull lust, and there shall never be such a deluge again.[25]

Also:

> the Indians make account the world shall have an end, but not till a great drought come, and as it were a burning of the aire, when the Sunne and Moone shall faile, and lose their shining, thence it is, that in the Eclipses of those two greater Lights, they make such yellings and out-cries, as if the end of all things were upon them.[26]

The representation of the Indians as simple, rustic and

even childlike, with their 'yellings and out-cries', gives a primitivist depiction of the Native Americans as they are imagined to be at an earlier stage of cultural and religious development.

Indeed Amerindians could be seen as 'natural children' who, though they cannot exercise reason in their childhood state, possess the potential to be rational in the future. 'Natural children', according to Spanish Dominican Francisco de Vitoria's text of 1537 *De indis recenter inventis*, were heirs to the state of true reason.[27] As such their possessions could be held in trust until they reached maturity. For de Vitoria maturity entailed, of course, Amerindian conversion to Catholicism. This Catholic argument was subsequently appropriated by Thorowgood to support his specifically Protestant conversion principles. While the text avowedly claimed to describe similarities between Native Americans and Hebrews, the implicit agenda was the converse; similarities between 'customs' were described in a manner that revealed differences between the peoples described. Thorowgood's hierarchy of terms corresponded to a belief in racial superiority: the American Indians possessed 'customs' that were a mere shadow of those of the Hebrews while the puritan missionaries possessed a 'civilisation', a term which placed them at the pinnacle of a racial hierarchy.

The imposition of a Jewish identity onto the Native Americans functioned as a way of bridging the gulf between the culture of the Puritan settlers and that of the Indians. It also had an overt political purpose. The construction of a Jewish identity for the Native American peoples established English territorial interests in the New World. Thorowgood presented the relationship between the different cultures in terms of an exchange of the Puritans' spiritual culture for the Indians' temporal wealth. The Puritans' aims were:

not to satisfie humane curiosity, but to promote mans salvation; not to see diversitie of places, but to seeke and finde, and save lost mankinde. And if such be the aim of our Nation there, we may with more comfort expect and enjoy the externalls of the Indians, when we pay them our spirituals, for their temporals, an easie and yet most glorious exchange.[28]

Elsewhere Thorowgood expressed this policy of exchange even more forcibly:

The inhabitants of the first England, so Versegan calls that part of Germany where our Ancestors came hither with the Saxons and Iutes, derive their Christianity from Iewry – tis but just therefore, *lege talionis*, that we repay what we borrowed, and endeavour their conversion who first acquainted us with the eternall Gospell.[29]

In this case the affiliation, and consequently the exchange, was between the Christians and the Jews. The motif of Jewish identity was being used as an intermediate term with which to connect Native Americans and the English settlers. As the English had a special relationship with the Lost Tribes due to mutual ancestors in Germany then, according to Thorowgood's argument that the Native Americans were Jews, English Puritans could claim that Native Americans shared the same lineage. The construction of a Jewish Amerindian identity was pivotal in this relationship of exchange; the English nation 'owed' a debt to the Jewish nation, and this debt was to be repaid by converting the native Americans to Christianity.

As Thorowgood had represented the American Indians as descendants of the Lost Tribes, with the special relationship with the English nation that this entailed, this could be used as a basis with which to substantiate an English claim to territory in the New World. The common genealogy proved that, as a nation state, England had a

superior claim to territory in the New World than had any
other colonial power. A shared Jewish ancestry between
the English nation and the Native American peoples was
used as an argument to support the territorial interests of
the English state.[30] When discussing the issue of state
formation in early modern Europe Michael Braddick
writes, 'territorial interests may override class interests and
thus result in a degree of autonomy'.[31] In a sense,
Thorowgood's text conformed to this statement; territorial
state interests were deemed so important that differences
in religion between Jew and Christian, previously emphasised by the usage of the hierarchical terms 'civilisation'
and 'custom', were, in the same text, now overridden by
the desire for colonial expansion. In the same way that
Garcia's text of 1607 had married ostensibly mutually
exclusive arguments for a shared heritage between
Spaniards and Amerindians with the belief in a racial
superiority, Thorowgood fused both these positions in
order to justify English expansion. The tension between
these opposing positions was ignored by Thorowgood as
the vindication of English territorial interests was the
paramount concern. Moreover, it should not be forgotten
that in 1650, officially at least, there were no Jews living in
England. This is even more indicative of the strength of
Thorowgood's desire for territorial expansion; a desire so
powerful that he was prepared, momentarily at least,
to construct the Jews as the authoritative primogenitor
from whom Christians had derived their religion. This
potentially radical statement – radical in the same way as
Winstanley's text – was, of course, immediately defused
by Thorowgood's articulation of the Protestants' mission to
convert these Jewish Native Americans.

The identification of the Native Americans as Jews thus
served a dual purpose; it confirmed the English claim for
territory in the New World and, because of the approach of
the apocalyptic years 1650–56, marked the Amerindians as

imminent converts to Protestantism. The final section of this paper will explore the ways in which Thorowgood's text had changed by the time it was re-published in a new edition in 1660, and suggest some reasons for those changes.

CATHOLICS, JEWS AND PURITANS: THE ENGLISH COMMONWEALTH AND REPRESENTATIONS OF AMERINDIANS IN 1660

In 1651 the theologian and historian Hamon L'Estrange had published a text disagreeing with Thorowgood's identification of the Native Americans as descendants of the Lost Tribes of the Jews.[32] L'Estrange provided an alternative history for the Amerindians, arguing for a less specifically Jewish genealogy. Amerindians were descended from Noah and his sons (particularly Shem) whom, he argued, peacefully migrated eastwards. According to L'Estrange, the Native Americans could not be descended from the Lost Tribes because they were placed in captivity under the Babylonians after this migration.

> Thus far I have offered my weak conceptions, first how America may be collected to have bin first planted, not denying the Iewes leave to go into America, but not admitting them to be the chief or prime planters therof; for I am of the opinion, that the American originalls were before the Captivity of the Ten tribes, even from Sems near progeny.[33]

L'Estrange's text offered a cryptographic critique of the role of Cromwell in the immediate past of the Civil War. L'Estrange argued that the movement eastwards of 'Sems near progeny', even into America, took place in a climate of peaceable openness, in a world before Babel, before the tyranny of Nimrod and before the resulting afflictions of civil war and disputes over territory. He wrote, 'I suppose that mankind having then (as we use to say) all the world before them, and room enough, spread, dilated and extended into that same moderate and temperate clymate, Eastward'.[34] Consequently the history of America could be represented as Edenic as it had bypassed the genesis of civil war which L'Estrange's transcription of biblical narrative described as violently splitting the rest of the world into two factions. In this turbulent division we can see an analogy with the political situation of the 1640s. Excluding America, the world was filled with 'so great a swarm of men ... who were like to be infected with continnuall broyles and warres, by the pride, cruelty, insolence, and usurpation of Idolatrous Nimrod'.[35] This representation of the biblical figure Nimrod served as a watermark for L'Estrange's political orientation. The figure of Nimrod can be seen as double-edged: his fabulous reputation as a 'hunter', 'builder' and founder of 'kingdoms' was based on biblical descriptions (Gen.10:8–12). However, the verse 'he began to be a mighty one in the earth' (Gen.10:8; I Chron.1:10) complicates this heroic description as it could mean he was considered the originator of the military state based on arbitrary force.[36] Superficially and surprisingly, it seems, royalist L'Estrange uses the motif of monarchy to condemn the figure of Nimrod. Yet, it is the word 'usurped' that can be seen to be decisive in L'Estrange's description. It is with this word that the analogy with Cromwell is constructed:

> He reigned not as king untill after the Confusion, but when he saw his hopes and purposes dashed, and a solstice of the work, and that now he was arrived at the Hercules Pillars, the nil ultra of his great action and adventure, and could not reach home to say with Nebuchadnezar, Is not this great Babel that I have built? yet he was unwilling to remove from the place where he had erected such a monument to his aspiring mind, but there he meant to stay and

abide, expecting the dawning of another day, and how so
great a wonder and miracle should conclude.[37]

Previously, L'Estrange's praise of the American Indians'
'records of the series and succession of their kings' and the
resulting artifacts of 'goodly buildings, and magnificent
monuments of Antiquity' revealed that it was not the
institution of monarchy that he censured; rather, it was the
'usurpation' of the institution of monarchy and the
foundation of a system of government based on military
coercion for which Nimrod was renowned which was
castigated by the text. L'Estrange created a distinction
within the institution of monarchy. A positive version of
monarchy was located in Edenic America; but his description of a distorted and unnatural monarchy established in
the rest of the world – which the figure of Nimrod with its
correlation to the role of Cromwell suggested – indicated
his political allegiances. Importantly, for L'Estrange,
America was a world that had escaped the turmoil of Babel
and civil war.

In the 1660 edition of *Jewes in America* Thorowgood both
answered the criticisms of Cromwell that L'Estrange
implied and reiterated his belief concerning the indelible
connection between Native Americans, Jews and the
English which L'Estrange had explicitly denied.
Thorowgood utilised the same historical paradigm as
L'Estrange, but provided a different reading of those
biblical characters and events. His description of Nimrod
was much more sympathetic. As in L'Estrange's text, the
figure of Nimrod was analogous to Cromwell, but there
was an attempt, partially at least, as might be expected
from a man that had been connected with the Republic, to
justify Nimrod's rebellion. Nimrod's rebellion was
motivated by 'impatience' with the tedious and
unimaginative patriarchal authority that thwarted his plan
to recolonise Eden.[38] Nimrod was presented as an

adventurous, enterprising colonial explorer who, because
he was dissatisfied with the hegemonic regime, revolted
and took the law into his own hands. Even the project
which Nimrod undertook, to build the Tower of Babel –
traditionally described in purely negative terms – was
presented by Thorowgood as partially explicable. It was
built to

> procure themselves a Sem, a great name to balance the
> potent name of Sem, and secondly to keep the people
> together from being scattered from him, having with him
> both greatnesse, strength and safety.[39]

Thus Babel was represented as a project of defence and as
an attempt to protect Nimrod and his nation from hostile
parties. The Babel project was described as an action of
necessary statesmanship within a context of uneasy
relationships between different peoples and states rather
than as an illegitimate attack upon God's power. Unlike
L'Estrange's text, where Sem was represented as the
original ancestor of the Native Americans, Thorowgood's
text described Sem as the leader of a hostile nation state. In
Thorowgood's text, competition between Sem and Nimrod
for power and authority can be seen as a reflection of the
unease between the emerging nation states of England and
Spain over colonial influence. Though the figure and
actions of Nimrod were not presented as totally legitimate
in this text, he was treated with some sympathy. The
project to recolonise Eden and the uneasy relationship
with the hostile Sem both figure as problems which faced
an emerging nation state as it sought to expand and
consolidate its position within a concert of powers.

However, Thorowgood's choice to include a defence of
Nimrod, a figure habitually associated with an illegitimate
rebellion against the just authority of God, surely figured
as a weak argument for Republicanism. The descriptions of
a stagnant, conservative regime which obstructs Nimrod's

natural ambitions partly redeemed Nimrod and his actions; but the redemption was not complete. This seemed due more to the failure of Nimrod's project rather than the intrinsic iniquity of the scheme itself. This subtle and complex representation of Nimrod was motivated by Thorowgood's attitudes to Cromwellian foreign policy. The political events against which Thorowgood's text were constructed were the strategies by which Oliver Cromwell attempted to further English territorial interests in the Caribbean, a series of policies known as the Western Design.

On 5 October 1655 war officially broke out between England and Spain. On 25–26 October in that year, Cromwell's Council of State framed the Protectorate's defence in a document entitled, *A Declaration of His Highness, By the Advice of his Council; Setting Forth ... the Justice of their Course Against Spain.*[40] This document described Spain's violation of both English and Amerindian natural rights. The Spaniards' despotic claims that they possessed 'the sole Signiory of that New World' were shown to be intolerable. The Declaration demonstrated that the Spaniards' cruelties against the *jus gentium* and the *jus naturale* of the English and natives 'in whose blood (the Spanish) have founded their Empire' demanded revenge.[41]

The military and naval Protestant expedition which Cromwell optimistically sent to capture Caribbean Spanish colonies in 1655 was trounced on the island of Hispaniola. The expedition only managed to avoid total defeat with the seizure of Jamaica, an acquisition of dubious economic benefit.[42] The failure of Cromwell's campaign became an important factor in rallying opposition to the Protector's rule as the regime seemed to be over-extending itself in both foreign and domestic spheres. At home his imposition of the rule of the Major-Generals had proved an unpopular policy and, when coupled with the failure of the

Western Design abroad, became a turning point in contemporary attitudes towards Cromwell. Theologians and
Commonwealthmen alike began to question the role of the
Protector, the godly basis for the Republic, and the reasons
behind its desire for enlargement. Thorowgood's text not
only engages with Hamon L'Estrange's royalist encoding
of the systems of government and peoples in America but
it also reveals his attitude to Empire.

In the 1660 edition of *Jewes in America* Thorowgood's
attitude to America can be seen as a reflection of the disappointment and disillusion he felt at the failure of the
Commonwealth. America was represented as a refuge for
the godly from 'not the violence of enemies so much as our
own national and personal sins'. The threat now came not
from the 'violence of former innovations' of Laudian
practices, perceived as quasi-Catholic by Puritans in the
1630s and 1640s; rather, the danger came from the 'false-
hood and hypocrisy, the backsliding and apostasy, the
avarice and selfishness, the pride and security' which had
accompanied the last years of the 'reign' of Cromwell and
which 'do portend no less than a deluge of destruction'
unless the English nation repent.[43]

Yet Thomas Thorowgood's 1660 edition of *Jewes in
America* still embraced an expansionist foreign policy.
Thorowgood disagreed with royalist L'Estrange's version
of the migration of the generations of Sem into America.
Rather, Thorowgood argued that there was no distinction
between the peoples that colonised America and those that
lived in the rest of the world. According to Thorowgood's
reasoning America had not bypassed the inception of what
L'Estrange called 'the continnuall broyles and warres'
which raged through all the world except America.[44] In
Thorowgood's text, America was just as much a part of
this post-lapsarian world as anywhere else. In fact
Thorowgood argued for the opposite as he represented the
Native Americans as particularly degenerate. In the 1660

edition of his text as well as expressing his beliefs of racial superiority with an etymological hierarchy moving from 'custom' to 'civilisation' as in the 1650 *Jewes in America*, Thorowgood now presented the Native Americans as barely human.

> When I was directed, at houres diverted from other studies, to look into the books that write of the New World, and saw therin the most degenerate spectacles of humane nature in those poor Indians, little of man was found in them, beside shape, and body, few impressions of reason were left, fewer of religion, I had no thought, at first to observe among them any semblance of Judaicall rites, and customes, but by some instinct, or providence upon further reading, and consideration, such cogitations increased in mee, that those, now despicable, and forlorne people might long agoe have had some other kind of being and condition, and yet may happily, by divine appointment, be restored and recovered.[45]

It is the degeneracy of the Americans, their 'despicable condition', that Thorowgood dwells upon. In this later text the American Indians are represented now as exhibiting only a 'semblance of Judaicall rites and customes'. This alteration in the representation of Native Americans from 'primitives' in 1650 to 'degenerates' in 1660 was motivated by the disappointment Thorowgood felt with the failure of the Commonwealth and, in particular, with Cromwell's betrayal of his Republican principles. The 'deluge of destruction', as Thorowgood so pessimistically described the situation of 1660 in England, seemed to have travelled across the Atlantic ocean to be repeated in the New World where Amerindians were mindlessly described as succumbing en masse to Catholic blandishments. These joint bogeys of Romanish practices and Indian credulity become the focus of Thorowgood's ire in his chapter, 'The Indians docible nature and the Spaniard's Cruelties'.[46] This

representation of Native American degeneracy can be seen
as a comment upon the contamination Thorowgood
believed they had received from contact with the
Catholics. American Indian contact with the Spanish and
their resulting idiotic conversion – 'that blinde, easy and
Spanish way (so much magnified in the Records of Charles
the Fifth, one of their Priests baptizing 70,000 of them,
another 30,000, a third 10,000)' – acted as a spur to the
orthodox Puritan to join in what Thorowgood saw as a
holy war against Catholicism.⁴⁷ In 1660 the native
Americans were represented as 'degenerate' instead of
'primitive' precisely because of Amerindian contact with
Catholicism; consequently Thorowgood's Puritan mission
to 'restore' and 'recover' the Indians became much more
urgent. As in the 1650 edition of *Jewes in America*, in 1660
Thorowgood continued to construct the Jew as an intermediate term between Puritan English colonial interest
and Spanish imperial designs. Because of Native American
contact with Catholicism, according to Thorowgood, the
affinities between the Indians and the Jews had become a
mere 'semblance' and it was the duty of the godly Puritan
to stem this tide of degeneracy.⁴⁸

In the critical months following Charles II's return to
England as monarch, it is impossible not to see such
marked usages of the word 'restoration' as politically motivated. Thomas Thorowgood dedicated the 1660 edition of
his text to the newly restored monarch. The dedication
functioned as a plea for tolerance towards a subject who
might have appeared, as a member of the assembly of
divines appointed by Parliament in 1643, to have been less
than outspoken in his previous support of the monarchical
cause. Couched in terms of an appeal for forbearance
towards those who were 'driven from their affection to
Episcopacy' by 'former innovations' (Laudian practices),
nonetheless, his request that 'your Highnesse will follow
the example of Great King James, who did equally love and

honour the learned and Grave men of both Opinions, and left the Councel to his Royal Successor, so to be beneficial to the Ministry' served as an apology for his own part in the ousting of the monarch.[49] The dedication to the new king can be seen as being politically expedient. In the confused months following the Restoration when nobody knew whether the Declaration of Breda, where the monarch collectively forgave the English nation – except the named regicides – for executing his father, would be upheld, it was not surprising to find Thorowgood attempting to shore up his own position.[50] Within this plea for royal forgiveness there seemed to be a desire to deflect monarchical displeasure from oneself by highlighting the guilt of someone else. Thus the blame for the Revolution was laid firmly at the feet of the Catholics: 'the hearts, and heads, and hands of the Jesuites have contrived and wrought these distractions in your Kingdomes'.[51]

This animosity towards Catholics in England was perfectly consistent with Thorowgood's attitudes to Spanish Catholics in the New World. In both situations it is Catholicism that is demonised as the real threat. Consequently, Puritan theologians like Thorowgood were represented as innocent of the charge of provoking the Revolution, and Native Americans were represented as Jews as a way of establishing the pre-eminence of an English claim to territory in the New World. Both at home and abroad, Catholicism was presented as the threat to the English nation. And in both cases these representations can be seen as a retreat to an intellectual, theological and political conservatism.

Thorowgood's representation of the Native Americans as Jews was an attempt on the part of a Puritan writer to claim territory for his country. The description of Native Americans as 'acceptable' Jews figured as a rhetorical strategy of a colonial discourse that was incapable of describing an alien culture on its own terms. Native

American culture was translated into a Jewish culture so that it could be understood – as inferior of course – by the hegemonic discourse of Puritanism. It was the same partisan discourse that in 1660 sought to provide a critique of the recent past. Thorowgood identified the Catholics, more specifically the militant Jesuits, the secret army of the Catholic Church, as the agitators who conspired against Charles I. Moreover, America was represented as the new terrain upon which to wage the perpetual war against Catholicism. According to Thorowgood, Catholics caused the Revolution in England and they could now be punished for their sins by avenging Puritans in America.

The aggressive foreign policy against Spain that Thorowgood supported in *Jewes in America* in 1660 was designed to distract attention from and cover the past of a Puritan and Republican sympathiser. Assertive foreign policies were a safe political topic in the early days following the Restoration. Also, and perhaps this was what was so subtle about Thorowgood's text, the author never retracted his Republican sympathies. The very foreign policy that he so dogmatically maintained, by which he pointed to someone more guilty than himself, was precisely the course that Oliver Cromwell had so persistently followed. Aggression against Spain in 1660 allowed the Republican sympathiser to both assert his loyalty to the newly restored monarch and continue the policies established under Cromwell and the Commonwealth. It was with this same subtlety that Thorowgood's analogy of Cromwell with the biblical figure Nimrod operated. Nimrod was condemned only because his project failed, not because the project itself was iniquitous. Thus the 1660 edition of *Jewes in America* functioned as a deliberate rewriting of the recent past and also, perhaps, as a deliberate continuation of the policies of the past.

Acknowledgements

For helpful critical readings of earlier drafts I would like to thank the following: Anthony Archdeacon, Ruth Gilbert, Siân Jones, Tony Kushner, Richard Maber, John McArdle, John Peacock, Carola Scott-Luckens, and Kevin Sharpe. I would particularly like to thank Sebastian Mitchell and Jonathan Sawday for their astute observations. I am grateful to *The Seventeenth Century* for permission to reproduce this chapter.

Notes

1. This chapter is a revised version of a paper which was presented as part of the 1994 Parkes Library seminar series at the University of Southampton, and published by *The Seventeenth Century*, Vol. 10 (1995), pp. 101–19.
2. T. Thorowgood, *Jewes in America, or, Probabilities that the Americans are of that Race* (London: W.H. for The Slater, 1650); T. Thorowgood, *Jewes in America, or, Probabilities that the Americans are of that Race* (London: H. Broome, 2nd edn, 1660).
3. For more information concerning the advocates of these different opinions see A.M. Hyamson, 'The Lost Tribes, and the Influence of the Search for Them on the Return of the Jews to England', *Publications of the Jewish Historical Society*, (1903), pp. 19–20.
4. B.A. Simon, *The Ten Tribes of Israel, Historically Identified with the Aborigines of the Western Hemisphere* (London: Thames Ditton, 1836), p. 41.
5. G. Garcia, *Origen de los Indios de el nuevo Mondo, e Indias Occidentales*, 3 Vols (Valencia, 1607), III, pp. 119–23.
6. See Bartoleme de las Casas, *Historia de las Indias*, 3 Vols (Mexico: Fondo de Cultura Economica, 1951).
7. For a full discussion of the legal and religious status of the Amerindians in Spanish debates during the fifteenth and sixteenth centuries see A. Pagden, 'Dispossessing the Barbarian: the Language of Spanish Thomism and the debate over the property rights of the American Indians', in A. Pagden (ed.), *The Languages of Political Theory in Early-Modern Europe* (Cambridge: Cambridge University Press, 1987), pp. 79–98.
8. For further details concerning this debate between Protestant theologians concerning the timetable for the end of the world see C. Hill, 'Till the conversion of the Jews', *Collected Essays*, 2 Vols (Amherst: University of Massachusetts Press, 1965), Vol. I, pp. 269–300.
9. Hill catalogues a register of subscribers for the calling of the Jews. From Andrew Willet in 1590, through William Perkins, Richard Hooker, Thomas Brightman and many others, the notion of Jewish conversion had a growing currency through the seventeenth century. After the breakdown of censorship in 1640, Thomas Brightman's influential but illegal *Revelation of the Revelation* was republished. Brightman's texts together with Joseph Mede's *Key of the Revelation* form the basis from which a host of millennial texts were spawned as these ideas circulated more widely and the apocalyptic years approached. Hill, *Collected Essays*, Vol. I, pp. 273–6.
10. For a more detailed account of the diversity and intensity of this debate see Hill, *Collected Essays*, Vol. I, pp. 274–7.

11. Though writing after the first publication of *Jewes in America*, Margaret Fell is a prime example of a writer who addressed the Jewish community in Amsterdam urging them to convert to Christianity. She wrote two pamphlets addressed to the Jews. The first, *For Menasseh-ben-Israel the calling of the Jews out of Babylon* was published in 1656. This pamphlet was written at the height of the debate concerning the possible readmission of Jews to England. In 1657, following the breakdown of these discussions between the Amsterdam Jews and Cromwell's government, Fell published another pamphlet, *A Loving Salutation to the Seed of Abraham amongst the Jews*, now bemoaning the absence of a 'home' for Jewish peoples. In both texts the Jews were constructed as proto-Christians. For a biographical study of Fell see I. Ross, *Margaret Fell, Mother of Quakerism* (London: Longman, Green & Co, 1949), pp. 89–97.

12. For more information on the relations between Christians and Jews in this period see D. Katz, *Philo-semitism and the Readmission of the Jews to England 1603–1655* (Oxford: Clarendon Press, 1982).

13. J. Sadler, *Rights of the Kingdom, or Customs of our Ancestours* (London, 1649).

14. G. Winstanley, 'The True Levellers Standard Advanced', in A. Hopton (ed.), *Gerrard Winstanley Selected Writings* (London: Aporia Press, 1989), pp. 7–23.

15. Winstanley, *Selected Writings*, p. 10.

16. Winstanley, *Selected Writings*, p. 10.

17. Winstanley, *Selected Writings*, p. 11.

18. Winstanley, *Selected Writings*, p. 16.

19. Between c. 598 BC and c. 538 BC the Hebrews lived in captivity under Babylonian rule. When Jehoiakim, king of Jerusalem, refused to pay tribute to Nebuchadnezzar, the Chaldeans marched on Judea; the unpopular King was killed; and Jehoichim, the eighteen-year-old son and successor of Jehoiakim, surrendered in 598 BC. The king, court, men of valour, craftsmen, and ironworkers were exiled to Babylonia. Only the poor and incompetent remained in Jerusalem. King Zedekiah, the new appointee of Nebuchadnezzar, rallied the remaining inhabitants, who moved into the abandoned homes of the exiles. Strong nationalist feelings led Zedekiah to rebel against Nebuchadnezzar. After a siege attended by famine, Nebuchadnezzar captured Jerusalem in August 587 BC, King Zedekiah was killed, the Temple and palaces were plundered and burned, and the entire population taken to Babylonia. The Exiles were usually placed in colonies, like Tel Abib by the River Chebar, near Nippur. The treatment they received and their reactions to their new home varied. Some possessed houses, married, made money, obtained high position in the state: others, probably the poor, suffered harsh treatment. For further details of this history see T.K. Cheyne and J. Sutherland Black (eds), *Encyclopedia Biblica: a Critical Dictionary of the Literary, Political and Religious History, the Archaeology, Geography and Natural History of the Bible* (London: A. & C. Black, 1914), pp. 177–8.

20. Biographical information about Thomas Thorowgood is scarce. Thomas Thorowgood (or Thurgood) was educated at Queen's College, Cambridge, receiving his B.A. degree in 1613–14, and his M.A. in 1617. He was incorporated at Oxford in 1622, and awarded the degree Bachelor of Divinity in 1624. He was ordained in 1618 and became Rector of the parish of Little Massingham in Norfolk in 1620. In 1625 he became Rector of Grimston as well; and in 1661 added the parish of Great Cressingham, also in Norfolk, to his duties. He was a member of the Assembly of Divines in 1643, and at Christmas 1644 he preached a sermon before the House of Commons. The

sermon was published the following year. See Thomas Thorowgood, *Moderation Justified, and the Lords being at hand Emproved: in a Sermon ... before the hon. House of Commons. Preached at the late Solemne Fast, Dec 25 1644* (London: [n.pub.], 1645). Thorowgood continued his duties as rector in Norfolk until his death in 1669. For more information see: J. Foster (ed.), *Alumni Oxonienses: The Members of the University of Oxford 1500–1714: Their Parentage, Birthplace, and Year of Birth, with a Record of their Degree,* 2 Vols (Nendeln: Kraus, 1968), Vol. II, p. 1482; F. Blomefield, *History of Norfolk,* 11 Vols (London: William Miller, 1805–10), Vol. VIII, p. 201. See also S.A. Allibone, *A Critical Dictionary of English Literature and British and American Authors,* 3 Vols (Philadelphia: J.B. Lippincott & Co, 1880), Vol. III, p. 2411; and Anthony à Wood, *Athenae Oxonienses: An Exact List of all the Writers and Bishops who have had their Education in the most Ancient and Famous University of Oxford from 1500 to end year 1690,* 2 Vols (London: Thomas Bennet, 1691), Vol. II, p. 224.

21. The Jews had been officially expelled by Edward I on 18 July 1290. For more detail of Jews living in England in the Renaissance and the readmission debate see D. Katz, *The Jews in the History of England, 1485–1850* (Oxford: Clarendon Press, 1994), pp. 15–189, esp. pp. 107–44.

22. Thorowgood, *Jewes in America* (1650), sig. B3v.

23. Thorowgood, *Jewes in America* (1650), sig. C2r.

24. For further details of the etymology of the term 'culture' see J.A. Simpson and E.S.C. Weiner (eds), *Oxford English Dictionary,* 20 Vols (Oxford: Clarendon Press, 2nd edn, 1989), Vol. IV, pp. 121–2. See also R. Williams, *Keywords: A Vocabulary of Culture and Society,* (London: Fontana Press, 2nd edn, 1983), pp. 87–93.

25. Thorowgood, *Jewes in America* (1650), sig. C2r.

26. Thorowgood, *Jewes in America* (1650), sig. C2v.

27. See Pagden, *The Languages of Political Theory in Early-Modern Europe,* pp. 84–6.

28. Thorowgood, *Jewes in America* (1650), sig. I2v.

29. Thorowgood, 'The Epistle Dedicatory', *Jewes in America* (1650), sig. B2r.

30. Michael Braddick describes the problem of defining the state and pinpointing a date for its emergence in this period. Though discussing the internal dynamics of state formation, Braddick points out the central importance of inter-state rivalries in the process of state formation. See M. Braddick, 'State formation and social change in early modern England: a problem stated and approaches suggested', *Social History,* Vol. 16 (1991), pp. 1–16.

31. Braddick, 'State formation', p. 7.

32. H. L'Estrange, *Americans no Jewes, or, Improbabilities that the Americans are of that Race* (London: W.W. for Henry Seile, 1651). Hamon L'Estrange, 1605–60, was the second son of Sir Hamon L'Estrange of Hunstanton in Norfolk. Interestingly the L'Estrange family was resident in the same parish over which Thomas Thorowgood was rector, suggesting a more personal and intimate knowledge between the two than has previously been acknowledged. Hamon L'Estrange fought as a Colonel in the Royalist Army. From 1643–51 he was declared a delinquent and his property was sequestered by the state. See H. L'Estrange, *The Charge upon Sr Hamon L'Estrange together with his Vindication and Recharge* (London, 1649). Among his other writings, he published *The Reign of King Charles, A History faithfully and Impartially delivered and disposed into Annals* in 1655. For further details see L. Stephen (ed.), *Dictionary of National Biography,* 63 Vols (London: Smith, Elder & Co, 1885–1900), Vol. XXXIII, pp. 115–16.

180 *Cultures of Ambivalence and Contempt*

33. L'Estrange, *Americans no Jewes*, p. 11.
34. L'Estrange, *Americans no Jewes*, p. 9.
35. L'Estrange, *Americans no Jewes*, p. 9.
36. *Encyclopedia Biblica*, p. 492.
37. L'Estrange, *Americans no Jewes*, p. 7.
38. T. Thorowgood, *Jewes in America, or, Probabilities that the Americans are of that Race*, (London: H. Broome, 2nd edn, 1660), p. 9. All subsequent references in the text are to this later edition.
39. Thorowgood, *Jewes in America* (1660), p. 9.
40. For this history I am indebted to D. Armitage, 'John Milton: Poet Against Empire', in A. Hiny and Q. Skinner (eds), *Milton and Republicanism* (Cambridge: Cambridge University Press, 1995), pp. 206–25.
41. T.O. Mabbott and J.M. French (eds), *The Works of John Milton*, 18 Vols (New York: Columbia University Press, 1931–38), Vol. XIII, pp. 513, 517, 555.
42. For a more detailed account of Oliver Cromwell's policy see, S.A.G. Taylor, *The Western Design: An Account of Cromwell's Expedition to the Caribbean*, (London: Solstice Productions, 2nd edn, 1969).
43. Thorowgood, *Jewes in America* (1660), sig. B1r.
44. L'Estrange, *Americans no Jewes*, p. 9.
45. Thorowgood, *Jewes in America* (1660), sig. B2v.
46. Thorowgood, *Jewes in America* (1660), sig. H2r–L2v.
47. Thorowgood, 'Epistle Dedicatory, To the King's Most Excellent Majesty', *Jewes in America* (1660), sig. A2r.
48. Thorowgood's arguments for the degeneracy of the Native Americans and their partial loss of a Hebrew identity has correspondences with the arguments 'J.J.' constructed in his text, *The Resurrection of Dead Bones, or the Conversion of the Jews*, published in 1654–55 on the eve of the crucial date in the apocalyptic calendar of 1656. 'J.J.' believed that the retrogression of the Jews was a sign that their conversion was imminent. Thus he stated: 'So according to human censure, Israel is past recovery, but according to the supernatural promises of God, they were never so near to their restoration as now, because they have fallen into the greatest desolation.' J.J., 'Preface to the Christian Reader', *The Resurrection of Dead Bones, or the Conversion of the Jews*, (London, 1654–55), sig. A3v.
49. Thorowgood, *Jewes in America* (1660), sig. A2r.
50. See J. Sawday, 'Re-writing a Revolution: History, Symbol and Text in the Restoration', *The Seventeenth Century*, Vol. 7 (1992), pp. 171–99, 174.
51. Thorowgood, *Jewes in America* (1660), sig. A3v.

8

In England's Green and Pleasant Land: James Parkes and Jerusalem[1]

TONY KUSHNER

The East End of London at the end of the nineteenth century became a symbol representing the problems associated on a general level with late Victorian society as a whole and, more specifically, the mass immigration of East European Jews. Hostile contemporaries believed that the area was being swamped by aliens: 'there is no end of them in Whitechapel, Mile End. It is Jerusalem.' Indeed, the Jerusalem metaphor was used powerfully and repetitively by anti-alienists to argue their case for the ending of free movement of peoples into Britain. The new Jerusalem, the anti-aliens were explicit, should not be confused with the utopian future 'of which they sung, but [to quote the *East London Advertiser*] ... the Jerusalem which ... exist[s] in Whitechapel, St George's and Stepney ... street upon street of overcrowded houses, filled by a foreign population.'[2] By the inter-war period, even in the East End, the vast majority of Jews in Britain were British-born – yet the alien tag remained: 'Jews should go back to Jerusalem and leave us alone. There are too many foreigners here now.' Such comments were not infrequent in British society during the inter-war period and as late as the 1940s. They were heard in casual conversations but also in asides aimed at Jewish MPs in the House of Commons itself. One such remark by Earl Winterton, which was aimed at a Labour backbencher in the chamber, makes clear that such abuse did not come from a convinced Zionist position. Winterton, as an important British government figure in the Jewish refugee crisis in the 1930s and the Second World War, had been a fierce opponent of Jewish immigration into Palestine and bitterly resented the idea that Jerusalem was somehow a Jewish city, because it was 'sacred for Christians'.[3] In fact, Winterton and others, in making the Jerusalem/Palestine connection, were simply articulating their distaste for Jews in Britain and emphasising their alien 'otherness' rather than revealing any favour of a Jewish return to the 'Holy Land'. Indeed, it will be stressed how marginalised the once mainstream views about Jewish restoration had become in British society by the Nazi era. In a survey carried out in 1947 it was found that only four per cent of those approving of a Jewish national home in Palestine did so for religious reasons, representing less than two per cent of the British population as a whole. Paradoxically, however, the whole subject of Palestine and Zionism had 'religious associations for people, however meaningless it may be to them otherwise'.[4] This paper will explore this paradox and the nature of the religious significance of Jerusalem to the British population through the career of James Parkes. As a Church of England clergyman, Parkes was almost totally isolated from the rest of British Christianity, yet his outsider status makes him an ideal figure through which to view 'mainstream' attitudes and responses to the myth and reality of the Jewish presence in Jerusalem in the 1930s and 1940s.

THE LAST DAYS OF THE BRITISH MANDATE

By the autumn of 1947 the British public was tired and frustrated by events in Palestine. It was reported from public meetings on the subject that 'Great Britain should get out of Palestine quickly'. After a long war, many were asking 'what are the lives of "our boys" in Palestine being wasted for?'.[5] The Labour government, crippled by financial crisis at home and annoyed that one of its key stages of decolonisation was being thwarted by Zionist activities (which in turn led to embarrassment on the international scene, especially conflict with the USA), was anxious to withdraw from its responsibilities in Palestine. On one level – that of practical considerations in a depressed and austerity-ridden country – both British state and public wanted nothing more to do with this troubled area. On a cultural and ideological level, however, Palestine could not so easily be forgotten and the crux of such considerations lay with the question of Jerusalem.[6]

As a symbol, Jerusalem has occupied a central place in western thought from the Middle Ages through to the modern period. As the Israeli writer Amos Elon suggests, 'in the imagination of believers, Jerusalem became more than a city. She became a metaphor.' The power of its image partly represents its religious significance for Christians, but it also reflects Jerusalem's importance in terms of the historical power relationships between 'East' and 'West'. As we will see, for the Christian world in Britain, the ideological legacy of the Crusades lasted well into the twentieth century.[7] The events in the last years of the British Mandate in Palestine and the first days of the newly independent Jewish state created a crisis for Christians as they faced for the first time the *reality* as against the myth of Jewish power. The strengths of their fears were so great that even the possibility of *partial* Jewish control of 'Holy Places' sent shock waves through the

Christian community in Britain. In November 1947 the United Nations passed a resolution in support of partition in Palestine and the creation of an independent Jewish state. The very prospect pushed Cyril Garbett, Archbishop of York, to write with specific regard to holy sites in Jerusalem that 'we cannot rely on the Jewish State giving adequate protection or showing impartial justice to Christians or Arabs'. This was the start of a concerted campaign by Garbett, second in the Church of England hierarchy. Garbett was in no way isolated amongst the leaders of the British Christian community. Indeed he had the full support of the Archbishop of Canterbury over the control of Jerusalem in the period immediately before and after the formation of the independent Jewish state.[8] This paper will analyse why the question of Jewish control over Jerusalem caused so much anguish and agonising for Christians in Britain and why, in contrast, the Reverend Dr James Parkes, accepted the concept and reality of this possibility not only with ease but with enthusiasm and satisfaction.

JAMES PARKES – RELIGIOUS PHILOSEMITE?

James Parkes' life and his involvement in Christian–Jewish relations has been well-charted and it is not necessary to cover all the details of his career here.[9] There are, however, several key features which need to be identified which make sense of Parkes' position on Jerusalem. They shed light on why so many Christians in Britain felt threatened by events in the last days of the Palestinian mandate and the struggle for Jewish independence. First, Parkes believed that antisemitism in the twentieth century was one of the most dangerous developments in the modern world. Parkes realised the potential of antisemitism even before the Nazi rise to power and the subsequent exterminatory programme was executed. Second, although Parkes accepted that modern antisemitism had an anti-religious, racist tendency, he was insistent that the roots of such contemporary hatred rested with Christian anti-Jewishness.[10] Third, Parkes, although a practising Christian (indeed a minister in the Church of England), acknowledged the validity of Judaism as a faith. By accepting the integrity of the Jewish faith, Parkes totally rejected all Christian attempts at proselytisation. Fourth, Parkes saw Judaism as a live religion – one that needed freedom to develop within its own dynamic traditions. Judaism was not, therefore, to Parkes simply a forerunner to Christianity which reached its fulfilment in the latter religion. His interest in Judaism and the Jewish people was thus not only to understand the roots of Christianity – Judaism as a museum piece – but also to appreciate its own integrity in a truly tolerant way. Parkes believed all religions were dynamic and that they could co-exist in a non-combative or competitive way. They could in turn learn from one another in an atmosphere of tolerance and not toleration.[11]

As we move through these points, Christians in Britain found it increasingly difficult to accept his views. There was even some difficulty in accepting Parkes' first premise – the danger of antisemitism in the modern world. Nevertheless, by 1939 and even more so by the end of the Second World War, leading British Christians (both Protestant and Catholic) had protested and were undoubtedly sincerely shocked by the increasing persecution and then wholesale destruction of European Jewry. Garbett, the leading campaigner against any Jewish control of Jerusalem, called for the 'dealing out of retribution to those responsible for the massacres' and later spoke with passion calling for the government to rescue those 'doomed simply because of belonging to the race from which the prophets came and of which Christ and his disciples were members'. Garbett, in his battle over Jerusalem, was, in his own words, accused of 'stirring up prejudice against the Jews'. He replied, not without foundation, 'that [he] hate[d] anti-Semitism; it is a sin against God and an offence against man'.[12] It was indeed Christian revulsion against the crimes committed against the Jews during the war which acted as the final catalyst to the formation of the Council of Christians and Jews (CCJ) in 1942 – an organisation which had been in the minds of activists such as James Parkes for over a decade. It was formed to create goodwill between Jews and Christians and to combat antisemitism.[13]

After some major internal diplomacy particularly on behalf of William Temple, Archbishop of Canterbury and a patron of Parkes since the 1920s, the Chief Rabbi and the Catholic Archbishop of Westminster were persuaded to join the Executive of the CCJ. In the three years before the end of the war many local branches were formed indicating that there was some popular support for this initiative.[14] Yet there were serious limitations in the CCJ approach which reflected more general tendencies in the Christian community – ones that were to resurface in the debate about the future of Jerusalem. Strangely, although the plight of European Jewry acted as the stimulus needed for its formation, the CCJ after an initial interest, had, by 1943, lost all sight of the Jewish disaster. No lead was given in terms of a popular protest against British government inactivity over the Jews of Europe. Instead, much time was spent on discussing the domestic roots of British anti-semitism. Here, through the input of Parkes, some consideration was given to the misrepresentation of the Jews in Christian teaching, but a far greater stress was placed on Jewish activities themselves. In short, Christians had great difficulty accepting Parkes' now unremarkable maxim that antisemitism was 'a problem for non-Jews'.[15] The difficulty stemmed in part from a tendency to view antisemitism as inevitably coming out of, and related to, the Jewish refusal to accept the authority of Jesus Christ. Antisemitism, many

Christians in Britain still believed, was the Jews' punishment for their killing of Jesus and their continuing stubbornness to accept the true faith. A British Christian visitor to the 'Holy Land', Leonard T. Pearson, expressed such sentiments bluntly in a work published in the late 1930s. In a section on Jerusalem, Pearson wrote that:

> Tradition blinded the Jew at the coming of Christ.... It also brought about the rejection and death of the Messiah, and ever since the Jew has been in darkness, hating the name of his own Saviour, and so grovelling in darkness as a result.[16]

Few in Britain were prepared to accept the fruits of Parkes' researches on the mediaeval world. Parkes placed the Church firmly at the centre of a persecuting society with regard to the Jews.[17] For many Christians, solving the problem of antisemitism rested with the Jews themselves. William Temple was, as Bishop of Manchester in the 1920s, the one leading Church figure to support James Parkes. Temple was exceptional in his willingness to accept Christian responsibility for past intolerance towards the Jews and in his recognition that such hatred had a continuing legacy in the modern world. In the late 1920s and early 1930s, he had allowed and even encouraged Parkes to engage in his controversial research. Yet he was unwilling to follow Parkes beyond this point. In 1942, Temple was appointed to the Archbishopric of Canterbury, the highest position in the Church of England. Parkes hoped that Temple would move beyond condemning antisemitism and take a strong stance on Christian attempts at conversion of the Jews (which Parkes realised created tremendous insult, fear and unease in the Jewish community). Temple responded in clear terms:

> I do not think I could interpret my interest in promoting Christian–Jewish friendship as in any way precluding an equal interest in attempting to convert Jews, because that

does appear to me be a Christian obligation; and if I had to choose it would take precedence of the other.[18]

Such a response from his close friend, Temple, was unacceptable to Parkes. Yet in his outright rejection of conversionism Parkes remained in a tiny minority. With specific regard to the Holy Land, Mona Swann, author of *Jerusalem: A Bible Drama* (1933), was far more typical of much Christian thought in Britain.[19] Swann's play was based almost exclusively on references to Jerusalem in the 'Old' and 'New' Testaments which flowed into one another in her text. These were selected to show their prophetic nature concerning the return of the Christian Messiah to Jerusalem. It was imperative, she wrote, that 'the action of the drama remains continuous and unbroken throughout ... no exigencies of circumstance [must] be allowed to disturb this continuity'. The Jews and Jerusalem were simply a precursor to the Jerusalem of Jesus and then for the 'new Jerusalem' in the Messianic age. In contrast, James Parkes opposed antisemitism not only because it resulted in crimes against humanity which no decent Christian could condone, but also as it hindered the prac-tice and development of Judaism – in the historic city of Jerusalem or elsewhere. As Parkes stated at the outbreak of war: 'Our immediate duty to the Jew is to do all in our power to make the world safe for him to be a Jew'.[20]

PARKES AND JERUSALEM

It was this open perspective that allowed Parkes to develop a position on Palestine and specifically on Jerusalem that was almost unique amongst Christians in Britain during the war and after. Moreover, Parkes was immediately aware of the implications of what had happened to Jewish life and culture during the war. In both these areas Parkes' views were (and to an extent remain) decades ahead of the rest of British Christian opinion. That Judaism was not only a live but also a valid religion did not occur to Parkes' Christian contemporaries. It also took many years for the British population to realise that six million Jews on the continent had been killed – let alone what this meant in terms of the destruction of the Jewish heritage. On both a secular and religious level the dominant British solution to the Jewish problem in the 1930s and 1940s was for the Jews to assimilate to their local culture and religion. This would save the Jews from further persecution; that the Jews had any history, customs or traditions worth preserving was thus inconceivable to the vast majority of British society.[21]

As early as January 1945, Parkes published a review of the impact of the war on the Jews.[22] In it Parkes wrote that for the Jews on the continent 'the survivors ... are to be numbered only by hundreds of thousands, the casualties by millions'. He recognised immediately the full significance of this disaster, particularly the destruction of Polish Jews which 'mark[ed] the end of an epoch'. Its impact was much greater than that of the previous mass expulsions of the Jews in history: 'for Polish Jewry has not been expelled: it has been exterminated as a living force'. Parkes realised that it was not simply the numerical strength of Polish Jewry that gave it significance for, in his own words, Eastern Europe was, since the sixteenth century, 'the religious, and at the same time the national, centre of the world-wide community'. Parkes was able to recognise even before the end of the Second World War that behind the statistics of millions killed (figures that most of the British state and public had difficulty in accepting), a way of life, such as that of the little-town Jews of Eastern Europe, had 'perished, and that particular form of Jewish life can never be re-established'.

To many of Parkes' British contemporaries, the remnants of European Jewry after the war were perceived as refugees or, more frequently, as 'Displaced Persons' – aliens who, by their lack of clear status, created immense administrative headaches. There was not necessarily an absence of sympathy, but ultimately issues of national and international policy would come first (with limited lip-service to humanitarian considerations) when dealing with the survivors of the attempted genocide.[23] In Parkes' view, however, the problem of those left in Europe went beyond issues of compassion, strong as they were in his considerations (he had established too many human links with the Jews of Central and Eastern Europe for this not to be the case). His overriding concern was with the *continuation* of Jewish life in the post-war world. Parkes realised that because of the sheer destructive power of Nazism, the centre of gravity of the Jewish world had shifted towards the USA and to Palestine. Parkes had stated in 1946 after his first visit to Jerusalem, that he had been concerned initially 'with the Jewish question from the European end'. As he added, 'that seemed a sufficient task for one man' and he left issues of Zionism and Palestine to one side. Even so, his close involvement with the refugee movement in the 1930s 'inescapably forced the Palestine issue to the fore'. Moreover, during the war and immediately after it Parkes began to believe that Palestine was more than just the 'most successful centre for the acceptance and absorption of refugees'. The disaster of the war years pushed Parkes into the conviction that 'Palestine [was] the *one* land in which a Jewish form of life was being reconstituted', although strangely he still did not regard himself as a Zionist as late as 1946.[24] To Parkes, both Christian and Jewish religious life could continue and develop in Palestine – even if it became a Jewish state. This was indeed essential to him, for he believed Judaism and Christianity were complementary: 'Neither was an incomplete form of the other'. As a socialist with strong utopian leanings, Parkes was deeply impressed with Jewish agricultural developments in Palestine. Parkes thus supported 'the independence of the Yishuv as much as because I want to see a *Jewish* life worked out in a modern society as for other and more normally "political" reasons'.[25]

Parkes spent a considerable length of time in Jerusalem during his first visit to Palestine during the summer of 1946. This factor, in addition to his religious and political interest in the Jewish future and the increasingly bitter debate about Palestine in Britain, forced Parkes to consider the issue of Jerusalem. Shortly after his return to Britain in the autumn of 1946, Parkes wrote for the first time about his solution to the 'problem' of Jerusalem. He believed in partition on two grounds. First, '[he could] not conceive of an Eretz Israel without Jerusalem'. Second, partition was not only politically possible, but it would force close relations between rival groups – ones which might eventually 'become fruitful and friendly' out of a background of hostility and bitterness. Parkes, believing as a Christian that Jerusalem was a special city, hoped that it could act as a model for his belief in religions that co-existed, sharing ideas from a position of respect and mutual tolerance, realising similarities *and* differences.[26]

PARKES, JERUSALEM AND CHRISTIAN OPINION

The battle for Jerusalem in 1948 and the growing Christian campaign for the internationalisation of *all* the town forced Parkes to expand and clarify his views. He had welcomed the formation of the independent Jewish state in 1948. The isolation of his position within the Christian world was shown by the reluctance of even the majority of the CCJ to share Parkes' enthusiasm for this new development.

Indeed, the debate in the CCJ revealed an important shift – power relations between Jews and Christians had now fundamentally changed. Initially the CCJ had been formed because of Christian sympathy towards the helpless Jews of Europe. After 1948 there was a possibility not only of the Jews having control of their own affairs, but also of those of other faiths. Out of this transformation came the bitterness of leading British Christians' attacks over partial Jewish control of Jerusalem in 1948 and early 1949.[27] In turn it gave an urgency to Parkes' defence of the Jews. Parkes was convinced that letters in *The Times* on the future of Jerusalem from 'our religious leaders, York especially but also Canterbury ... talk religion [but] they mean politics – and anti-Israeli politics at that'. Out of Parkes' concern came his first major writing on the city: *The Story of Jerusalem*. Parkes believed that the Jewish claim on the city was irrefutable. First, Parkes argued in terms of secular history and contemporary reality:

> the city of Jerusalem today, as a city in which men live and work and express their ideals in practical living, is preeminently a Jewish city – a city of Jewish homes, streets and shops, of Jewish factories and professions, of Jewish institutions of religion, learning and philanthropy ... Ever since Jerusalem began to grow from a medieval walled city, Jews have formed two-thirds of its population.[28]

The statistical reality of Parkes' arguments could not be denied but Arabists in Britain such as Robert Graves stressed that the majority of Jews in Jerusalem were newcomers and that the Jews had 'no superiority over the Arabs in respect of the area which they occupy'. Few agreed with Parkes in this area and there was an almost total lack of British appreciation of the post-Biblical Jewish links with Jerusalem and Palestine. As the 1947 annual report of the British Association for the National Home put it: a 'sympathy for the mythical Arab of fiction [as against the real Jewish presence]' led to a 'complete lack of appreciation of the importance of the establishment of the Jewish State'.[29]

The second aspect of the Jewish claim to Jerusalem stressed by Parkes concerned the political sphere. Jews had survived the bitter siege of 1948 and had done so with 'their own valour and endurance'. The lack of support given to the Jews in these desperate months convinced Parkes not only of the moral but also the security case of Jews having a direct stake in the control of Jerusalem.[30] The moral arguments outlined by Parkes made little headway in the contemporary debate in Britain and his concern over the security of the Jews was even more isolated. In such questions, the importance of what was at best a patronising and at worst a derogatory and imperialist attitude towards Judaism surfaced. Christians, with Jews in partial control of Jerusalem, felt threatened by the fresh status quo represented by the newly-independent Jewish state. Arguments were produced to suggest that the Jews were not morally fit to take care of Christian and Muslim Holy sites. These varied from claims made in *The Times* and in the House of Lords that Jews would engage in 'Old Testament' style revenge for earlier persecutions. It was even argued in terms reminiscent of *The Protocols of the Elders of Zion*, that Jews were agents of an atheistic Soviet plan, a view frequently expressed by British officials in the period after the First World War but still lingering after 1945, especially with regard to East European Jewish immigration to Palestine.[31] Harold MacMichael, High Commissioner for Palestine and Transjordan from 1938 to 1944, made clear the sense of fear many Christians were suffering: 'Can it be that the conscience of mankind is now able, with only a passing qualm, to regard the fate of Jerusalem as a matter of bargaining or fighting between the bickering races of the Levant?' No wonder that Jewish and pro-Jewish observers pointed out the crusading discourse that appeared to be at work in Christian public pronouncements.

Lord Altrincham, after predicting the danger posed by
Jewish fanatics, was rebuked by Lord Strabolgi and pictured
'as a descendant of Peter the Hermit, preaching a new crusade for the liberation of the Holy City, not from the
Moslems but the Jews.'[32]

The moral case against Jewish control of 'Holy Places'
reflected in turn the rejection of any Jewish religious claims
on the city. If Judaism was not a valid religion it could have
no real rights over the city. Harry Sacher, a leading British
Zionist wrote of the Christian and particularly the Catholic
world's apprehension of a Jerusalem as the capital of a
reborn Jewish nation. Like Parkes, he believed that those
Christians who were creating such a fuss about the future
of the 'stocks and stones' of the Holy Places, were looking
for an excuse to discredit 'the pulsing life of the New
Jerusalem, the Jerusalem of Israel' where Jews had shaped
their own destiny.[33] Parkes believed that the Jews had a
much greater religious claim to Jerusalem than the
Muslims. Furthermore, to argue that Jews could not be
trusted to control the 'Holy Places' reeked of Christian
arrogance. Parkes countered such views by stressing the
relative lack of a Jewish tradition of religious intolerance in
comparison to the Christian and Muslim faiths.[34]

A friend of Parkes in 1949 pointed out to him that
within the Christian hierarchy he was 'not exactly a
persona grata'. Parkes repeatedly stressed that he was not
interested in Jerusalem as a museum piece but as a potential new centre of Jewish life and a truly ecumenical
religious centre. Few in the Christian world could accept
this position. There had, it is true, been a religious philosemitic tendency in England since the early modern period
which had a limited impact in the readmission of the Jews
in the seventeenth century. Yet its impact by the twentieth
century, and certainly by 1945, should not be exaggerated
and certainly its role in the creation of the Balfour
Declaration has been distorted by romantic historians.

Issues of international diplomacy and the mistaken belief in widespread Jewish power were of much greater importance in the British decision to support a future Jewish state in Palestine.[35] Nevertheless, this philosemitic tradition survived into the post-1945 period, and the importance of millenarianism in creating a favourable ideological climate in this process should not be totally dismissed. Some of the leading members of the (non-Jewish) British Association for the Jewish National Home in Palestine, formed in 1943, were motivated by a religious fervour that was based on the premise that the Messianic age would occur with the restoration of the Jews. Such beliefs, it must be emphasised, were dissimilar to those of Parkes. Millenarians saw the Jews as especially important in that they would prepare the ground for the return of the Messiah. Judaism itself thus had no internal integrity – the Jews would ultimately convert. This form of religious philosemitism is a highly important aspect of Christian Zionism in North America today.[36] It did not, I would argue, play a very significant role in Britain. Parkes got support from some sects such as the Scottish 'Wee Frees', but their number and certainly their influence was limited. Leonard Stein suggested that even in the mid-nineteenth century, when such views were common in Britain, they did not necessarily represent 'a widespread popular movement'. By the middle of the twentieth century their marginality was even greater, almost in the category of crankiness. Indeed of perhaps greater numerical importance was the 'British Israelite' movement which believed that the English had replaced the Jews as the Chosen People or were actually the Lost Tribe of Israel. Antisemitism amongst these strange but numerous groups was common and they were generally bitter opponents of Zionism and the new Jewish state. Catholics in Britain as elsewhere shared the same views on Christian succession to the status of Chosen People and thus followed a basic anti-Zionism.[37]

Most people in Britain were, however, concerned with more down-to-earth matters concerning the Jews and Jerusalem. Robert Graves writing in *The Times* warned about the dangers of the Jews gaining control permanently of a greater Jerusalem. If they were not stopped soon, warned Graves, they would persist 'until either the Holy City is recovered in a Cross-Crescent crusade, or until the Jews are converted to Christianity, which, as the poet Marvell foresaw, will be a longish process'.[38] Religious philosemitism in support of the new Jewish state and of Jewish control of Jerusalem was only of marginal significance in terms of popular opinion and most certainly British government responses. In contrast, religious and more secular antisemitism was not insignificant in postwar Britain when considering the Palestine and Jerusalem issue. A Mass-Observation survey found that there was strong disapproval of Zionism (as opposed to a national home for the Jews), because Zionism was seen as representing the threat of Jewish power. It concluded that

> the religious associations of Zionism are [seen as] especially objectionable, [there is] dislike [of] anything reminiscent of Jewish insistence on their special religious role ... people are irritated by the mention or thought of the Jewish religion ... by the Jewish insistence on themselves as the Chosen People ... and the *claim* to Palestine on religious grounds.[39]

Parkes was thus almost alone in Christian Britain in having broken free of such crusading, patronising and frequently anti-Jewish ideologies. He managed to do so *not* through religious philosemitism, which regarded the Jews as something special (but only as a museum piece or a symbol of changes to come), but by accepting Jews on their own terms as a live, often conflicting and developing religious, political and cultural group. His support for a Jewish home and at least part Jewish rule of Jerusalem was based on historical, political and religious grounds. All three aspects demanded an adjustment of Christianity which most of the British population found at the time largely unacceptable even after the massive secularisation of society that had occurred after the First World War. Christianity was still an essential if increasingly vague ingredient in the formation of British national identity and the Jews were thus viewed as an alien and dangerous people. Jews at home or abroad (especially in the value-laden land of Palestine) could not be trusted. The Jerusalem question in the years immediately following the end of the Second World War brought Christian fears to the surface and exposed the isolation of James Parkes. That his views, including those on conversionism, have now gained some credence, certainly in his own Church, is an indication of the positive changes that have taken place since the late 1940s. Yet there is a danger in believing that the situation has fundamentally altered. Today in Britain many Christian groups and individuals show a real concern for issues concerning the Israeli state and its treatment of the Palestinians. Much of this interest comes from a genuinely humanitarian impulse (although it is noticeable that the intensity of this concern far outstrips the equivalent Christian response towards the victims of Nazi persecution in the 1930s and 1940s). Behind some of the Christian attacks on individual Israeli actions, however, is a much more sweeping rejection of the integrity of Israel as a *Jewish* state. It is indicative that there is still a long way to go in terms of British Christian acceptance of the reality of Jewish power. James Parkes died in 1981: his stance on the Jews whether as a people or a group, thus remains, in much of the Christian world in Britain and beyond, decades ahead of its time.[40]

NOTES

1. This chapter is based on a paper delivered as part of the Parkes seminar series at the University of Southampton in 1994.
2. See D. Feldman, 'The importance of being English: Jewish immigration and the decay of liberal England', in D. Feldman and G. Stedman Jones (eds), *Metropolis London: histories and representations since 1800* (London: Routledge, 1989) pp. 56–84 for general comment; William Walker, an ex-shopkeeper in Jubilee Street quoted in *Report of the Royal Commission on Alien Immigration*, Vol. 2, *Minutes of Evidence* (Cmd 1742, London, 1903), p. 298; *Eastern Post*, 19 Oct. 1901, cited in B. Gainer, *The Alien Invasion* (London: Heinemann, 1972), p. 43; C. Holmes, *Anti-Semitism in British Society 1876–1939* (London: Edward Arnold, 1979), p. 17 for the use of Jerusalem or Palestine in anti-alien rhetoric.
3. For the inter-war transformation in terms of the origins of East End Jews see H. Llewellyn Smith, *The New Survey of London Life and Labour*, Vol. 6 (London: P.S. King, 1934), pp. 269 and 293; for later comments on Jews and Jerusalem see Mass-Observation Archive, University of Sussex (M-O A), TC Food Box 6, File C, June 1946; for Winterton's Commons remarks see *Daily Telegraph*, 30 Nov. 1945; *Jewish Chronicle*, 27 Dec. 1946; *Daily Worker*, 24 Oct. 1947; for his comments on Jerusalem see *Hansard* (HC), Vol. 326, col 2263, 21 July 1937; A.J. Sherman, *Island Refuge: Britain and refugees from the Third Reich 1933–1939* (London: Elek, 1973), *passim* for Winterton's role in the refugee crisis. See also Earl Winterton, *Orders of the Day* (London: Cassell, 1953), p. 251.
4. M-O A: FR 2515, Sept. 1947.
5. Nov. 1947 report of the British Association for the Jewish National Home in Palestine and report for summer 1947 by Captain Sinclair-Thomson in Parkes' papers, 15/012, Southampton University archive (SUA).
6. For the Labour government and Palestine see W.M. Louis, *The British Empire in the Middle East 1945–1951* (Oxford: Clarendon Press, 1984); R. Ovendale, *The Foreign Policy of the British Labour Governments 1945–1951* (Leicester: Leicester University Press, 1984); and K. Morgan, *Labour in Power: 1945–1951* (Oxford: Clarendon Press, 1984). For public opinion and Palestine see T. Kushner, 'Anti-semitism and austerity: the August 1947 riots in Britain', in P. Panayi (ed.), *Racial Violence in Britain, 1840–1950* (Leicester: Leicester University Press, 1993), pp. 149–68.
7. A. Elon, *Jerusalem: city of mirrors* (London: Weidenfeld & Nicolson, 1990), p. 27. See also, F.E. Peters, *Jerusalem: the Holy City in the eyes of chroniclers, visitors, pilgrims, and prophets from the days of Abraham to the beginning of modern times* (Princeton: Princeton University Press, 1985) and M. Grindea, *The Image of Jerusalem: a literary chronicle of 3,000 years* (New York: Rochester University Press, 1968). Grindea, p. 208, comments that 'the image of Jerusalem has sometimes come to signify more at times than the Jerusalem of actuality from which it sprung'; on the persistence of the crusading image see, for example, Bernard Partridge's cartoon 'The Last Crusade' in *Punch*, 19 Dec. 1917 depicting General Allenby as Richard the Lion Heart re-taking Jerusalem.
8. Archbishop of York in Diocesan leaflet, December 1947 reported in Council of Christians and Jews (CCJ) Executive minutes, 3 Dec. 1947 in CCJ archives, 2/3, SUA; Canterbury and York letter to *The Times*, 27 Feb. 1948; see comments of James Parkes on York and Canterbury in letter to Rachel Heath 21 Feb. 1949, Parkes' papers, 7/10/1, SUA.
9. J. Parkes, *Voyage of Discoveries* (London: Gollancz, 1969); R. Everett, 'James

Parkes: historian and theologian of Jewish–Christian relations' (Columbia University Ph.D. thesis, 1983) and idem, *Christianity Without Antisemitism: James Parkes and the Jewish–Christian Encounter* (Oxford: Pergamon Press, 1993).

10. For his 'discovery' of modern antisemitism see Parkes, *Voyage of Discoveries*, Chps 5 and 6, *The Jew and His Neighbour: a study of the causes of anti-Semitism* (London: Student Christian Movement Press, 1930), and *The Conflict of the Church and the Synagogue: a study in the origins of antisemitism* (London: Soncino Press, 1934).

11. Parkes' views on contemporary relations between Judaism and Christianity can be followed in his sermon delivered at Oxford University before the outbreak of war, in Parkes' papers, 17/10/1, SUA and J. Parkes, *Jewish Christian Relations* (n.pub., 1939) in Parkes Library.

12. For a positive assessment of the British churches and the persecution of the Jews see R. Gutteridge, 'The churches and the Jews in England, 1933–1945', in O. Kulka and P. Mendes-Flohr (eds), *Judaism and Christianity under the Impact of National Socialism, 1919–1945* (Jerusalem: Historical Society of Israel, 1987), pp. 353–78. T. Kushner, 'Ambivalence or antisemitism? Christian attitudes and responses in Britain to the crisis of European Jewry during the Second World War', *Holocaust and Genocide Studies*, 5 (1990), pp. 175–89 provides a more critical analysis as does A. Wilkinson, *Dissent or Conform? War, Peace and the English churches 1900–1945* (London: SCM, 1986); Garbett's attacks on Nazi antisemitism can be found in *Hansard* (HL), Vol. 125, col 486, 9 Dec. 1942 and J. Snoek, *The Grey Book: a Collection of Protests Against Antisemitism and the Persecution of Jews Issued by Non-Roman Catholics and Church Leaders During Hitler's Rule* (Assen: Van Gorcum, 1969), pp. 243–4; for Garbett's position on Jerusalem see *Hansard* (HL), Vol. 162, cols 1329–35.

13. T. Kushner, 'The beginnings of the Council of Christians and Jews', *Common Ground*, Nos 3 and 4 (1992), pp. 6–9 and M. Braybrooke, *Children of One God: a history of the Council of Christians and Jews* (London: Vallentine Mitchell, 1991).

14. CCJ Executive minutes, 1943–45, CCJ archive, 2/2, SUA.

15. T. Kushner, 'Ambivalence or Antisemitism?', pp. 182–3 further developed in T. Kushner, *The Holocaust and the liberal imagination: a social and cultural history* (Oxford: Blackwell, 1994), Chp. 6; J. Parkes, *A Problem for the Gentiles* (London: Peace News, 1945).

16. M-O A: DR June 1939 for Christ-killer associations; L.T. Pearson, *Through the Holy Land: a fascinating tour with the Bible in hand* (London: Victory Press, 1937), p. 88.

17. J. Parkes, *The Jew in the Medieval Community: a study of his political and economic situation* (London: Soncino Press, 1938); for an indication of how Parkes' views have become accepted by some scholars more recently see R. Moore, *The Formation of a Persecuting Society: power and deviance in western Europe, 950–1250* (Oxford: Blackwell, 1987), but see C. Richmond, 'Englishness and medieval Anglo-Jewry', in T. Kushner (ed.), *The Jewish Heritage in British History: Englishness and Jewishness* (London: Frank Cass, 1992), pp. 42–59 for a powerful critique of many post-war British historians dealing with the subject.

18. A. Suggate, *William Temple and Christian Social Ethics Today* (Edinburgh: T. & T. Clark, 1987) and F. Iremonger, *William Temple* (Oxford: Oxford University Press, 1948); Parkes, *Voyage of Discoveries*, pp. 58–9, 65, 75–6, 84; Parkes to Temple, 16 April 1942, and Temple to Parkes, 19 April 1942, in Parkes' papers, 17/10/2, SUA.

19. M. Swann, *Jerusalem: A Bible Drama* (London: Gerald Howe, 1933), p. 3. It is significant with regard to the symbolism of Jerusalem that a work based purely on Bible quotations should nevertheless begin by quoting Blake's words on Jerusalem. The Jerusalem of past, present and future was located for her just as much 'In England's Green and Pleasant Land' as it was in contemporary Palestine.

20. Parkes' sermon, Oxford University, summer 1939 in Parkes' papers, 17/10/1, SUA.

21. T. Kushner, 'The impact of the Holocaust on British society and culture', *Contemporary Record*, 5, 2 (Autumn 1991), pp. 349–75; for the continuing belief in assimilation as the answer to antisemitism see M-O A: DR July 1946.

22. J. Parkes, 'The Jewish world since 1939', *International Affairs*, 21, 1 (Jan. 1945), pp. 87–105, esp. p. 90; idem, 'Life is with people: the story of the little-town Jews of eastern Europe', *Common Ground*, 6, 5 (Aug.–Oct. 1952), pp. 16–21.

23. See, for example, debates within government circles on survivors being given permission to enter Britain in Public Record Office, LAB 8/92 and 99; HO 213/618, 695, 781, 782 and 1360.

24. J. Parkes, 'Palestine in the Spring of 1946', *The New Judea*, 22, 9 (June 1946), pp. 162–3; see also his 'Judaism and Palestine', *Chayenu*, 10, 10 (Oct. 1946), pp. 7–8.

25. Parkes, 'Palestine in the Spring of 1946', p. 162.

26. Parkes, 'Judaism and Palestine', p. 7.

27. J. Parkes, 'In My View', *Jewish Chronicle*, 26 Nov. 1948 and 'The Emergence of Israel', *The Christian News-Letter* No. 338 (25 May 1949), pp. 167–76; Parkes was not part of the CCJ Middle East Group – see Parkes' papers, 15/034, SUA. For the impact on the CCJ of the new Jewish state see the Executive minutes, 9 Nov. 1948, 11 Jan. 1949, 6 Sept. 1949, 19 Oct. 1949 in CCJ papers, 2/3, SUA.

28. Parkes to Rachel Heath, 21 Feb. 1949 in Parkes' papers, 7/10/1, SUA; J. Parkes, *The Story of Jerusalem* (London: Cresset Press, 1949), p. 7.

29. R. Graves, letter to *The Times*, 11 Feb. 1949; 1947 Report of the British Association for the Jewish National Home in Parkes' papers, 15/012, SUA.

30. Parkes, *The Story of Jerusalem*, p. 8.

31. See letter of Sir Ronald Storrs in *The Times*, 25 April 1949; *Hansard* (HL), Vol. 162, cols 1329–66, 1 June 1949; for earlier conspiracy theories concerning Jews and Palestine see D. Cesarani, 'Anti-Zionist politics and political anti-semitism in England, 1920–1924', *Patterns of Prejudice*, 23, 1 (1989), pp. 28–45 and similarly B. Wasserstein, *The British in Palestine: the mandatory Government and the Arab–Jewish conflict* (Oxford, 2nd edn, 1991), pp. 66–7 and 225–38; A. Kochavi, 'Britain and the Jewish exodus from Poland following the Second World War', *Polin*, Vol. 7 (1992), pp. 161–75.

32. H. MacMichael, letter to *The Times*, 14 Feb. 1949; Lord Strabolgi (a Christian Zionist) in *Hansard* (HL), Vol. 162, col 1346, 1 June 1949, and similarly H. Lewis in *Jewish Review*, 2 Dec. 1949.

33. H. Sacher in *Jewish Chronicle*, 16 Dec. 1949.

34. Parkes, *The Story of Jerusalem*, p. 8 and synopsis of the book in Parkes' papers, 7/10/1, SUA; idem, 'The religious future of Jerusalem', *The Hibbert Journal*, 47, 4 (July 1949), pp. 328–34.

35. Helena Charles to Parkes, 7 March 1949, in Parkes' papers, 7/10/1, SUA; D. Katz, *Philo-Semitism and the Readmission of the Jews to England 1603–1655* (Oxford: Clarendon Press, 1982); F. Kobler, *The Vision Was There: a history of the British Movement for the Restoration of the Jews to Palestine* (London:

Lincolns-Prager, 1956); L. Stein, *The Balfour Declaration* (London: Magnes Press, 1961) and M. Levene, 'The Balfour Declaration: a case of mistaken identity', *English Historical Review*, 100 (Jan. 1992), pp. 54–77 for accounts that stress international diplomacy and the belief in Jewish power. S. Kochav, 'The Advent Testimony Movement and the Balfour Declaration', paper delivered at International Center for University Teaching of Jewish Civilization conference, Jerusalem, July 1992, and workshop on 'Jerusalem in the mind of the western World' provides an alternative perspective.

36. The minutes and correspondence of the British Association can be found in the Parkes' papers, 15/012, SUA. In 1947 Parkes was commissioned to write a paper on Britain and Palestine emphasising its importance to English Protestants from Cromwell through to the present in loc. cit.; D. Katz, 'The phenomenon of philo-semitism', in D. Wood (ed.), *Christianity and Judaism (Studies in Church History*, 29) (Oxford: Blackwell, 1992), pp. 327–61, for its impact in modern American society. I would suggest that issues of geography and the importance of small-town/country life in the United States explain the greater continuation of Christian fundamentalism (including philosemitism) than in the United Kingdom where urbanisation is more complete and accepted.

37. Helena Charles to Parkes, 2 Oct. 1946 in Parkes' papers, 15/012, SUA, on the Scottish 'Wee Frees'; Stein, *The Balfour Declaration*, p. 15 and L. Kochan, 'Jewish restoration to Zion: Christian attitudes in Britain in the Late 19th and Early 20th Centuries – a comparative approach', in M. Davis (ed.), *With Eyes Toward Zion – II* (New York: Praeger, 1986), pp. 102–21; for the British Israelites see T. Kushner, *The Persistence of Prejudice: Antisemitism in Britain During the Second World War* (Manchester: Manchester University Press, 1989), p. 113; for Catholics see, for example, *The Tablet*, 17 Dec. 1949.

38. Graves, letter to *The Times*, 11 Feb. 1949.

39. M-O A: FR 2515, Sept. 1947.

40. For the formation of British national identity in modern Britain in terms of race, see P. Gilroy, *There Ain't No Black in the Union Jack: the cultural politics of race and nation* (London: Hutchinson, 1987); T. Kushner, 'Heritage and ethnicity: an introduction', in *The Jewish Heritage in British History*, pp. 1–28 also stresses the importance of religion in identity making and exclusion of minorities. Perceived notions of the alien 'nature' of Jews (even in the 'Holy Land') were widespread in British culture. In the summer of 1947 Richard Crossman visited Palestine and came across British officials in Jerusalem who refused to educate their children in local schools. Their objections were on the grounds that their children would 'mix with strange people'. As Crossman added, what they 'meant by strange people, of course, were Jewish people', R. Crossman, *Palestine Mission: A personal record* (London: Hamilton, 1947), p. 141. T. Kushner, 'James Parkes, the Jews, and conversionism: a model for multi-cultural Britain?', in D. Wood (ed.), *Christianity and Judaism*, pp. 451–61, for the legacy of Parkes and recent developments concerning the Church of England and conversionism. Parkes' influence can be seen most clearly in the 'Lambeth document': *The truth shall make you free: the Lambeth Conference, 1988* (London: Church House Publishing, 1988); on the problems for Christians posed by the existence of Israel by a protégé of James Parkes, see A.R. Eckhart, 'Antisemitism is the Heart', *Christian Jewish Relations*, 17, 4 (1984), pp. 43–51.

JEWS AND
ANTISEMITISM

9

Parkes, Prejudice and the Middle Ages[1]

COLIN RICHMOND

In memory of Gunther Lys

'No man,' says a Rabbi, by way of indisputable instance 'may turn the bones of his father and mother into spoons' – sure that his hearers felt the checks against that form of economy. The market for spoons has never expanded enough for anyone to say 'Why not?' and to argue that human progress lies in such an application of material. The only check to be alleged is a sentiment, which will coerce none who do not hold that sentiments are the better part of the world's wealth.

George Eliot, *Daniel Deronda* (Harmondsworth: Penguin edition, 1967), epigraph to Ch. 33.

I once heard the eighty-year-old Heiko Obermann at Kalamazoo not give a lecture. Kalamazoo is, once a year, the town of a thousand lectures, as once a year the Medieval Academy of America holds its international conference in that town of slow-moving, night-whistling, enormously long freight trains. Obermann is the Dutch (or Dutch–American) doyen of Reformation studies. He announced that he was not going to give a conventional lecture, but that he would state nine propositions on the advertised topic: which was, I seem to recall, Reuchlin and the Jews.

I shall follow Obermann's august example except that my propositions will be questions.

There is another reason: trying to find a lecture mode to fit the age – the age since 1916: a fragmented world, a world of dissonance, which modern music captures better than anything. How to lecture inelegantly I term it, not to be rounded, not to move smoothly from one point to another, not to be polished (and therefore superficial), not to be brilliant – the code-word deployed by writers to describe the work of their friends and lovers. To give, perhaps a Zen lecture: to speak discordantly, not to shirk contradictions, even to cultivate them, to avoid asking questions let alone arrive at answers, not to succeed but to fail.[2] Oh well: here goes.

You should know two other things. One, that I shall begin and end with George Eliot, and two, that there will be, in homage to Walter Benjamin and because others always say things better than oneself, a good deal of quotations.

1. Is Mr Mallinger Grandcourt a typical English gentleman? I use him because for over 30 years I have been studying his type when the type begins to take on shape, that is in the England of the later Middle Ages – and remember the gentleman is an English phenomenon – while myself becoming Daniel Deronda.

> If this white-handed man with the perpendicular profile had been sent to govern a difficult colony, he might have won reputation among his contemporaries. He had certainly ability, would have understood that it was safer to exterminate than to cajole superseded proprietors, and would not have flinched from making things safe in that way.[3]

Neal Ascherson's young Southern-English gentleman of the 1890s who went out West for fun, sport and adventure should be interposed here.[4] One of the young man's letters in a box in a village attic Mr Ascherson stumbled on 40 years ago:

> Then I came to another letter. The Indians in the territory, it said, had begun to dance. This was bad news, presaging rebellion and war. Alarm had gone around the isolated ranches of the white man who had taken the Indians' land. But the ranchers, helped by Mexicans from across the border, had taken preventive action. A party of squaws and children had been intercepted, making for the border of the reservation where they would be safe from whatever might be about to happen. By luck, they had been overtaken just before they reached the reservation. All were slaughtered.
>
> The young Englishman had not been present. But he was excited and pleased. He wrote about the massacre in his usual racy, high-spirited way. The capital thing about it, he explained, was that the Indian breeding stock had been destroyed; to have killed male braves would not have been nearly as effective ... The letter turned to other things: his health, enquiries about the family back in England.

This is intriguing in the light of *The Tablet*'s contemporary criticism of *Daniel Deronda*:[5]

> the author commits a literary error when she makes Deronda abandon on learning the fact of his Jewish birth all that a modern English education weaves of Christianity and the results of Christianity into an English gentleman's life.

And also, where an English education is concerned, the obituaries on Nicholas, Lord Ridley last year: 'Truly, he was a great Englishman', said Lady Thatcher; 'Fortunately for me', said Tam Dalyell, 'I was never his fag at Eton. I say fortunately, because, as the late Tom Brocklebank's first house-captain, he was rough with tongue and cane on those whom he considered less than perfect.' Ah, the Grandcourt *de nos jours*.

Henry James has the customary last word:[6]

> *Pulcheria*: It is extremely unlikely that Grandcourt should not have known how to swim.

> *Constantius*: He did, of course, but he had a cramp. It served him right. I can't imagine a more consummate representation of the most detestable kind of Englishman – the Englishman who thinks it low to articulate. And in Grandcourt the type and the individual are so happily met: the type with its sense of properties and the individual with his absence of all sense. He is the apotheosis of dryness, a human expression of the simple idea of the perpendicular.

2. Was James Parkes a gentleman? Not like that he wasn't, you will say. And truly: the 'industrious decency' of Parkes is what Grandcourt did not have. Yet, his emphasis on continuities, which is the way Frederic Raphael characterises Parkes' life's work, was very English. Those continuities, not those over-worked English ones which serve unhistorical politicians so well, or in the case of John Major so badly, but the continuities of antisemitism, not disrupted ('ruptured' says Raphael) in the lifetime of Parkes, even if Parkes' own life was not. 'Fearing, yet proceeding, the *Shoah*, he can hardly be derided for not taking it into account', concludes Raphael.[7]

Parkes was perhaps less prophetic than another great European, Henry Bergson, who wrote in his will of 8 February 1937: 'I should have become a convert, had I not seen in preparations for years ... the formidable wave of anti-Semitism which is to sweep over the world. I wanted to remain among those who tomorrow will be persecuted.'[8] Still, it might be said, Bergson was Jewish.

Neither English gentleman nor French philosopher could have predicted the Final Solution, which was, after all, German. The not–imaginable was not imaginable. But, if Parkes did not take the *Shoah* into account then who else can realistically be presumed? Who else can we deride if not him? We could certainly be critical if not derisive of his *Observer* profilist of 18 September 1960, who begins with the *Shoah*, but in his anecdotal piece never returned to it. By 1960, aged 21, I had already written a short story about Auschwitz. And derisive too of *The Times* obituarist of August 1981 (the obituary a measly nine-inch double-column affair), who had read the *Observer* profile of 20 years before and little else, which does not mention the *Shoah* at all. Had it happened, one is obliged (over and over again) to ask? That obituary ends with a platitude which, given the omission of the *Shoah,* is strikingly inapt: 'Parkes belongs to the procession of men who in dangerous ages urge upon their fellows the need to practise a degree of honest realism that alone will enable them to save mankind.' On such as that obituarist compare Jakov Lind, that survivor *extraordinaire*, at Hampstead in the 1950s: 'I had landed in a circle of intellectuals I didn't think it possible could exist after all that had happened'.[9] Honest realism: did Parkes have it? If he did he cannot have been a gentleman – as not one of them had it before, during, or after the Second World War, and as almost all of them were close to doing a deal with Hitler in March 1940. I do not wish to deride Parkes for not seeing the future, but as I do not want to be deprived of being able to condemn those Englishmen who did not see (did not want to see) what was immediately staring them in the face in the 1930s *they* have to be gentlemen.

Can a historian ever be other than derisive of the type? Take Arnold Toynbee's story of Namier, or Bernstein as he then was, and Lord Robert Cecil in 1918.[10]

On Armistice Day, 1918, Lord Robert Cecil, who had been the United Kingdom's war–time Minister of Blockade, kept his vow that he would resign from the government, as soon as the war was over, as a protest against the disestablishment of the Episcopalian Church in Wales. He had then promptly been appointed head of the section of the British delegation to the forthcoming peace conference in Paris that was to deal with the setting up of the League of Nations. Lord Robert wanted to equip himself for his new task, so he sent to the Political Intelligence Department of the Foreign Office for a map of Austria–Hungary. This was Bernstein's job, and he went to Lord Robert's room, map in hand. 'That map must be wrong', Lord Robert said to Bernstein after glancing at it. 'Well, no, it is correct, sir', Bernstein answered. 'But surely that long straggling piece ought to be yellow, not red'. Lord Robert had his finger on Bernstein's native Austrian Crownland, Galicia. (On Bernstein's map, Hungary was coloured yellow, Austria red, and Bosnia green. I saw the map a few minutes later, when Bernstein came staggering into my room, still holding the map, with a dazed look on his face.) 'Well, no, you see, sire, Galicia is part of Austria, not of Hungary'. There was a moment's pause, and then: 'What a funny shape Austria must be', Lord Robert said ruminatively, half to himself. This from a Minister of the Crown who had been engaged in blockading the Hapsburg Monarchy for the last four years! Bernstein never got over the shock of that interview. 'The English: are they human?' The query would seem to be justified by Bernstein's experience [concludes Toynbee].

Or what about this – Grandcourt, extermination, and an English education in mind? Anthony Wood is describing his eldest brother Thomas Wood:[11]

About a yeare before that time, viz. in 1650, he returned for a time to Oxon, to take up his arrears [of study] at Ch. Church, and to settle his other affaires; at which time being often with his mother and brethren, he would tell them of the most terrible assaulting and storming of Tredagh [Drogheda], wherein he himself had been engaged. He told them that 3,000 at least, besides some women and children, were, after the assailants had taken part, and afterwards all the towne, put to the sword on the 11 and 12 of Sept. 1649; At which time Sir Arthur Aston the governour had his braines beat out, and his body hack'd and chop'd to pieces. He told them, that when they were to make their way up to the lofts and galleries in the church and up to the tower where the enimy had fled, each of the assailants would take up a child and use it as a buckler of defence, when they ascended the steps, to keep themselves from being shot or brain'd. After they had kil'd all in the church, they went into the vaults underneath where all the flower and choicest of the women and ladies had hid themselves. One of these, a most handsome virgin and arrai'd in costly and gorgeous apparel, kneel'd downe to Tho. Wood with teares and prayers to save her life: and being strucken with profound pitie, took her under his arme, went with her out of the church, with intentions to put her over the works and to let her shift for herself; but then a soldier perceiving his intentions, he ran his sword up her belly or fundament. Whereupon Mr Wood seeing her gasping, took away her money, jewels, &c., and flung her downe over the works, &c.

Is this, then, how the conversation used to go among the rattle of teaspoons? We may say with absolute certainty that, whether Parkes was or was not a gentleman, he was not to be found either in the corridors of power or in Oxford sitting rooms: he did not measure out his life in such ways.

3. Why wasn't Parkes a Dadaist? Or, alternatively, bearing in mind the half-remembered story of Parkes and the

greengages, was he? The simple answer might be that he was not because he was a gentleman. Even if he was not, even if his work, both his activity out of Geneva to combat antisemitism and his writing about, and in opposition to, it was against the grain, he somehow was not: he was (paradoxically as he was a Channel Islander) very much an Englishman: his passion for gardening and architecture, for example, whatever the Voltairean nature of the former. I no doubt do him an injustice: the son of a Guernsey tomato grower is unlikely to be anything other than interesting: witness the story of the greengages. Perhaps, we should see him as the Matthew Le Tissier of Jewish Studies. Nonetheless, that industrious decency of Frederic Raphael's and the sturdy Anglicanism, are they not typically English? They are not Dadaist. And that was despite the Trenches. As someone has said: the Holocaust really began in the trenches of the Great War. Or another: I grew up to the sound of the drums of the First World War, and our history since that time has remained murder, injustice, and violence. We all have our definitions of Dadaism, and you may think that Parkes' narrative of how he did not win the Military Cross, especially his description of the event which ought to have produced it for him but did not as 'an immensely successful trench raid in which we captured a loaf of bread with only about 80 casualties', is about as Dadaist as an Englishman can get: the loaf of bread, for instance, is reminiscent of (and may be synonymous with) that brioche which Hans Arp had up his left nostril at the birth of Dada in Zurich on 6 February 1916.[12]

Yet, he was too well mannered to be a true Dadaist. Indeed, show me an English Dadaist. Think how unhappy Kurt Schwitters was in England: Dada/Merz and the Lake District do not go together. I am also thinking of how the war did not change Parkes in the way it changed, say, David Jones or Ludwig Wittgenstein, to name but two. Of how Verdun and the Somme mark a watershed in

European history and of how the Dadaists – those seismographic (seismoscopic) souls – perceived that shift into Modernity, modern murder, modern barbarity, quicker than anyone else, and whose perception of twentieth-century immoderateness is marked by their immoderate language. Here is a quotation from that book on twentieth-century history too little used by twentieth-century historians: Greil Marcus, *Lipstick Traces*. This is Huelsenbeck in 1920.[13]

> We had all left our countries as a result of the war. ... We were agreed that the war had been contrived by the various governments for the most autocratic, sordid and materialistic reasons; we Germans were familiar with the book *J'accuse*, and even without it we would have had little confidence in the decency of the German Kaiser and his generals. Ball was a conscientious objector, and I had escaped by the skin of my teeth from the pursuit of the police myrmidons who, for their so–called patriotic reasons, were massing men in the trenches of Northern France and giving them shells to eat. None of us had much appreciation for the kind of courage it takes to get shot for the idea of a nation which is at best a cartel of pelt merchants and profiteers in leather, at worst a cultural association of psychopaths who, like the Germans, marched off with a volume of Goethe in their knapsacks, to skewer Frenchmen and Russians on their bayonets.

Or whichever Dadaist it was who, when challenged from the floor at a public meeting in the 1920s by a voice which asked what had he done in the war, promptly replied: 'avoided getting killed for shits like you'. Kurt Schwitters did a whole lecture tour of Holland in which the lectures consisted of his admittedly wide range of dog-barks: fitting comment on what had happened when the human dogs of war had run amok. As fitting a comment on the First World War as Marcel Duchamps' urinal of 1917 signed Mutt, presumably for all the mutts who had been sacrificed (been pissed on) by their government. What was there to say after Verdun? *That* was when poetry ought to have been finished with. What to say after Verdun in 1921 became a package tour? I quote the brochure.[14]

> Not only to the French mind is [Verdun] the battlefield *par excellence* . . . . If the entire war cost France 1,400,000 dead, almost one third of that number fell in the sector of Verdun, which comprises but a few square kilometers. The Germans suffered more than twice the number of casualties there. In this small area where more than a million men – perhaps a million and a half – bled to death, there is not a square centimeter of soil that was not exploded by grenades . . . details which at Verdun combine into an unprecedentedly phenomenal panorama of horror and dread . . . wine and coffee and gratuities included.

I am suggesting only that Parkes was still too much in the grain; he was not against it like the Dadaists, or rather had not detected the deeper, truer grain of European culture as they had: like the state of Denmark it stank. Too few of us can be sufficiently against the grain to be a Sophie Scholl, an Oskar Schindler, a Yitzak Zuckerman, a Maria Stromberger, an Anton Schmidt, and Ariadne Skryabina – twentieth-century heroes and heroines: the list is much longer and most of the names on it are known only to God. But, why oh why don't the English shed just a little of their 'in the grain-ness'. Why aren't there more Englishmen like Thomas More and Thomas Cranmer?

I wish James Parkes had not been so bloody polite. Did he ever entitle a lecture as I did the other day on élites and hoi-poloi in history 'All car-drivers are wankers'. I ask too much. I wish, nevertheless, Parkes had been like Eric Linklater (oh, but he was a Scotsman) who, when learning that his German publisher would not use the usual translator of his books, said: 'If Goverts Verlag refuse to employ him simply because he is a Jew, you can tell them to stuff a large bag of tin swastikas up their fundamental orifices and ride a tandem bicycle to hell'.

On the other hand, he was all too ready to have echoed the Polish-Jewish poet Julian Tuwim – in the following simply substitute Englishman for Pole and English for Polish: 'I am a Pole because my hatred of Polish Fascists is greater than my hatred of Fascists of other nationalities. And I consider that particular point as a strong mark of my nationality'.[15]

4. Was Parkes a philosemite? Short answer: he could not have been because he was too much of a gentleman. Frederic Raphael said that Parkes realised and wrote and taught that the Jews are the margin which runs down the middle of the page of European history. And I say, as everyone is bound to, with what clarity he set that before us. Achievement enough. He recognised that the Christian 'teaching of contempt'[16] underlay modern antisemitism and facilitated, though it did not enable, the *Shoah*. The good-hearted Robert Everett tells us, though only in footnotes,[17] that Parkes' grasp of the uniqueness of Christian anti-semitism and its dire consequences either underpins the contemporary work of Rosemary Reuther, Franklin Littell, Gavin Langmuir, and Bob Moore (but without being given recognition), or is ignored by mainstream historians, who criticise me for trying to get Jews more into the middle of the page of mediaeval English history. All I wonder is: did he go far enough? I do not think he saw how corrosive such contempt has to be. From the twelfth century European culture becomes a persecuting, a victim-ising culture.[18] What I call a culture of contempt was born: it was Christian and classical and a disaster for us one and all. Modernity has escaped neither the corrosion nor the contempt.

I suppose that is another mark against Parkes: he

believed both the Renaissance and the Enlightenment were good, not bad: see further below.

Because, until very recently, Jewishness escaped West European culture, while contributing to it – was in other words counter-cultural – its attractions have to be enormous for someone coming to it from that culture. If one has come to loathe European culture (West European culture anyway: who can listen to Beethoven or Bach after perceiving what the *Shoah* really amounts to?[19]), then one has to love the Jews. That is the theme of Spielberg's remarkable text for our time, *Schindler's List*:[20] watch Oskar's development from no views at all, apart from capitalist ones (which amounts to the same thing), to becoming a Jew-lover. Myself: I wonder if you can really be neutral. Either you are an antisemite or you are philosemitic. As General Ironside said of Orde Wingate: his supreme crime [was] of favouring the Jews too much.[21] Whereas, the whole point is: if only Jews had been favoured too much Europe might have had a culture Dadaists could have believed in. General Ironside sums the fourth proposition up for us nicely: there is no such thing as a philosemitic English gentleman. It is a contradiction of terms. Where does that leave Parkes? As a contradiction.

5. Why am I not Parkes? The answer to the question you are saying to yourselves is because he is not a gentleman and he is philosemitic. I remain more puzzled than that. Born in Sidcup, I am quintessentially suburban English. Or am I? Do I really feel more at home these days in what was once Jewish Cracow? Why do I like to be in Warsaw where once Krockmalna Street was? Am I only pretending that I prefer Chelm to Chislehurst? Or Lviv to London? And is it only because, as Nick Hornby has commented, being suburban means desperately wanting to come from somewhere else?[22]

But, for me, there is also the *Shoah*. Where did that come

from? What memories return unbidden – Proust's test of what counts? The Regal cinema, Sidcup High Street, Spring 1945, and those newsreel, as well as newspaper,[23] images of Bergen–Belsen and Buchenwald? Reading Anne Frank's Diary in 1954: *The Diary of a Young Girl* is the Pan Book title and like any young girl, Jewish or not, Anne had her order of priorities aged 11 in 1939 exactly right: laughing, history, and movie stars seem to sum up the quality of ordinary, normal life the *Shoah* snuffed out. Seeing the memorial to the murdered Jews of Prague in the old cemetery in 1964: name after name after name after name. The exhibition of Jewish religious 'objects' at the Whitworth Art Gallery in Manchester in 1980: objects I hated then but love now and ponder the transformation – like the once grating sounds of a .cantor praying which now are beautiful. Yad Vashem in 1982: I come out of the Bunker of Remembrance and from the depths of my English, my Sidcup–English, ignorance exclaim to the custodian, who has responded to my first enquiry in halting German as to where he comes from with Cracow, oh yes, I exclaim, as if I know something, oh you are Polish then, and am met with the angry, anguished, withering reply I deserve: Ich bin Jude. And: did it ever cross my mind what it might have cost him to speak in German? Perhaps the last dozen years are an attempt never to be so stupid again. There I am like Parkes: he too was resolved upon teaching himself what no one else had bothered to teach him.

One final memory, which is also determining because it is about where to put one's trust: it is high above Haifa and the blue, Camus-like Mediterranean; we are at the house of Gunther and Ruth Lys; he is German, a diminutive and skeletal German, skeletal because he was a Humanist and a Pacifist and in the camps throughout the war because he would not fight in it; she is Jewish, and they were childhood sweethearts in pre-war Hamburg; after the war he advertised for her in Israeli newspapers, found her, and they married; here they are in 1982 active in the Israeli peace movement. Gunther and Ruth were like Sister Wanda in Lithuania or Mother Catherine Crowley in Zamocs of whom it has been said: someone had to be honest for the world to continue. It takes half a lifetime to learn the platitudes: the just women and men are always to be found in out-of-the-way places, the unjust in the seats of authority.

For so personal an approach to the pursuit of history I have the warrant of Parkes himself. As John Pawlikowski has said of Parkes – hold your breath:[24]

> If we were to describe the movement in Parkes' method, it would be from personal experience to history (corporate experience) to theology to meaning. And if we were to describe Parkes' methodological orientation from the philosophical-theological viewpoint especially, we could characterize it as Buberian, progressivistic, historical, transcendental, neo-orthodox and holistic.

That quotation also shows you why I am not Parkes, or for that matter not Pawlikowski.

6. How anthropological was Parkes? I do not think he would have agreed with the Solomon Islander who said to Beatrice Blackwood in the 1930s: 'White man he capsize altogether something belong before'. I take that acute summary of Modernity from the 1993 guide to one of the saddest yet most exhilarating museums I know of: the Pitt Rivers at Oxford. We are all anthropologists these days, or ought to be, must be indeed, or the world is lost, that plural world which is being destroyed by us Moderns almost at a faster rate than God created it: one language disappears every day, taking a whole way of life with it. I do not see how Parkes could have been expected to do other than still believe in Western man and Western

civilisation, especially when even in the Pitt Rivers the anthropologists got things wrong. Here is David Weiss, scientist and scholar.[25]

> They were lying among a rather disordered assortment of tribal philtres, talismans, and amulets in a glass-enclosed case bearing the simple legend 'Asian and African Fetishes'. They were very old, the cracked cowhide thongs still wound about the small faded-black receptacles of hard leather to form the folded wings, and I wondered how they came to rest here, in the image-choked vaulted hall of the Oxford University Museum's anthropological collection. I had passed casually through the museum's rooms during a lunch break from my laboratories down the road on that spring day in 1956, and my eye was caught, startled, by the familiar object in such strange company. Bending over the case, I saw yellowed slips of heavy paper describing each of the fetishes. The one placed at the side of the tefillim explained that these are a representative specimen of the phylacteries ritually worn in the past at worship by males of certain Jewish sects, a phallic archetype of the Israelitic Jehovah cult, and − the author was undoubtedly an academic, scrupulously cautious to leave no possibility unreckoned with − to ward off the evil eye.

After that, try to tell me that the drive behind the *Shoah* was not Modernity. Nor are Oxford academics always a hundred years behind, for here they are caught anticipating by a century the Nazi museum in Prague where Jewish religious 'objects' were displayed. Truly, as Camus said, it is not in the museum that we must seek reasons to hope.

Parkes, by all accounts, believed in Western Civilisation, believed in its superiority and in what it had to offer other civilisations. I do not blame him. I was taught to believe such things in the 1950s. Despite the Dadaists, despite the Trenches, despite the other superficial disillusion of some writers, and because Fascism had to be resisted in the end, belief in Western Civilisation remained an unexamined assumption of almost everyone until the 1970s: witness the University of Keele's Foundation Year Programme, whose demise is due not only to the grey-suited men with cannibal minds, but also because we teachers have come to see at last that a year's canter through Western History, Western Science, Western Philosophy, and Western Religion is really a justification for those men's grey suits, mobile phones, and unsavoury minds.[26] Post–Verdun, post-*Shoah*, post-Vietnam, we have begun to realise the genocidal damage we have done in the Americas, Australia, Africa, and Asia, because at last we are listening to Americans, Australians, Africans, and Asians. The myth of European benevolence is becoming as sharply delineated as is the myth of European superiority – in everything except bottled drinks, denims, and the arms trade. It has been a downright swindle we say. I am sure Parkes did not say that – moral being to the hilt though he was. The age of cultural anthropology had not dawned when his mentality was formed.

7. Why was James Parkes not Gershom Scholem? In one sense he was: he studied the irrational, antisemitism being defined, without the shadow of a doubt, as fantastical. Both were great men who looked at what others had refused to look at or averted their faces from in distaste or disgust, and were pioneers in doing so: the 'what' which was not considered *wissenschaftlich* – folklore, popular fact and fable, mysticism and magic in Scholem's case; the dark side of Christianity in the case of Parkes. Where, I think, they depart from one another, even if we may want to discern similarities in the manner in which each radically and deliberately altered course as young men, where they differed fundamentally, was in attitude or outlook. Does not Parkes always remain reasonable, although he is in pursuit of the greatest unreason of all: antisemitism?

Would he, for instance, have agreed with the following:[27]

> *Scholem*: Yes I think that people generally use the instrument of Reason to criticize a tradition or a milieu. This is a very legitimate use, because the instrument of Reason developed in man largely on the critical, destructive side. When Reason is isolated from the other possibilities in the complex of human urges, in the whole psychological network, it transpires that its task is to criticize. In history it has done so quite successfully. In the area of construction, Reason has had relatively few successes. Other forces have had far more outstanding and decisive successes in construction than Reason. Reason is a dialectical tool that serves both construction and destruction, but has had far more notable successes in destruction. The devotees of Reason have tried to build networks of positive thought – but these networks are far less enduring than criticism; that is creative destruction. I know that this is a very painful point, and many admirers of Reason (of whom I am one) do not like to hear this. But I am inclined to think – in summing up my researches in history, religious history, philosophy and ethics – that Reason is a great instrument of destruction. For construction, something beyond it is required.
>
> *Muki*: What is that?
>
> *Scholem*: I don't know. Something that has – something moral. I don't believe there is an enduring rational morality; I don't believe it is possible to build a morality that will be an immanent network for Reason. I confess that in this respect I am what would be called a reactionary, for I believe that morality as a constructive force is impossible without religion, without some Power beyond Pure Reason. Secular morality is a morality built on Reason alone. I do not believe in this possibility. This is an utter illusion of philosophers, not to speak of sociologists.

Shapira: Was this the view of Walter Benjamin? We got onto this subject via Walter Benjamin.

Scholem: I am not Walter Benjamin. I am Gershom Scholem.[28]

The dilemma here is straightforward and not new: strange allies may be won when reason is attacked – no doubt because the liberal tradition is part and parcel of the rationalist tradition. You may not want Ezra Pound on your team, but do you want Emmanuel Kant, he who defined marriage as a contract for the mutual exchange of genital organs? We are back with the great twentieth-century debate: The Hannah Arendt Debate. Is the mess we have been in since 1916 a culmination of the Enlightenment or a reaction against it? One thing is sure (and here Scholem and Parkes agree): humanism is not enough. Our century demonstrates that truism. Still, as Parkes showed, again and again, nor is religion. As Jacob Katz put it:[29] 'It is genuine religious exhilaration which engenders aversion towards the visible symbols of an alien religion.' In a pluralist world religious over-enthusiasm (exhilaration) brings only suffering: see contemporary Sudan, for example. So what is left: morality says Scholem. Yet, here we are again: morality based on reason, based on human-ity has failed – whatever the valiant attempts of Camus to make morality existential. Scholem says religion has to come in somewhere – even if it has failed in the past, we necessarily add. Damn: but then, as Skvorecky says: who was ever consoled by history? Thus, Robert Everett's summing up of Parkes and Israel,[30] 'his belief that the solution to the problem requires both sides to deal honestly with the historical facts of the attachment to the land of both Jews and Palestinians, make his work in this area an important source for any future negotiations', is naïve and not in the least consoling. Think about the phrase 'both sides to deal honestly with the historical facts', with Bosnia in mind: 'In the War of Maps and of the *narod*, there is no such thing as objective history'.[31] Or, to return to George Eliot:[32] 'to judge wisely I suppose we must know how things appear to the unwise; that kind of appearance making the larger part of the world's history'.[33] Even that statement presupposes that someone somewhere is capable of wisdom. Which brings me to the eighth proposition.

8. How on earth could James Parkes have been a progressive, or, as I believe the technical, theological jargon has it, a modernist? An alternative title might be: how to avoid the redemptive ending. Even Alan Bullock's vast book of 1,158 pages on those ogres of our time *Hitler and Stalin* ends with the Avenue of the Righteous at Yad Vashem. Parkes lived in a malign world 1896–1981 and recognised that he did:[34]

> Our obscene politics, our waste and pollution, our dehumanization of the person, alike proclaim our past failure ... mankind is still very young. As an infant prodigy he has reached the moon; but his political activities would be perfectly comprehensible to Nebuchadnezzer ... I do not believe that an adult humanity is automatically secularized or atheistic. But I am quite sure that not one of the religious institutions of the world, eastern or western, is in its present form capable of guiding us through the dangers and difficulties which lie ahead, though I believe equally that all have amassed experience in the past which is essential for the future.

Parkes wrote in 1972; his words, nonetheless, are not without hope. Such optimism, says Robert Everett is unconvincing today – at best naïve at worst outdated and useless: 'Modernism put a good deal of faith in reason, education, and science, and it appears to have been

betrayed by all three'.[35] It may be that out of sheer decency
(or his sort of Dadaism?) Parkes averted his face from the
atrocities of his time; I mean: philosophically averting his
face. If hardly any English people went to see Claude
Lanzmann's film *Shoah* in 1987, was that because one does
not go to that sort of film if you are English? Observe the
following exchange on the letters page of *The Independent*.
M.G. Farrell and K.K. Hedinger-Farrell asked, 'Why is it,
we wonder, that the British media and public have shown
so little interest in this unique documentary which is as
much part of our history as that of our European neighbours? Our question is not rhetorical; we would like an
answer.' Back it came from David Mackintosh, 'Five
decades ago our nanny taught us that two topics were
barred from civilized conversation: money and the state of
one's health. Were she *in loco parentis* today, I am sure that
she would add a third – last night's television programme
of *Shoah*'. Well: *are* the English human? Let Andy
Charlesworth, historical geographer *extraordinaire*, answer
David Mackintosh:[36]

> One geographer with a visible sign of distaste has asked me
> how can I take students to a place like Auschwitz-Birkenau.
> No such distaste would have been expressed if I had taken
> them through the monumental imperialist landscapes of
> Berlin. Yet the heart and the anus of European civilization
> was inextricably linked. To turn away from one is to cheat
> intellectually.

Am I accusing Parkes of intellectual cheating?
I recall buying Goya's *Disasters of War* in the Charing
Cross Road in 1954, while I was still a schoolboy. I do not
think I am a voyeur any more than Andy Charlesworth is.
Nor am I morbid; at any rate, my family and friends will
tell you I am not. Surely, it is straightforward: the historian,
like the historical geographer, has to look some things,
everything indeed, as straight in the eye as possible. 'For

the historian', says Charles S. Maier, recalling Walter Benjamin's Angel of History, 'a steady gaze at the wreckage is vocation enough'.[37] Blindness, like ignorance, may not be pleaded – although everywhere it is. When I, as an unlikely Head of the History Department at Keele, suggested that in a proposed joint degree with the Department of Foreign Languages and Politics, to be called European Studies, the *Shoah* should feature, the Professor of Politics said it was not that important, whereas the formation of the European Economic Union was. In other words, if you do a David Mackintosh or a Martin Harrison, you are an intellectual cheat. But that is exactly what English gentlemen have ever been; it is what their nannies (and their public schoolmasters) teach them to be.

Does looking evil straight in the eye lead to madness? For those who survived the *Shoah* – that is those who saw it face to face, eye to eye – it has often led to suicide: let Paul Celan and Primo Levi stand for all the others. Nevertheless, more survivors survive than do not. They live with the bleak memories of evil witnessed. Donald and Lorna Miller, who have written a history of the Armenian genocide from first–hand accounts, put it perfectly:[38]

> We acknowledge that the discovery of something redeeming in these tales of human tragedy has been our defence against despair. We refuse, however, to allow these examples of good to turn our attention from the awful reality of the genocide itself.[39]

Living with inhumanity is what we have to live with. As the great historian W. G. Hoskins once said, sitting on our sofa: 'well, the grass will remain. Now, we are not even sure of that, hence we have to think the way Einstein did: "I am thinking that, after all, this is a very small star".'

9. What is Dorothea Brooke doing here? Or: the redemptive ending is unavoidable after all. What an Englishman is

hopeless at, but James Parkes was good at, is putting himself in the place of someone else: principally Jews in the case of Parkes. That is what historians, and not only historians, ought to be doing all the time; putting themselves in the place of others. That is what morality consists of, compassion consists of, love *is*. I need not labour the point. Nor is it my final one; although it is obviously what Dorothea does all the time.

Robert Everett says at the end of his study of Parkes:[40] 'I remain amazed by the relative obscurity of his writings'. I am more amazed at their number: 239 in the biography of 1977.[41] And whatever I have said, or inferred, to the contrary – in an attempt not to be merely pious – James Parkes was a wise and perceptive man. Spot the wisdom as well as the progressivism in the following. Here he is in 1961 after the Eichmann trial verdict:[42]

> It is possible to treat any group as Jews were treated only if the link of common humanity is broken. Millions of Europeans did not show pity; tens of thousands showed cruelty; thousands indulged in every bestiality ... There is a brute in every man [and would he have added woman, if writing today?] which needs control and restraint ... It is there ... it can be controlled by intelligent and continuous action, beginning in the home and the school.

Here he is again, in the same year, reviewing Raul Hilberg's great book *The Destruction of the European Jews*:[43]

> The Eichmann trial has gradually forced a minority of the more thinking Jews, Christians, and humanists to realize how profoundly the whole structure of human thought, theological and philosophical, as well as in the more modern disciplines, is affected by events which 'only a generation ago would have been considered ... inconceivable'. It is not that men can no more be optimists, can no more devote themselves in hope of success to work for

human betterment, but that the whole idea of an inevitable betterment based on the nature of the universe itself has to be ruled out of the picture. Nature is not on the side of progress; perhaps it is not even neutral. Here is a long factual record of what man could organize and do, could watch and plan, and could find allies in the whole operation among all the 'civilized' countries of Europe. Only if these factors are taken into account dare men hope for a better future for humanity.

Parkes hoped the *Shoah* had made a difference. We know it has not. Robert Everett is amazed that Parkes' writing is not better known. We are not: a lifetime of words – always compassionate, whatever else they were – which have made no difference to the world. That, at any rate, is what I had begun to think; had begun to think I would write; had begun to believe I would end with. Then, two things happened. First, a mature student, whom I had taught in my Thomas More course last year, came to see me. I had to see you, he said, to tell you that the meditation on litter you gave out to us in the Thomas More class after you had shown us *Witness* has influenced my partner greatly; she says it sums up all she has thought; she says it sustains her; she is a very active woman: Israel, Romania, now Africa. Secondly, I read again the last paragraph of *Middlemarch* and there was Dorothea Brooke:

> Her finely-touched spirit had still its fine issues, though they were not widely visible. Her full nature ... spent itself in channels which had no great name on the earth. But the effect of her being on those around her was incalculably diffusive: for the growing good of the world is partly dependent on unhistoric acts; and that things are not so ill with you and me as they might have been, is half owing to the number who lived faithfully a hidden life, and rest in unvisited tombs.

How could Gunther Lys ever know when he conscien-
tiously objected to the Second World War in Hamburg that
over 40 years later in Haifa he would give an Englishman
from Sidcup such an example of moral goodness that one
Englishman at least has contrived ever since to attempt
unhistoric acts.

• • • • •

Until now I have neglected the mediaeval: not inadver-
tently but under the weighty pressure of modernity. Here
I shall seek to rectify that.

In a report on the commemoration of the 1190 massacre
at York in 1995 my newspaper got one thing right and
another wrong. What it got right was that 'the tragedy was
largely forgotten in Britain until five years ago, when a
plaque and a Jewish–Christian service of reconciliation
marked the 800th anniversary'. Half-right anyway: the
tragedy was not forgotten by Jews, English and European.
What it got thoroughly wrong was that 'incited by city
merchants in debt to Jews, a mob slaughtered any Jews it
could find'. How newspapers (the police, politicians, the
government) love a mob. Whatever the composition of the
one which burned, robbed, and murdered at York in March
1190, the identity of its leaders is not in doubt. Far from
being urban businessmen they were Yorkshire gentry.
Their animosity was calculated and it was that of debtors
for creditors: the neuralgic point for them was money not
religion. It is impossible to regard Richard Malebisse and
his fellows as in any manner religious, unless being antisemitic (and nothing much else) may be considered
sufficient to define Christianity – as for these lesser barons
setting out on Crusade it probably was. Rosalind Hill wrote
in 1946: 'The population of the diocese of Lincoln in the
thirteenth century was, in fact, not unlike that of England
today – that is to say, most people were essentially pagan

in thought and behaviour in spite of a long training in the outward observances of Christianity, some were generally silly and a few habitually criminal.'[44] The only issue for the historian is of the criminality of those Yorkshire gentlemen. They were the major criminals in March 1190, but were they habitually criminal? In other words, was their behaviour in March 1190 aberrant, or were they a criminal class? The question seems ideological; in fact, it is moral. Put another way, in the way that Thomas More posed it in *Utopia*, who are the mob? Thomas had an unequivocal answer: those who indulged themselves in what they, though never he, called noble pursuits, like hunting, were the mob.[45] Those whose pleasures were brutal were the killers: they killed Thomas More in 1535. They were the killers at York in 1190.

The newspaper has a photograph of the daffodils blooming on the castle mound at Clifford's Tower in York. Is it a picnic place? No doubt tourists rest there even if they do not eat lunch there. Here is an entry from James Bartholemew, *Inside the Tower: The Alternative Guide*, published in 1990:

> Execution Site, Tower Hill: very close to Tower Hill Underground station, in Trinity Gardens, this is the site of the 112 public executions which took place between 1381 and 1747. The gardens make a pleasant place for a picnic lunch.

One of those executed (legally murdered) at that pleasant place for a picnic lunch was Thomas More. None of us is Funes the Memorious. None of us would want to be. None of us could be. Complete recall, comprehensive sensitivity, total awareness are beyond us. Thankfully. Nor is there any getting away from it: yesterday's killing sites are today's picnic places. Like yesterday's house is today's restaurant. Here is an advertisement from a guidebook to Lincoln:

> The Jew's House Restaurant. Dine in the exclusive
> surroundings of this twelfth–century house. Open six days
> a week for lunch and dinner.

No harm in that, we are likely to say, so long as the tragic
history of the Jewish community of Lincoln in the thirteenth century is known to lunchers and diners. But what
if it is not made available, what if it is suppressed (in the
good cause of a pleasant dinner)? I am thinking of the
excellent dinner I had at the Stikliai Restaurant, 7 Gaono,
Vilnius, one evening in July 1994, or rather was having,
until I remembered that we were enjoying ourselves in the
heart of the ghetto and walked out. Nothing had been said,
there was nothing to tell you where we were. What you
had been told was that we were in the picturesque Old
Town of the Lithuanian capital. The moral must be not that
history is to be avoided by those running restaurants, and
certainly not deliberately avoided, but that in the siting of
restaurants it is to be carefully enquired into. I can no more
imagine James Parkes lunching at the Jew's House,
Lincoln, than I can see him dining at The Glass Makers,
Vilnius. His sensitivity has to be the measure of ours.

James Parkes might have been, could have been, should
have been, the historian of antisemitism in England. Zefira
Entin Rokeah has said that the subject 'still awaits its
historian'. It ought to be her. In a sequence of papers she
has clarified the life of Jews in England during the twelfth
and thirteenth centuries. The most remarkable of them is
about Christians: 'Unnatural Child Death among
Christians and Jews in Medieval England'.[46] If there was
child abuse in thirteenth-century England (and there was)
it was undertaken by Christian parents. Jews had no word
for infanticide and did not practise it, least of all on adoles-
cent Christian boys. What is one to make of this extra
dimension to the charge of ritual murder which Christians
made against Jews? Such inventiveness goes beyond that

of Bob Moore's *clerici* creating a fictional identity for Jews out of the need to displace them from, and to replace them in, lucrative positions of bureaucratic authority. That was a matter of one group ousting another and turning them into non-humans in order to do so. Where the ritual murder charge was concerned, the persecuting group was as large as parenthood extended and the identity issue was not one of creation but transference: we accuse you of doing what we ourselves do. Nothing is so simple. Nor so complicated. Antisemitism, after all, is one of the most complex aspects of Christian culture, while also being brutally straightforward. By 1290 most English Christians could not abide Jews – one might think; so why four years earlier did they attend a Jewish wedding at Hereford in such numbers that they came to the notice of their indignant bishop?[47]

Two of the issues raised here require further comment. I will take the Englishness of the ritual murder charge first, postponing until the next paragraph discussion of the responsibility of the *clerici* for the genesis of antisemitism. The durability of the charge is not in doubt. A survey carried out in Poland between 1976 and 1980 discovered that 'eighty percent of the inhabitants of rural areas believed' it.[48] It has also been exported. I quote from *Al Fair*, the Jerusalem Palestinian Weekly, of 23 January 1983:

PALESTINIAN
BOYS STABBED

ACRE – The bodies of two 15-year-old youths were found in the village of Tamra in the Nazareth region. They had been repeatedly stabbed with a sharp instrument. The bodies of the two youths were taken to the forensic laboratory in Abu Kbir for examination.

It is, however, the origin of the myth at Norwich shortly

after 1144 which commands attention. James Parkes commented that 'the account of the death of St William of Norwich makes it quite clear that people were slow to believe in ritual murder.'[49] In this instance it is not chivalrous knights who are to be held responsible, but peace-loving monks. At this juncture we need to listen closely to one of the most sensitive interpreters of the Middle Ages:

> The case of St William of Norwich [writes James Campbell[50]] is of sharp interest in the history of Europe because it marks the point at which the deadly lie of Jewish ritual murder comes to the surface: and does so in a big, well-endowed, not unsophisticated house of Black Monks. One need not be an enemy of the Black Monks in saying: 'They should have known better'. One would be less than a friend if one did not say: 'One wishes they had known better'. It is important that some of the monks of Norwich did indeed know better. It is clear from [Thomas of] Monmouth's book that there was opposition within the monastery to the adoption of the cult ... I would maintain that there is a parallel between those decent doubters at Norwich and William of Newburgh who would not swallow Geoffrey of Monmouth ... It may be contended, and understandably contended, that it is anachronistically beside the point to criticise the imaginative flights of medieval hagiography. Understanding, rather than condemnation, may be called for. At least in such an extreme case as that of the monks of Norwich and St William the force of another approach can be felt, one well summed up in an observation by the Duc de Broglie which Lord Acton was fond of quoting: 'We must beware of too much understanding lest we end by too much forgiving' ... Too much had been composed in the spirit of Geoffrey of Monmouth. Lies about saints were not new to the twelfth century; but the literary development of the age enabled them to be supplied on a larger scale and in a better style.

Geoffrey of Monmouth created the myth of King Arthur in his *Historia Regum Britanniae,* composed at Oxford in the first half of the 1130s. What may have been an academic joke became a phenomenal international success. Thomas of Monmouth's *De Vita et Passione Sancti Willelmi Martvris Norwicensis* was not written as lightly (it had after all an entirely different purpose), nor did it become a best-seller. Thomas, however, treated evidence with as little regard for its reliability as did his fellow–townsman, and his lies were, as James Campbell says, far, far more deadly. When intellectuals take the *Liberty Valence* option – publishing the myth and not the truth – we know not what we are about: opening Pandora's Box releases the Beast as well as Beauty.

What was the role of the monk Theobald of Cambridge, a converted Jew, in the creation of the ritual murder myth at Norwich in the mid-twelfth century? It is often said that he contributed the theme of Jewish conspiracy. Where he got such an idea from, if it was his contribution to the story, remains as great a mystery as why the crucifixion myth surfaced in England, or (more accurately) why it was connected by literate monks to the corpse of a tanner's apprentice in a wood outside Norwich at Easter 1144. What induced them to make such a connection? What was in their heads? Here is Benedicta Ward discussing the veneration of the Virgin Mary in England in the early twelfth century:[51]

> A story was told of the feast of the Assumption and its celebration in Spain. After the mass of that day, a voice was heard saying that the Son of the Virgin was again being crucified by the Jews; this experience led to violence against the Jewish community and the discovery of a wax image, pierced and crowned with thorns. The story was the first in the series collected by Anselm of Bury; as retold by William of Malmesbury, it is given a setting as historically precise as the stories of the Conception and the Purification.

Anselm of Bury's collection of 'The Miracles of the Virgin' was made soon after 1100; William of Malmesbury composed his 'Miracles of the Virgin' about 1140. Was it that story about the feast of the Assumption which was in the heads of Thomas and Theobald and came to mind when (or some time after) William's mutilated body was found in Thorpe Wood? I see no reason why not: monkish heads were stuffed with such stories, which, as Benedicta Ward reminds us, monkish minds regarded as 'historically precise'. James Campbell, at the close of the passage from which I have cited, says that 'William of Malmesbury often stood for the pursuit of truth, zealous supporter of the cult of the saints though he was'. In other words, what was history and what myth, who was an historian and who was not, and what was truth and what were lies, are more complicated matters than at first appears.

I believe there may have been another ingredient of the lethal concoction brewed at Norwich between 1144 and 1150. Here is Bob Moore:[52]

> Another reminder of the special enthusiasm of the convert is supplied by Petrus Alfonsi, at some time doctor to Henry I of England, who confirmed, in his *Dialoqus Petri et Moysi Judaei* of 1110 the opinion that his erstwhile co–religionists had organized the Crucifixion out of malice, not ignorance.

The 'new view' of the motives of Christ's killers may not have caught on at once in the academic circles of the first half of the twelfth century, but evidently it was known in England. Is it not a possibility that dislike of Jews in monkish circles was transformed into hatred by an awareness that they had deliberately murdered the Lord, who now (in those monkish minds) had become their lord? In the feudal code killing one's lord was the most heinous of crimes, as the stir caused by the murder of Galbert of Bruges demonstrated. If the Jews had known Jesus was their lord and had knowingly tortured and killed him they were the basest of men. Intellectually, was this not a major transformation in their position and an important step towards their dehumanisation? Put another way: if they could behave thus towards their lord they were capable of the most bestial behaviour, like *rustici*, like the serfs who had murdered Galbert while he was praying in church. Perhaps, before they became demons, who also knew who their lord was, Jews had to become peasants. Peasants after all were no better than brutes – or so intellectuals liked to think.[53]

Which brings us to reason and irrationality: Bob Moore's *clerici* now reappear. If we are bound to regard them as in some measure intellectual, being the product of the schools and universities, it is a half-baked intelligence that confronts us. They were the administrators and managers of their world; they were not historians, scientists and theologians. They were careerists not truth-seekers. Wandering they may have been, scholars they were not. Whatever else these upwardly mobile young men were they were not original thinkers, though they seem to epitomise (and undoubtedly themselves believed, if their verse is anything to go by) what those thinkers had come to hold as self-evident by 1200: that the urban, upper-class, white, Christian male was superior to any other being on earth. It has been argued elsewhere that the racism of a Grosseteste is not that of a Schoolman; his ruralistic bigotry is more akin to that of those Yorkshire gentlemen who massacred the Jews of York in 1190, or to that of Simon de Montfort, which may have been picked up in southern France; it is not the scientific racism of the university lecture hall, recently brought to our attention by Peter Biller in a paper which needs to be read by anyone interested in the human condition.[54] It was in the lecture hall and not on the street corner where it was first proclaimed that 'After the death of Christ all Jewish men, like women, suffer menstruation.' The diffusion of anti-semitism is not like cultural diffusion; it goes one way only:

it may be 'of the gutter' but that is not where it had its origin. That is why, whatever the way men and women who are less sure of themselves regard and treat those who are very much more aware of who and what they are, which is how the late Professor Wallace-Hadrill viewed the relationship of Christians and Jews before the watershed of the eleventh century,[55] it is the development of university education in the twelfth and thirteenth centuries which inaugurates antisemitism. It is the highly educated, as Anna Sapir Abulafia has shown,[56] who, coming to believe in a God of Love on the one hand, and in Christianity as a rational faith on the other, characterise Jews as unreasonable in not responding to what God did out of Love on the Cross. Men of the calibre of Peter the Venerable and Rupert of Deutz hated Jews with a more than reasonable hatred for that very reason: if Love of such a kind is offered how can it be rejected – save by those who lack humanity, a humanity after all which is in the image of God? Such fear and loathing on the part of the best and brightest of their age, while beginning in reason goes beyond it. It is no wonder, therefore, that such reasonable men are ready to believe in 'irrational' Jewish behaviour, because their reasoned Christian faith is itself an intensely emotional commitment, more atavistic than rational, and far more 'irrational' than anything observable or not observed in Judaism and Jewish behaviour.

How would one classify Guibert of Nogent? He is a worrying figure. He fits uneasily, if at all, into the simple configuration of the previous paragraph. Guibert, monk, historian, autobiographer, and 'rationalist', died in 1124.[57] Here is Anna Sapir Abulafia on him:[58]

> In Guibert's mind Jewish rejection of the Christological interpretation of the Hebrew Bible and Christian doctrine were intimately connected and the implication of that rejection was that Jews were filthy and carnal in a material sense.

In turn, their beastly filthiness made it impossible for them to stop rejecting what they needed to accept in order to become clean. In short, there is precious little hope for Jewish redemption in Guibert's writings. Guibert is not really seeking to convert Jews. His concern seems to be to ferret out the reason why Jews will not become Christians notwithstanding all the information they are offered about that faith. The conversion he describes at length in his autobiography is one of force not conviction. It is the conversion of the Jewish boy who was saved from death at the hands of the (popular) crusaders who attacked the Jewish community of Rouen in 1096. The boy consented to baptism out of fear for his life. Guibert was, in fact, surprised he turned out so well, overcoming what Guibert dubbed 'his evil nature'. The boy became a monk at Fly, Guibert's monastery, before Guibert became abbot of Nogent.

It is that phrase 'evil nature' which in 1116 seems disturbingly early.[59] I have not the Latin to hand; here, however, is John Benton's translation of the Guibertian passage:[60]

> Once he was assigned to the monastic discipline, he showed such love for the Christian life, drank in whatever divine learning he could acquire with such keenness of mind, endured all that was put on him by way of discipline with such calm, that the glory of the victory over his worthless nature and his recently disturbed character drew from all the greatest respect .... His naturally acute intellect was so sharpened daily that although many well educated men flourished there, not one was thought to show greater distinction of understanding. Although many feel this way, he turns no one to envy or backbiting, since his behaviour always appears cheerful and of special purity.

The phrase is less striking *in situ*: clearly a Jew (like any other man?) could triumph over nature. Or: was it baptism which worked the miracle? After all, there was a miracle at Guillaume the converted Jew's 'forced' baptism; a drop of wax falling in the water formed a tiny cross; 'therefore', concludes Guibert, 'the cross at his baptism seems to have been formed not by chance but by Providence, as a sign of the future religious faith of a man of Jewish origin, which in our days is unusual'. I would like to have the Latin of 'origin' as well as of 'nature'. Hard to say (even if I did have the Latin, and knew what to do with it when I had it) whether Guibert is of his time or ahead of it. He appears here not so that matters may be simplified, but that they shall be made more complicated. The one point all can agree on where Guibert is concerned is that he impels us to think (and think again).

The same might be said of Herman, the Jew of Cologne who became a Christian in 1129, and who wrote about it in what has been called an autobiography.[61] And here, at last, we come to Bob Moore's *clerici* and their key role in the creation of the antisemitic stereotype of 'The Jew.' As Arnaldo Momigliano summarises the story, 'Hermannus pointedly opposes the barrenness of his controversy with Rupert of Deutz (which is also the barrenness of Rupert's controversy with him) to the spiritual fruitfulness of the kind concern shown to him by a domestic of bishop Egbert [of Munster]. If the bishop had allowed it, that domestic would have submitted himself to an ordeal for the sake of the Jew's soul.' The domestic was Ricmar, purveyor of the bishop's household, who gave to Herman the white bread and roast pike bishop Egbert 'in the midst of dinner [had] sent him ... as lords do'; Ricmar, 'because he was completely filled with feelings of piety, set before me [continued Herman], with love's supreme alacrity, what had been sent to him (for I was sitting beside him).' Herman was bowled over (converted we might say) by considerate behaviour on the part of a Christian. He goes on:

Not only did I greatly rejoice on account of this deed, but I was also powerfully wonderstruck that a man whom thus far I thought beyond the Law and without God could have the virtue of charity in such great measure, especially toward me. For he could likewise have detested me as the enemy of his sect, rather than loving me.... . Wherefore, he assiduously showed his love to me in good deeds, although I was unworthy of them, and he laboured tirelessly with gentle conversations, both exhorting and beseeching, to draw me away from the error of my fathers and to win me for Christ.

Was Ricmar a true Christian, a true Jew, or simply a mensch?[62] More to the present point (though not the eternal one), is what was Ricmar's social standing? I presume that purveyors were not *clerici*. In Ricmar, surely, we are confronted by that familiar figure, the devout layman. It was a *laicus* not a *clericus* who converted Herman, and by that early Christian method, famously observed by Tertullian, namely love. So far so good.[63] The rationality of a *clericus*, Rupert of Deutz, was ineffective. However: was Rupert really trying? Was he, like Guibert of Nogent, 'not really seeking to convert Jews'? Is all that controversy literature really not academic hot air? I am inclined to believe so.[64] Twelfth-century Schoolmen were not interested, in the way Ricmar was interested, in saving souls. Twelfth-century *clerici* (as they have been defined above) were not interested either. It is not that both groups (overlapping and interpenetrating) were not interested in the opposition: the former responded to the intellectual challenge presented by Judaism, the latter to the threat Jews posed at the Job Centre. At any rate theoretically.

Yet, where are the Jews in Goliardic verse? It is a long time since I have read any so I may be making a mistake; besides, if Jews do not feature, that may be only a tiny spanner in the works. Bob Moore has stoutly maintained that he remains 'unembarrassed' by the lack of evidence of 'jealousy in the courts of northern Europe' (as so he ought to be),[65] yet in those after-hours poems would one not expect to find it? Take the Arch-poet of Cologne's 'Confession of Golias'; it is all the standard stuff of women, wine, and gambling, and might just as well have been written yesterday by a young man in the City of London. Rainald of Dassel no doubt enjoyed it as a relief from reading business papers: it is all harmless fun he duly reported to Frederick Barbarossa. Perhaps that is it: it is exactly because these are after-hours poems that one should not expect to find serious invective in them. I would, however, like reassurance on that score.

It also seems that the Premonstratensians of Cappenberg did not resent Herman-Judah's presence in their community – any more than the monks of Ely had been jealous of Guillaume's prominence in theirs; moreover, Herman went on to hold leading positions in the Church. Still, he was by then a Christian: wasn't he? Considering identity: there is an admirable example of its imposition in the story of Godeliva and the Jewess told by Michael Adler (for a different purpose); the story is in *Materials for the Life of Thomas Becket* and dates to 1193:[66]

> It is related that a Christian woman named Godeliva was one day carrying a bucket containing water that had been sanctified by the martyred St Thomas and was passing the inn of a certain Jew. At the invitation of a Jewess who suffered from a weak foot, Godeliva very kindly entered the inn for the purpose of 'charming the foot', being skilled in charms and incantations. 'But', continues the tale, 'scarcely had her foot entered the cursed house when the bucket flew into three pieces, and by the loss of the water she learned the wicked intuitions of her own mind, and understanding that she had committed a fault, she returned no more to that Jewess'.

We are faced once more with the notions of the learned; here they are producing *apartheid* in twelfth-century Canterbury. Which is only to be expected.

What of the unexpected? Joseph the *Hasid* of Bungay is a surprise.[67] How many other *zaddiks* were there in the small country towns of thirteenth-century England? What were the links, if there were any, between them and the German Pietists? It is also a surprise to read Richard Hunt writing post-1945, 'Controversial literature directed against the Jews reappeared at the end of the eleventh century and was vigorously maintained throughout the twelfth, as the Jewish problem became more acute.'[68] I do not think James Parkes would have cared for 'Jewish problem'. What he would have enjoyed is Michael Hilton's *The Christian Effect on Jewish life*, which appeared in 1994, a book as courageous as was Charles Dugmore's *The Influence of the Synagogue upon the Divine Office* which came out exactly 50 years previously. It ought to seem astonishing that Oxford University Press in the early 1930s refused to publish what Gavin Langmuir has called a 'courageous and singularly prescient book', namely *The Conflict of the Church and the Synagogue*, but to anyone who knows the England of the 1930s it does not.[69] It is no more unexpected than that there is not a biography of James Parkes. There is particular need for one because his autobiography is so unassuming it reveals virtually nothing about a great English eccentric, eccentric because he was not only 'against the grain', but was also an activist: he was one for whom thinking was not enough.

NOTES

1. This chapter is a revised version of a paper delivered as the 1994 Parkes Lecture at the University of Southampton.
2. Prior to the lecture I went to Venice; after it I read John Ruskin, *The Stones of Venice* (fifth edition, Orpington & London: George Allen, 1893), Vol. II, pp. 164–6. The incomparable Ruskin there discusses the matter: 'And her history, so far as it was thus in her desolation graven, is indeed in this book (as now

put into the traveller's hand, free of the encumbrance of minor detail) told truly, and, I find on re-reading it, so clearly, that it greatly amazes me at this date to reflect how no one has ever believed a word I said, though the public have from the first done me the honour to praise my manner of saying it; and, as far as they found the things I spoke of amusing to themselves, they have deigned for a couple of days or so to look at them, helped always though the tedium of the business by due quantity of ices at Florian's, music of moonlight on the Grand Canal, paper-lamps, and the English papers and magazines at M. Ongaria's ... .

'Allowing to the full for the extreme unpleasantness of the facts recorded in this book to the mind of a people set wholly on the pursuit of the same pleasures which ruined Venice; only in ways as witless as hers were witty; I think I can now see a further reason for their non-acceptance of the book's teaching, namely, the entire concealment of my own personal feelings throughout, which gives a continual look of insincerity to my best passages. Everybody praised their "style", partly because they saw it was stippled and laboured, and partly because for that stippling and labouring I had my reward, and got three sentences into pleasantly sounding tune. But nobody praised the substance, which indeed they never took the trouble to get at; but occasionally tasting its roughness here and there, as of a bitter almond put by mistake into a sugar-plum, spat it out, and said, "What a pity it had got in".'

3. George Eliot, *Daniel Deronda* (Harmondsworth: Penguin edition, 1967), p. 655.
4. 'The bad and the indifferent', *The Independent on Sunday*, 10 Oct. 1993.
5. Barbara Hardy, 'Introduction', *Daniel Deronda*, p. 14.
6. '*Daniel Deronda*: A conversation', *Atlantic Monthly*, 1876, reprinted in F.R. Leavis *The Great Tradition: George Eliot, Henry James, Joseph Conrad* (London: Chatto & Windus, 1948).
7. Frederic Raphael, *The Necessity of Anti-Semitism* (The Parkes 25th Anniversary Lecture, University of Southampton, 1989), p. 21, for all the citations in this paragraph.
8. Lucy S. Dawidowicz (ed.), *The Golden Tradition: Jewish Life and Thought in Eastern Europe* (Northvale, NJ: Jason Aronsen, 1967), p. 349.
9. Jakov Lind, *Crossing: the Discovery of Two Islands* (London: Methuen, 1991), p. 55.
10. Arnold J. Toynbee, *Acquaintances* (London: Oxford University Press, 1967), pp. 65–6.
11. Llewelyn Powys (ed. and abr.), *The life and times of Anthony à Wood* (London: Wishart & Co., 1932), pp. 41–2.
12. For an alternative explanation of the genesis of Dada, see Colin Richmond, 'The Day Henry James Discovered Dada', *Encounter*, No. 313 (Oct. 1979), collected in Colin Richmond, *The Penket Papers* (Gloucester: Alan Sutton, 1986), pp. 81–5.
13. Greil Marcus, *Lipstick Traces: a Secret History of the Twentieth Century* (London: Secker & Warburg, 1989), pp. 194–5. I owe my knowledge of this stimulating book to an old friend and pupil, Dr Ian Arthurson.
14. Marcus, *Lipstick Traces*, p. 229.
15. Julian Tuwim, *We, Polish Jews...* (1944, facsimile edition, Warsaw, 1993), p. 42.
16. Robert A. Everett, *Christianity without Anti-Semitism: James Parkes and the Jewish-Christian encounter* (Oxford: Pergamon, 1993), pp. 234–5.
17. Everett, *Christianity Without Anti-Semitism*, pp. 202, 207.
18. R.I. Moore, *The Formation of a Persecuting Society: Power and Deviance in Western Europe 950–1250* (London: Blackwell, 1987).
19. It amounts to this, and the 'this' is only the Preface of one book, Reuben

Ainsztein, *Jewish resistance in Nazi-occupied Eastern Europe* (London: Elek, 1974): 'To the Memory of my sexagenarian parents, Hannah and Zelman Ainsztein, murdered at Ponary; my eldest sister Frida and my youngest sister Zhenya gassed at Kaiserwald near Riga; my sister Mania Liff and her daughter Shoshana, who survived the Vilno Ghetto, Kaiserwald, Stutthof and the death march of January 1945, when with several hundred Jewish women and Red Army prisoners-of-war they were saved by a Red Army tank unit commanded by a Jewish officer from being burned alive by their SS guards in a barn near Chimow; Mania's only son Yosef, who did not join the partisans in order to be with his parents and was last seen alive by his mother at Stutthof; his father Isaac Liff, who survived the Vilno Ghetto, the labour camps of Estonia, Kaiserwald, Stutthof, Buckenwald and Halberstadt to be saved by American soldiers and die in Israel; my sexagenarian aunt Paula Stolar of Antwerp, who was removed with a broken hip from a Belgian hospital by Germans who sent her to one of the death factories in Poland; my uncle and aunt in Leningrad who died with over 600,000 civilians during the siege of their city by the Wehrmacht; and to all my other relatives and friends who were exterminated at Ponary and elsewhere.'

20. Based on Thomas Keneally's, *Schindler's Ark* (London: Hodder & Stoughton, 1982), later reissued as *Schindler's List*.
21. Christopher Sykes, *Orde Wingate* (London: Collins, 1959), p. 217.
22. That very funny and very wise passage in Nick Hornby's, *Fever Pitch* (London: Gollancz, 1992), pp. 47–51, describing how he re-invented Maidenhead as Islington.
23. I am thinking particularly of the photographs in D. Marley (ed.), *Daily Telegraph Story of the War*, Vol. V (London: Hodder & Stoughton, 1942–46), a book I bought second-hand in Charing Cross Road in the early 1950s; those photographs, especially that of the barn at Gardelegen near Magdeburg where more than 1,000 concentration camp prisoners were burned alive by their guards, haunted me. I opened that book rarely and with reluctance. At some stage my copy went missing; this morning (30 April 1994) I bought the book second-hand for the second time; these days I am more used to such photographs, but not that one.
24. John Pawlikowski, 'The Church and Judaism: the thought of James Parkes', *Journal of Ecumenical Studies* (1969), quoted in Everett, *Christianity Without Anti-Semitism*, p. 270.
25. David Weiss, *The Wings of the Dove* (Washington, DC: B'nai Brith Books, 1987), p. 159.
26. I have in mind here Gregor von Rezzori, chronicler of the Central European world of the day before yesterday, especially in *The Snows of Yesteryear: Portraits of an Autobiography*, (New York: Knopf, 1989). The following quotation, however, is from *The Orient Express* (New York: Random House, 1993): 'Thus here too in the world of Market-conscious technocrats – and above all in the world of their string-pullers – everything depended on the possession of cave-man survival skills. Researchers and scientists, the most brilliant minds of the age, poets, geniuses, and inventors were all being dictated to by troglodytes in charcoal-grey double-breasted suits beneath which beat cannibal hearts.' Identified here are the self-styled experts of our problem-oriented, 'problem-solving' world, on whom and on which Jorge Luis Borges has had the last (and predictably best) word: 'The word *problem* may be an insidious *petitio principii*. To speak of the *Jewish problem* is to postulate that the Jews are a problem; it is to predict (and recommend) persecution, plunder, shooting, beheading, rape, and the reading of Dr. Rosenberg prose', cited in Zygmunt Bauman, *Modernity and Ambivalence* (Cambridge: Polity, 1991), p. 260, n. 23.

244   *Cultures of Ambivalence and Contempt*

27. 'With Gershom Scholem: an interview', Werner J. Dannhauser (ed.), *On Jews and Judaism in Crisis. Selected Essays* (New York: Schocken Books, 1976), pp. 31–2.
28. Did Scholem agree with that great Russian scientist, scholar, and priest, Pavel Florensky, who condemned the Renaissance? When Western art became humanistic in the thirteenth century, repudiating iconic spirituality, all began to be lost. That is clearer now than it was in the 1920s. I owe my scanty knowledge of Florensky to Donald Nicholl. Scholem would not have gone as far as Dr Marek Edelman, who, one memorable morning in Warsaw in March 1991, told me that man had mistakenly mutated, the part of his brain which is technically inclined being over-developed, the part where compassion resides being under-developed. The judgement of someone who witnessed what Edelman did at the hospital beside the *Umschlagplatz* in 1942 and during the Ghetto Uprising in 1943 cannot be lightly put aside.
29. Jacob Katz, *Exclusiveness and Tolerance: Studies in Jewish-Gentile Relations in Medieval and Modern Times* (London: Oxford University Press, 1961), p. 96.
30. Everett, *Christianity Without Anti-Semitism*, p. 309.
31. Ed Vulliamy, *Seasons in Hell: Understanding Bosnia's War* (London: Simon Schuster, 1994), p. 5
32. *Daniel Deronda*, p. 380.
33. Take Bosnia again: 'At the back of the dank dugout, Dragan, a good-looking young man, was talking to the radio. Dragan was joking and laughing and exchanging friendly insults; we wrongly assumed he was bantering with his men on the lines. He was talking into Vukovar; the translation went something like this: "Is that you, Davor, you Ustasha bastard, you all OK there?" "Fine Chetnik scumbag. When did you last see a bar of soap?" "Your wife still there? Good! Here's one for her", and he puts down the receiver and goes out to the little huddle around the mortar, who duly load their weapon, push their fingers in their ears and fire. "Didn't even hear it", comes the crackly voice from Vukovar some time later, "You're useless". They knew each other from the local shoe factory, in which they had worked as packagers until six months previously.' Vulliamy, *Seasons in Hell*, p. 20.
   Until historians grasp that war is more appealing than packaging, that killing may be a pleasure, and that many modern young men, like the two jolly killers in Bosnia, need no other reasons for doing either, they will not be able to get to grips with the twentieth-century history of Europe. For more on this subject see Klaus Theweleit, *Male Fantasies*, 2 Vols (Minneapolis: University of Minnesota Press, 1987 and Cambridg: Polity, 1989), and Ernst Klee, Willi Dressen and Volker Riess, *'Those were the Days': the Holocaust Through the Eyes of the Perpetrators and Bystanders* (London: Hamish Hamilton, 1991).
34. Everett, *Christianity Without Anti-Semitism*, pp. 154, 159.
35. Everett, *Christianity Without Anti-Semitism*, p. 132.
36. Andrew Charlesworth, 'Towards a geography of the Shoah', *Journal of Historical Geography*, Vol. 18 (1992), p. 469.
37. Charles, S. Maier, *The Unmasterable Past: History, Holocaust and German National Identity* (Cambridge, MA: Harvard University Press, 1988), p. 159.
38. Donald, E. and Lourna Touryan Miller, *Survivors: an Oral History of the Armenian Genocide* (Berkeley: University of California Press, 1993), p. 5.
39. The inscription on the St Barbe family tomb of 1658 in Romsey Abbey, which I noted the day I gave the Parkes lecture, will not do for historians: THE MEMORY OF THE WICKED SHALL ROT BUT THE REMEMBRANCE OF THE JUST SHALL LIVE FORE EVER. Memory of the wicked must never be allowed to rot; the dead and only the dead may forgive; historians cannot forget.
40. Everett, *Christianity Without Anti-Semitism*, p. 130.

41. Sidney Sugarman and Diana Bailey (comp.), *A Bibliography of the Printed Works of James Parkes*, with selected quotations and biographical notes (University of Southampton, 1977). I am grateful to Tony Kushner for sending me a copy of this work. The quotations are an admirable introduction to Parkes.

42. Sugarman and Bailey (comp.), *A Bibliography of the Printed Works of James Parkes*, p. 68; it is a piece in the *Observer*, 17 Dec. 1961.

43. MS 60 Parkes Papers 10/2; a typescript draft of a review for the *Observer*, Nov. 1961, a copy of which was kindly supplied by the Archive Department, University of Southampton.

44. Miss R. M. T. Hill, 'Oliver Sutton, Bishop of Lincoln, and the University of Oxford', *Transactions of the Royal Historical Society*, Fourth Series, XXXI (1949), p. 6. For Richard Malebisse and his fellow criminals: R. B. Dobson, *The Jews of Medieval York and the Massacre of March 1190*, University of York, Borthwick Papers No. 45 (1974), pp. 31–7. For knights as the culprits in the Rhineland in 1096 see Jonathan Riley Smith, 'The First Crusade and the Persecution of the Jews', *Studies in Church History*, Vol. 21; W. J. Sheils (ed.) *Persecution and Toleration* (York: St Antony's Press, 1984), pp. 54–6, and for knights as perpetrators of the 'Rintfleisch' movement of 1298–1300 and of the 'Armleder' movement of 1336–38, both occurring in southern Germany and both of them terrifyingly murderous, see Miri Rubin, 'Desecration of the Host: the Birth of an Accusation', *Studies in Church History*, 29, Diana Wood (ed.), *Christianity and Judaism* (Oxford: Blackwell, 1992), pp. 177, 181–2. In that volume R. I. Moore elaborates the point I am urging here about antisemitism as a knightly pursuit: 'Anti-Semitism and the Birth of Europe', pp. 45–7.

45. Edward Surtz and J. H. Hexter (eds), *Utopia* (New Haven: Yale University Press, 1965), p. 172.

46. *The Journal of Psychohistory*, Vol. 18 (1990), pp. 181–226. I am indebted to Edmund Fryde for introducing me to the work of this most accomplished of the pupils of John Hine Mundy. Mrs Rokeah's comment on the lack of an historian of English antisemitism comes from her essay, 'The State, the Church, and the Jews in Medieval England', in Shmuel Almog (ed.), *Antisemitism Through the Ages* (Oxford: Oxford University Press, 1988), p. 102.

47. See the comments of Barrie Dobson, 'Jewish Women in Medieval England', *Studies in Church History*, Vol. 29, Wood (ed.), *Christianity and Judaism*, (Oxford: Blackwell, 1992), pp. 158–9.

48. Alina Cala, 'Contemporary Anti-Semitism in Poland', *Polish Western Affairs*, XXXII (1991), p. 167.

49. James Parkes, *The Jew in the Medieval Community* (London: Soncino Press, 1938), p. 127.

50. James Campbell, *Essays in Anglo-Saxon History* (London: Hambledon Press 1986), p. 226.

51. Benedicta Ward, *Miracles and the Medieval Mind* (London: Scolar Press, 1982), p. 161.

52. Moore, 'Anti-Semitism and the Birth of Europe', p. 52.

53. Alexander Murray, *Reason and Society in the Middle Ages* (Oxford: Clarendon Press, 1978), pp. 237–44.

54. 'Views of Jews from Paris around 1300: Christian or "Scientific"?', *Studies in Church History*, Vol. 29; Wood (ed.), *Christianity and Judaism* (1992), pp. 187–207.

55. J. M. Wallace-Hadrill, *Early Medieval History* (Oxford: Blackwell, 1976), pp. 6–8.

56. A. Sapir Abulafia, *Christians and Jews in the Twelfth-Century Renaissance* (London: Routledge, 1995), esp. Chps 5, 8, 9.

57. John F. Benton, in the introduction to his translation of Guibert's memoirs, *Self and Society in Medieval France* (Toronto & London: Medieval Academy of

America, 1984), p. 10, tells us, 'Nineteenth-century historians were drawn to Guibert by his rationalism, scepticism, and proto-nationalism. In that condescending fashion with which historians sometimes grant awards, Lefranc called him "practically a modern man." But other commentators have noted a dark side to his character ... . He was among the first anti-Semitic writers to accuse the Jews of witchcraft and black magic.' Nothing better illustrates the fact of one age's rationalism being another's black magic. I note that Colin Morris in his influential book - influential on me, that is – *The Discovery of the Individual 1050–1200* (New York: Harper & Row, 1972), p. 84, calls Guibert's autobiography 'something of a scrap-book, but an intelligent and enjoyable one.' Hmm.

58. Sapir Abulafia, *Christians and Jews in the Twelfth-Century Renaissance*, p. 113.
59. Rather as John Clare's description of Farmer Thrifty as 'An outside Christian but at heart a Jew' is disturbingly late: *The Parish*, written in the 1820s, line 1857.
60. Benton, *Self and Society in Medieval France*, p. 136.
61. Arnaldo Momigliano, 'A Medieval Jewish Autobiography', *History and Imagination. Essays in honour of H. R. Trevor-Roper* (London: Duckworth, 1981), pp. 30–6. The autobiography is now available in translation in Karl F. Morrison, *Conversion and Text. The Cases of Augustine of Hippo, Herman-Judah, and Constantine Tsatsos* (Charlottesville: The University Press of Virginia, 1992), pp. 76–113.
62. Against the cliché of the true this and that we have been warned by no less an historian than Gershom Scholem, *Sabbatai Sevi* (London: Routledge & Kegan Paul, 1973), p. 283.
63. Ricmar embodies the first (although not necessarily the second) part of Joseph Needham's famous saying, 'only the wholly other can inspire the deepest love and the profoundest desire to learn': *The Grand Titration* (London: George Allen & Unwin, 1969), p. 176.
64. So, I take it, is Robert C. Stacey, 'The Conversion of Jews to Christianity in Thirteenth-Century England', *Speculum*, Vol. 67 (1992), pp. 263–4, 'Serious theological discussion about Jewish conversion did not begin until the twelfth century, when Christian intellectuals turned the Christian-Jewish *disputation* into a veritable literary and philosophical genre. Even then, however, these disputational tracts continued to be aimed at a Christian rather than a Jewish audience.' *His* reference is to the work of David Berger. Saul Bellow puts it another way, *The Bellarosa Connection* (London: Penguin, 1989), p. 24: 'One can think of such things – and think and *think* – but nothing is resolved by these historical meditations. To *think* doesn't settle anything.' That is the point about Ricmar: he wasn't *thinking*.
65. Moore, 'Anti-Semitism and the Birth of Europe', p. 51.
66. Michael Adler, *Jews of Medieval England* (London: Goldston, 1939), p. 56.
67. V.D. Lipman, *The Jews of Medieval Norwich* (London: Jewish Historical Society of England, 1967), p. 148.
68. 'The Disputation of Peter of Cornwall against Simon the Jew', in *Studies in Medieval History Presented to Frederick Maurice Powicke* (Oxford: Clarendon Press, 1948), p. 146.
69. Gavin Langmuir, 'The Faith of Christians and Hostility to Jews', *Studies in Church History*, Vol. 29; Wood (ed.), *Christianity and Judaism*, p. 91.

10

Reporting Antisemitism: The *Jewish Chronicle* 1879–1979[1]

DAVID CESARANI

For over 150 years, the *Jewish Chronicle* has reported the incidence of antisemitism in Britain and abroad. In this lecture I want to survey how it covered antisemitism between 1879 and 1979, and try to show what determined its editorial position.

My starting point will be 1879 because that year saw the inception of so-called modern antisemitism on the continent and the coining of the term itself by Wilhelm Marr.[2] It was also a crucial period in the development of anti-semitism in Great Britain. The Bulgarian Agitation had still not burned itself out; Disraeli was Prime Minister and inspired a torrent of anti-Jewish doggerel as well as the more subtle opprobrium in which Gladstone specialised.[3] Finally, in July 1878, the *Jewish Chronicle* had acquired new owners and a new editor and by the following year had embarked on a period of fresh development.

I will end in 1979 because a hundred years of almost anything is quite enough, but also for more serious reasons. In 1977 William Frankel, who had been editor for nearly 20 years, retired and a new era began at the paper.

Two years later Margaret Thatcher's election victory broke the mould of post-war British politics which had been the matrix for issues of 'race', immigration and antisemitism.

Before proceeding any further it is necessary to say a word about terminology. The term antisemitism is as problematic as the subject itself. It is preferable to speak of a discourse about the Jews which operates through stereotypes that can be either positive or negative depending upon the intention of the agent employing them, something which can be deduced by careful attention to the context in which they are used. Hence the very same Jews can be either ruthlessly selfish, capitalist exploiters or thrusting, individualistic entrepreneurs. The point is not what such Jews are actually supposed to be or what they do, but how they are constructed in language and culture. Discourse about Jews is of ancient provenance, deeply rooted in western Christian culture and pervasive. So called philosemitism is part of this stereotypical system. Thus, when I use the term antisemitism I am using it within the framework of a complex discourse about Jews, fraught with ambiguities.[4]

The paper's new owners in 1878 were Israel Davis (1847–1927), who controlled its fortunes until 1907, and Sidney Montagu Samuel (1848–84), whose life and influence were of short duration. They appointed Asher Myers (1848–1902), the former assistant editor, to the editorial chair.[5] Myers was born in London and trained for a commercial career. He was drawn into newspaper publishing as a young man and after a financially ruinous involvement with the *Jewish Record* arrived at the *Jewish Chronicle* in 1870. Myers was well-connected with the Anglo-Jewish intelligentsia of the time and sensitively articulated the views, aspirations and anxieties of the Anglo-Jewish middle classes.

By 1879, the *Jewish Chronicle* had a well-oiled machine for foreign news gathering. Its correspondents quickly reported the phenomena of pseudo-scientific and political antisemitism which appeared first in Germany. In a series of three leading articles beginning in November 1879, the paper threw scorn on the so-called scientific basis of the new movement and shrewdly diagnosed it to be the political fall-out from the economic depression of the 1870s.[6] Initially, it was not inclined to take the antisemites seriously. However, when political antisemitism prospered at the polls and showed no signs of dying out it reflected at length on its causes.

The paper's correspondents (who have remained anonymous for the most part) reported that the Jews were a dominating force in German business, culture and politics and that the antisemites were reacting to this. Thus informed, the paper considered that German antisemites were motivated by jealousy of the Jewish 'race'. Such analysis led inexorably to blaming the victims of anti-semitism for its occurrence. A leading article on 14 January 1881, asserted that 'They [German Jews] have to a large extent, brought down all this envy on their heads by the ostentatious manner in which they have paraded their success.'[7]

Editorial advice to German Jews about how best to cope with the upsurge of racial hatred grew logically from the paper's perception of antisemitism. It advised Jews in Germany to behave in an exemplary fashion and avoid ostentation. An editorial on 4 November 1881 disparaged active communal defence: 'We are inclined to believe that much of the resonance caused by the antisemite's utter-ances of late years has been due to the ultra-sensitiveness of the Jews in Germany. For every pamphlet against the Jews there appeared seven in their favour magnifying the importance of the original attack sevenfold.'

The paper put its beliefs into practice three years later when Pastor Stoecker, the leader of the Berlin antisemitic party, visited London. Stoecker was prevented by a public

250 Cultures of Ambivalence and Contempt

outcry from using the Mansion House in the City for a rally, and his meeting at another venue was widely condemned. But the *Jewish Chronicle* stressed that this was 'entirely spontaneous and uninfluenced by any prompting of leading Jews'. It reiterated its aversion to demonstrations and polemics. 'We have never approved of laboured refutations of such charges. We have always thought that the best way for Jews to meet them was to make silent appeal from the traducers to their own lives. The imaginary Jew of the antisemite vanishes like the phantom it is when it is confronted with the Jew of real life. With Englishmen at any rate, the truth will prevail.'[8]

As we will see England was considered to be different. Underlying the coverage of anti-Jewish movements on the continent was the conceit that such occurrences would be impossible in this country. Much of the analysis of antisemitism was implicitly structured by this political and social differentiation. For example, the paper tended to blame political antisemitism in the Austro-Hungarian Empire, especially in Vienna, on the influence of the Roman Catholic Church. This was so even though its correspondents also showed that Karl Lueger, who finally became Mayor of Vienna at the head of the antisemites, was instrumental and opportunistic in his manipulation of Jew hatred.[9]

Ritual murder allegations defied such rational dissection. The paper dismissed the notorious ritual murder trial at Tisza-Eszlar in Hungary in 1882–83 as a temporary revival of 'mediaeval' Jew-hatred and the consequence of religious prejudice.[10] It was less easy to shrug off the 1892 Xanten Case in Germany, which could not be attributed to the prejudices of backward peasants. The paper despaired at the resurrection in a new form of the ancient blood libel: 'By pretending to use scientific methods they have arrested for a moment that dissolution of anti-Jewish prejudice and all its attendant superstitions which the enlightened spirit of the times was gradually working.' The *Jewish Chronicle* was at a loss to deal with antisemitic conspiracy theories according to which any contrary evidence to such claims could be disparaged as the product of Jewish machinations. It also apprehended the role of the press in blowing up and popularising such bizarre accusations.[11] Bereft of a way to explain how antisemites could use science and modern media to regenerate an ancient calumny, the paper ascribed the Polna case in Bohemia, in 1899, to a 'Clerico-Reactionary Conspiracy'.[12]

The same diagnosis of antisemitism in Germany and Austria was applied to the Dreyfus Affair. When, in 1894, Dreyfus was found guilty of the trumped-up charges against him the *Jewish Chronicle* was instantly suspicious. To its perpetual credit it declared that, 'For our part we decline emphatically to believe that any Jewish officer can have been guilty of the treasonable practices imputed to Captain Dreyfus, and we shall cling to this belief until it is made quite clear to us that the evidence against him was in itself conclusive and that its genuineness was properly tested.'[13]

Thereafter, silence descended over the matter. In France the Jews kept their heads down and Jewish communities abroad followed suit.[14] The *Jewish Chronicle* tacitly endorsed the policy of the French Jewish leadership and barely returned to the subject until the Affair was detonated by Emile Zola's famous exposé. Then, even though he disliked polemics, Myers acted with alacrity and published a specially commissioned translation of *J'accuse* in the *Jewish Chronicle* as a four-page supplement on 28 January 1898.

For the next two years the Affair dominated the paper's foreign coverage, but not without misgivings. At times it was almost apologetic about its reportage. An editorial commented in February 1898 that 'We are not blind to the dangers which beset Jewish interference in this matter …. Dignified, loyal and upright conduct is often the most effective reply to the shriek of the fanatic, the best antidote to the poison of the slanderer.' The motives for this reticence were revealing. 'People may regard it as an indication of the solidarity that is supposed to knit all Jews into a single whole. Our reply is that we said little or nothing in regard to the Dreyfus affair until an individual error was magnified into a *national crime* ... .'[15]

When Max Nordau criticised French Jews for their passivity, the *Jewish Chronicle* reproached him, saying that it would be a folly to 'rush as a body to the defence of Dreyfus, to identify themselves as a people with him'. The paper fully supported the official French Jewish organisations: 'The only rational course for the Jews of France to take was to hold aloof as far as they could from the agitation, to leave an ordinary offence to be dealt with in an ordinary way, and to refuse to give a racial colouring to the matter. ...' Never was a policy more justified by events.[16]

Although the *Jewish Chronicle*'s conduct mirrored the behaviour of French Jewry, evidence exists that the paper's stance was not universally approved. 'There have been some', it admitted on 9 June 1899, 'who have thought Jews and their press lax and halting in their resistance to the terrible injustice done to their coreligionist.' To these critics it repeated the argument that corporate agitation by Jews on behalf of Dreyfus would only have rebounded on their own heads.'[17]

Like much of the Liberal British press the *Jewish Chronicle* held French Roman Catholicism and the Jesuits, in particular, culpable for the Affair. On 6 January 1899, the leader writer stated that 'Jews have now to confront everywhere in Europe the Jesuit enemy; a bitter and relentless force which has pursued its course from generation to generation.' It stated daringly that: 'The Jesuits may be the irregular cavalry of the Catholic army, but that does not relieve the supreme commander from responsibility for their actions.'[18]

Length

The.

The preponderance of Roman Catholicism in France set that country apart from Britain and encouraged the conceit that such things could not happen here. However, if England was not Germany, Austria or France, what was the explanation for occurrences of antisemitism at home?

To begin with there was the continuing feud between Jews and the Liberal Party. In its survey for the Jewish Year in 1878, the *Jewish Chronicle* objected that, 'In this great country we have witnessed scurrilous and discreditable attacks on the Prime Minister, because his grandfather was a Venetian and a Jew' by men who claimed to be 'the champions of liberalism'. W. E. Gladstone was himself held to be guilty of 'strange extravagances ... a want of discretion'.[19]

Less subtle manifestations of hostility towards the Jews were more clearly discernible. The paper identified anti-Jewish currents running through the agitation against usury in the 1880s, 1890s and 1900s.[20] It attributed hostility to *shechita*, religious slaughter, to similar tendencies. Indeed, when the Liberal *Pall Mall Gazette* described *shechita* as 'fiendish inhumanity', in November 1882, the *Jewish Chronicle* observed that 'A remarkable change has during the past few years come over the outer world in relation to Judaism. Where previously all was good-will towards Jews and all that was Jewish, one finds in many quarters a tendency to criticise every point that can by any means be regarded as open to criticism.'[21]

Hostility was not merely verbal. In April 1884, the paper reported physical violence against Polish Jews, itinerant traders, in the Limerick area of Ireland. The editorial writer was 'not disposed to exaggerate the importance of the attack'.[22] However, the incident proved more than a flash in the pan. In 1888–89 a concerted campaign against Jews in Cork and Limerick got under way that lasted for over a decade, leading to the ruination of two Jewish communities.[23]

To what did the *Jewish Chronicle* attribute such developments? Broadly speaking the paper blamed Jews for antisemitism. In an editorial entitled 'Some Jewish Defects', on 2 June 1893, it warned:

> When the *Judenhetze* first broke out in Germany some years ago those who aided and abetted it were wont to point to the monopoly by the Berlin Jews of the best places at the theatres and to similar facts in justification of the new crusade. Here in England the same undesirable phenomena are to be witnessed. The obtrusion of Jewish luxury, the wearing of diamonds on inappropriate occasions and an abnormal profusion, dressing and talk alike which are 'loud' – all these things attract more attention than they deserve, but an attention which reflects unfavourably upon the Jewish character and upon Jewish interests.

The greatest blame was placed upon the immigrants from Eastern Europe. Myers thought that Russian and Polish Jews, with their 'hard shell', bore much of the responsibility for antisemitism in Britain. In a leading article on 25 October 1881 the paper reflected that 'They give rise to the Jewish Question everywhere; in their future amelioration lies the only hope of its permanent settlement.' It went on 'We have no desire to "wash linen in public", but it must be admitted that the raw unfledged "Polak" starts with manners which are likely to raise ill-feeling among the neighbours whom he calls "Goyim".'

Anti-alienism, the movement to restrict Jewish immigration, was taken to confirm this diagnosis. 'How long will it be', the paper asked in November 1895 in reply to the demands for legislation to restrict the influx, 'before the exclusion of other Jews than Russian and Polish immigrants is demanded? Already the Socialist press is asking why, if we are going to exclude pauper Jews because they compete with native labour, we do not exclude Jewish capitalists. We know whither this special legislation leads

... . Practically the whole of the agitation against the Russian and Polish immigrant is the result of an antipathy toward Jews, albeit racial rather than religious.'[24]

Between 1878 and 1902, when he died, Asher Myers perceived an alarming growth of antisemitism abroad and at home. His analysis tended to dismiss it as a mediaeval throw-back, the excrescence of Roman Catholicism, or the result of popular ignorance manipulated by unscrupulous politicians. The *Jewish Chronicle* at this time also attributed a good deal of antisemitism to the behaviour of its victims. This approach confirmed the fears of middle-class Anglo-Jewry and guided its response to the immigrants. Additionally, it helped to establish the notion that if Jews policed their own community they could mitigate anti-Jewish hostility. This conviction was a central tenet of the ideology of emancipation according to which it was held that the Jews had merited civic equality by virtue of their contribution to English society and concordance with English mores, and that conversely any deviation from accepted ways or 'parasitism' could jeopardise their civil status.[25] Myers was succeeded by Maurice Duparc, his assistant, but the real power passed to Israel Davis. A man of enormous energy and great intelligence, Davis had a distaste for unseemly polemics and tended to play down divisive issues or smother them in a mass of detail. Yet the spectre of antisemitism in Britain could no longer be ignored. During 1902 and 1903, there were disturbances in South Wales at Dowlais and Pontypridd during which Jews were physically assaulted. At Limerick the crippling boycott of Jewish traders continued.[26] However, the *Jewish Chronicle* maintained the policy which it preached to German and French Jews: lying low and hoping that the agitation would 'blow over'. This complemented the stand taken by the Board of Deputies. Despite criticism of this quiescence, a year after the Limerick affair started, the *Jewish Chronicle* declared: 'We are reluctant to stir up the

memories of a half-forgotten, if still continuing scandal
... .'[27]

Simon Gelberg (later Simon Gilbert), the paper's star
reporter, took a more robust position on antisemitism. He
was ever willing to denounce anti-alien politicians as antisemites and strongly influenced the paper's opposition to
the 1904 Aliens Bill. During this struggle the *Jewish
Chronicle* made free use of the suggestion that anti-alienism
was really antisemitism. It argued that legislation which
discriminated between British Jews and alien Jews would
inevitably colour perceptions of the former. The paper
warned that 'We cannot believe that the Home Secretary
has seriously considered the danger of generating such
dangerous distinctions in the popular mind, and of
creating the beginnings of an anti-Jewish sentiment under
government patronage.'[28]

In December 1906, the *Jewish Chronicle* was purchased
by Leopold Greenberg (1861–1931), who ran an advertising
agency, and a group of friends who were, like him, leading
activists in the Zionist movement. It now acquired a Jewish
nationalist slant which played into its handling of antisemitism. Like most Zionists who had read Pinsker and
Herzl, Greenberg regarded antisemitism as an inevitable
result of *galut* or exile. Jews were a national rather than an
exclusively religious group and were accordingly different.
In certain circumstances that difference could arouse irrita-
tion, but it should not become the cause for self-
effacement or apology. Without compunction Greenberg
pinned the label of prejudice on politicians, agitators and
journalists who indulged in negative comments about
Jews or Jewish practices. Conversely, he was willing to
publish material which former editors feared would be
exploited by antisemites. Greenberg saw no benefit in concealing the truth since he did not believe that Jew haters
would ever want for evidence, real or imagined, to fortify
their prejudices.

So, while debate raged throughout the Jewish world as to the merits and dangers of openly reporting Jewish involvement in crime, the *Jewish Chronicle* shed all its inhibitions. Greenberg explained that the role of Jews in 'white slavery' and other criminal activity stemmed from the oppressive treatment they had endured in Russia.[29] The same, unapologetic treatment was given to the series of terrorist incidents committed by Russian Jews in London between 1909 and 1911.[30] Other notorious criminal cases involving Jews were covered openly and without apology that the perpetrators were Jewish.[31]

Yet Greenberg was not wholly consistent. At other times he appeared to believe that the way Jews acted had a direct bearing on anti-Jewish feeling. He railed against certain types of Jew for their alleged proclivity for gambling, 'ostentation', low standards of commercial behaviour and propensity to resort to law in the course of business disputes.[32] This element in his thinking may be illustrated by a comment he made on an advertisement, printed in the *Hackney and Kingsland Gazette* in January 1908, which contained the phrase 'No Jews Need Apply':

> The very strangeness of features and habits of the Jewish new-comer sets up an antipathetic feeling in the insular Englishman, while the fact that to the Jew Sunday is not a day of rest tends inevitably to broaden the gulf. But sentiments of ordinary respect for others, to say nothing of self-interest, should lead the Jew to do his best to narrow rather than to broaden this gulf. He can and should avoid 'mowing' or 'washing' on Sunday. He ought to conduct his business on the Christian Sabbath as to give the minimum of annoyance to his Gentile neighbours. He must, in short, do his utmost to soften and minimise rather than exaggerate those incompatibilities which arise from differences of religious faith.[33]

Notwithstanding such advice, and perhaps as a rather

damming reflection upon its sagacity, during the years before the First World War anti-Jewish feeling in Britain intensified appreciably.

Hilaire Belloc, MP, and G.K. Chesterton were the leading figures in an overt form of political and racial anti-semitism. Rather than ignore their activities, Greenberg decided to interview them for the paper and interrogate them about their views. This was a breakthrough in Jewish journalism since until then the *Jewish Chronicle* had preferred to interview people who, on the whole, heaped praise on the Jews. His innovation was not without critics. Belloc took the opportunity to reiterate his belief that the Jews were unassimilable and should be legally segregated from the rest of society. The interview was followed by pained letters from readers who thought that it was fool-hardy to offer him a platform. Greenberg retorted that: 'Safety lies not in bottling up but in exposing the fallacies of the anti-semites ... . We sympathise with our corre-spondents' sensitivities, but, alas!, in this world did we only heed that which is pleasing, should we ever be pleased – or instructed?'[34]

Belloc's subsequent role in the 'Marconi Scandal', however, earned him Greenberg's undying hatred. In this affair allegations of parliamentary impropriety and corrup-tion centring on Jewish MPs were seized upon by Belloc's journal, *New Witness*. Chesterton, the editor, deployed the stereotypical images of Jews as clannish, conspiratorial and powerful to explain these admittedly murky transactions.[35] The *Jewish Chronicle* declared that the stories appearing in the press were 'significant of the lengths to which certain enemies of the Jews even in this country are prepared to go'. Yet, when reflecting on the parliamentary investiga-tions and their repercussions, the paper rebuked those whose indiscretions were responsible for the bad odour. Indeed, it came close to saying that because the main actors were Jewish they should observe a double standard of propriety: 'It cannot be gainsaid that an ordinarily prudent Cabinet minister would be expected to exercise more vigilance as well as more discrimination than Sir Rufus [Isaacs] appears to have displayed. When, however, it happens, too, that he is a Jew, it is clear that the exigencies of the Jewish position impose the necessity for extra-ordinary care, though it would be, of course, absurd to suggest that any higher standard of conduct is applicable to the Jew than to anyone of another faith.'[36]

The most dramatic eruption of antisemitism at this time occurred in August 1911, in the valleys of South Wales. For three days small, isolated Jewish communities endured a wave of rioting and vandalism. A special reporter despatched by the paper arrived in time to supply dramatic copy on the disturbances. Greenberg leapt on the riots to vindicate the Zionist argument that Jews, as a minority anywhere in the diaspora, were vulnerable to anti-Jewish attack. 'After the events of this week nobody can again say that, as far as the anti-Jewish malady is concerned, Great Britain shows a clean bill of health. ... Let us then dispose of the cant that the Jewish position in this country is essentially different from that elsewhere.'[37]

In the months before the First World War, Greenberg evinced growing apprehension about the rising tide of antisemitism in Britain. He mocked those like Claude Montefiore who asserted that there was none, or those like Morris Joseph who accepted that there was and recommended assimilation as a response. Expressing the characteristic Zionist diagnosis of antisemitism he wrote in July 1913 that 'if every Jew in the land could tomorrow become cultured, modest, righteous and well-behaved, they would be all the better as individuals, but they would not modify the anti-Semitic spirit, because they would not be less weak as a people politically.'[38]

The chauvinism and social tensions generated by the First World War led to a sharp intensification of anti-Jewish feeling and a corresponding decline in the stature of British Jewry. Jews were buffeted by an anti-alienism that was increasingly unable or unwilling to discriminate between enemy aliens and friendly aliens, foreign and British-born Jews. Greenberg was rattled and his response was frankly ameliorative. In the first weeks of the war, the *Jewish Chronicle* reported cases of discrimination and prejudice against Jews seeking to enlist. At the same time, it noted claims that Jews were not 'doing their bit'. In reply, it urged Jews to volunteer, denounced any form of prejudice, and publicised the number of Jews in the armed services by listing their names in an Honour Record.[39]

The rumours about Jewish reluctance to serve in the army failed to abate after conscription was introduced in 1916. Newspapers fastened onto stories about Jews seeking exemption as conscientious objectors. This led Greenberg to announce that 'The Jewish ideal of peace has no real connection with the doctrine of non-resistance.' The *Jewish Chronicle* asserted that 'In our belief no Jew ought or can claim exemption *qua* Jew.'[40] Greenberg bitterly resented the Russian-born Jews who used their anomalous status to avoid either voluntary enlistment or conscription and blamed them for anti-Jewish feeling. Although, unlike later commentators, he did not see this as the cause of the anti-Jewish riots in Leeds and London in 1917, he nevertheless ascribed the violence in Leeds to the aloofness, 'if not an absolute secession' of a rapidly expanded and highly visible Jewish population which aroused economic jealousies.[41]

During 1917–18, the paper anxiously monitored the growing volume of anti-Jewish comment in the press and in Parliament. Jews were accused of profiteering and job-snatching. When large numbers fled the East End to the Home Counties and South Coast to escape bombing raids, their migration attracted much adverse comment. Greenberg condemned these snide attacks, but he also asked in an exasperated tone, 'Is it not possible to impress upon these poor people a greater measure of self-restraint than is visible say, in the violent attacks of their assailants?'[42] In the post-war years anti-Jewish feeling remained at a high level. It took several overlapping and mutually reinforcing forms: anti-alienism, anti-Bolshevism and anti-Zionism, knitted together and informed by the myth of a Jewish world conspiracy. Greenberg deplored the 'rampant prejudice and the political weakness that truckles to it' when Parliament extended the wartime Aliens Act into peacetime and made it even more stringent. The paper reported the victimisation of, and systematic discrimination against, non-British-born Jews and Jewish aliens under the legislation, but its editorial protests were of little avail.[43]

With remarkable speed after the Russian Revolution of March 1917 the separate terms Russian, Bolshevik and Jew became interchangeable. The press and politicians played the game of bifurcating the Jewish minority into good and bad groups so as to legitimatise its prejudiced assault on some of its members and to deny a categorical hostility to the whole. The high-Tory *Morning Post* was prominent, but not unique, in this respect and challenged British Jews to repudiate Bolshevism. Greenberg saw the trap. If British Jews refused to condemn the Bolsheviks, they could be accused of covert sympathy with the revolutionaries. If they did, it would appear that Jews had a special reason to distance themselves from Bolshevism, which would only confirm the original fabrication.[44]

On the contrary, Greenberg was prepared to write that he saw much that was good in Bolshevik ideology. This only inspired more attacks by the *Morning Post* and calls on good British Jews to condemn such sentiments. In April 1919, ten prominent Jews rose to the bait and sent a letter to the *Morning Post* deploring Greenberg's sympathetic remarks. The signatories agreed with the *Morning Post* that

British Jews were 'being served very badly by their newspapers'.[45] Greenberg blasted the 'Ten' who had 'grovelled
abasingly before this antisemitic organ'. However, the
imputation of Jewish sympathy for Bolshevism spread ever
more widely. The *Jewish Chronicle* was soon battling against
The Times and even Winston Churchill, who also embraced
the myth of Jewish Bolshevism.[46]

Although the Balfour Declaration appeared to give
British endorsement to the Jewish National Movement,
anti-Zionism did not abate. The very success of Zionism
aggravated the deteriorating position of British Jews. A rich
vein of antisemitism ran through the propaganda conducted by pro-Arab forces in England. During 1922 to 1924,
Zionism was subjected to what Chaim Weizmann
described as an 'absolute barrage of detraction' in the
Northcliffe, Rothermere and Beaverbrook newspapers. It
was a vicious and unscrupulous campaign, drawing on
ancient antisemitic images and the more recent 'Protocols
of the Elders of Zion'.[47] The Jewish Press was naturally
inclined to dismiss the Palestinian-Arab case, but it did not
even have to engage with it seriously as long as anti-
Zionist propaganda was laced with vulgar antisemitism.
From this point onwards, but not always with such good
reason, antisemitism and anti-Zionism were associated
with one another and the former used as an excuse to
ignore the real issues contained within the latter.

The unifying element in all these emanations of post-
war antisemitism was the myth of an international Jewish
conspiracy distilled in 'The Protocols of the Elders of Zion'.
First published in England as *The Jewish Peril* in January
1920, by April it had attracted the attention of the press,
most notably the *Morning Post*. The watchful *Jewish
Chronicle* had also noticed its genesis and counter-attacked.
In a leading article on 14 May 1921, Greenberg jeered that
'The whole thing is a nightmare, the figment of a
disordered brain, the emanation of a man fit either for a

gaol or a lunatic asylum.'[48] Despite Lucien Wolf's exposé of the forgery, reprinted as a leaflet by the *Jewish Chronicle* for wider distribution, the lunatic idea of a world Jewish conspiracy continued to fascinate the right-wing Conservative press. Greenberg was at his wit's end to cope with the tide of vilification, which he dubbed 'Hebrabies'.[49]

This neologism reveals much about the way Greenberg perceived antisemitism. It suggests that he saw it as something external, an infection which was passed on by creatures already sick. It also implies a biological origin, a disease that led to madness. Consequently, what Jews did was of little relevance to its incidence. This does little to explain Greenberg's controversial decision to expose Jewish criminality to public scrutiny in a regular column devoted to law cases and crime news. The column, which began in April 1924, embodied the belief that Jews themselves contributed to antisemitism by their bad conduct. Publicity was necessary to make law-abiding Jews aware of the problem and shame the guilty ones. If Anglo-Jewry could purge itself of malefactors, then antisemites would be denied at least one pretext for attacking them. If such material was used by antisemites, it was of no odds since they would never lack for mud to throw at the Jews anyway.

The Board of Deputies disagreed. In January 1926, it passed a motion advising its Press Committee to request the *Jewish Chronicle* to discontinue the law and crime reports. The chairman of the Press Committee, Philip Guedalla, dissented and the committee later rejected the advice on grounds similar to those used by Greenberg to justify the column.[50]

The paper's foreign coverage during the 1920s was dominated by antisemitism in Germany, Poland and Russia. *Jewish Chronicle* readers first encountered Adolf Hitler in Spring 1923. The paper was one of the few English publications to pay close attention to his trial in April 1924, following his botched coup attempt in Bavaria.[51] Hitler's alarming rise to prominence in 1929–30 prompted Greenberg to send a special correspondent to Germany. The paper's excellent reporting of the German political scene left no doubt about the threat which Hitler posed to German Jewry. The *Jewish Chronicle* begged the world to take Hitler seriously and quoted extensively from the *Volkischer Beobachter*, the leading Nazi newspaper, to show the British people what the Nazis were saying about the Jews. Editorials in 1930–31 stressed that, on their own track record, the Nazi leadership meant exactly what they said. It was to little effect.[52]

Leopold Greenberg died in 1931, worn out by his exertions over the previous 20 years. He was a mercurial figure with an explosive temper, and it is perhaps too much to expect consistency from anyone, let alone a journalist, over a period of three decades. However, it must be said that his treatment of antisemitism was inconsistent. Putting these contradictions to one side, Greenberg was astonishingly forthright and strong. While he may have allowed the exuberance of Jewish East Enders to get under his skin, he reacted powerfully to any sign of intolerance in the majority society. Above all he was sensitive to the double-bind in which liberalism placed minorities. He demanded equal treatment for all Jews and refused to countenance the notion that the majority society could determine which were good and which were bad. That would only inveigle the minority into a self-policing action destined to accentuate its differences and force upon it a second-class status.

Following Greenberg's death, Jack Rich (1897–1987), the former secretary to the Board of Deputies, was invited to become editor at the behest of the paper's managing director, Mortimer Epstein (1880–1946). Rich never severed his ties with the communal leadership and was especially close to Neville Laski, President of the Board. This created severe tensions in the way the paper handled antisemitism and defence work.

The centre of antisemitic politics at this time was, of course, Germany, and the *Jewish Chronicle* tirelessly castigated British newspapers for swallowing pro-Nazi propaganda and not taking Hitler seriously.[53] Events in the Third Reich created a greater sensitivity to anti-Jewish activity in Britain. However, the response was confused, a bewilderment that was exemplified nowhere better than within the *Jewish Chronicle*. Simon Gilbert, now a leader writer and columnist responsible for 'In the Communal Armchair', believed that religion and tradition inevitably set Jews apart from their fellow citizens and it was, there-fore, futile to strive for total acceptance as Victorian Jews had thought was possible. The editorials took a quite different line and repeatedly urged Jews to conform to the expectations of a society that was ambivalent to Jewish differences.[54]

Finding an appropriate response to antisemitism became urgent after Sir Oswald Mosley formed the British Union of Fascists (BUF) in 1932. Individual BUF members were soon identified with anti-Jewish agitation and the *Jewish Chronicle* challenged Mosley to disown them. His response was equivocal. He declared that the BUF was not antisemitic and would 'never attack Jews because they are Jews'. However, if Jews attacked the BUF or were 'inter-national capitalists' or subversives, then the BUF would counter-attack. The paper found this reply 'a little perplex-ing' and deplored the references to 'international finance' and Communists.[55]

The BUF's East End campaign in 1935–36 and the erup-tion of widescale political antisemitism triggered a debate that split Anglo-Jewry.[56] Opinion at the *Jewish Chronicle* was no less divided. As early as 16 February 1934, Gilbert had argued that Jews were obliged to fight Fascism since, as an ideology, it was intolerant of minorities. By contrast, the paper's editorial line was resolutely against Jews forming themselves into or aligning with anti-Fascist organisations. It warned on 11 May 1934: 'That is our old friend the Jewish vote. It is perilous.' In August 1934, Gilbert favoured the deployment of Jewish anti-Fascist speakers at Speakers' Corner, Hyde Park, and urged the Board of Deputies to adopt an activist policy of self-defence. But a leading article on 7 September 1934 urged Jews to stay away from a major Fascist rally in Hyde Park. After more than a year of unchecked street meetings and disorder, on 17 January 1936 the *Jewish Chronicle* had to admit that notwithstanding its sympathy for Laski 'a great deal of dissatisfaction and anxiety exists in the community with this matter'. Four months later, with little more to show by the Board, the paper warned that 'while we have slept, young men among us have grown fretful, so that there is a danger of them throwing themselves into the arms of anti-Fascist groups ready to help in defence against attack'. In June 1936, Gilbert galvanised the defence debate with an article on 'The Question of Self-Defence'. He called for measures to organise and train speakers, a campaign of open-air meetings, and the printing and distribution of information sheets to counteract Fascist propaganda.[57]

The paper now began to collate news of antisemitic and Fascist activity, counter-measures and all aspects of the debate in a prominent news section under the heading 'Jewish Defence'. This feature often ran to four pages and in itself drew attention to the magnitude of the crisis. Regardless of Rich's association with Laski, editorials were now unsparing in their criticism of the Board's leadership.[58] A private letter written by Rich to Joseph Leftwich in September 1936 reveals some of the motives which animated him at this juncture. Leftwich had argued that the counter-campaign only amplified the effect of Fascist propaganda. He pointed to the example of German Jewry as a sign of how useless and even counter-productive such measures could be. Rich replied:

> The line which you take with regard to the present cam-
> paign that the Community is conducting against anti-
> semitism is quite familiar to me. I know what was done in
> Germany, but I believe that even if we knew that we were
> going to be unsuccessful in this country, we should have no
> right to sit with folded arms. Not only do we not know this,
> but I am convinced that an anti-Jewish [sic] defensive
> campaign has a much better chance of being successful here
> because this country is not Germany and because the
> Fascist movement has very little chance of success here. The
> Fascists have adopted the offensive by making antisemitism
> a main plank in their campaign and we are bound,
> consequently, to be on the defensive. We cannot help it. If
> we do not answer the numerous calumnies that are spread
> about, we shall present our adversaries with an extra
> argument. I have had many letters from non-Jewish well-
> wishers, expressing wonder that the Jews did not long ago
> take steps to answer antisemitic allegations.

Rich was convinced that the British public could be won
over against Fascism if only they were presented with the
facts, and he made the *Jewish Chronicle* into a platform for
enacting that belief.[59]

At the end of 1936, after a long board-room struggle,
Epstein's influence was broken and Rich, his protégé, was
ejected. He was replaced by Ivan Greenberg (1896–1966),
Leopold's son. Ivan was a right-wing Zionist and yet,
curiously, he had a long and warm relationship with the
non- or anti-Zionist communal leadership. His amity with
Neville Laski and his allies was based on their shared
distaste for the mainstream Zionist movement.
Consequently, the paper blended a defiant Zionism with
an apologetic stance on domestic matters, including antisemitism which continued to dominate home coverage.

An editorial on New Year's Day 1937, announced that it was necessary to stamp out 'the materialism which is rampant among some of our people' and the 'vice of vulgar display'. The paper next launched a campaign to expose 'sweating' in the London trades most closely associated with the Jews. Its special investigator, Maurice Goldsmith, made the round of Jewish workshops, exposing poor conditions of work and low rates of pay. The series caused an uproar at the Board of Deputies where the *Jewish Chronicle* was accused of giving ammunition to anti-semites.[60] In fact, this approach was shared by many prominent Jews, including Neville Laski. The series helped to establish as orthodoxy the argument that a good deal of antisemitism was related to the allegedly low ethical standards of Jewish businessmen and so contributed to the formation of the Trades Advisory Council of the Board of Deputies (TAC) in 1938.[61] As tension between Britain and Germany increased in the years before 1939, Mosley accused the Jews of wanting to push the country into a war to serve their interests. By exploiting anti-war feeling Mosley reinvigorated the BUF and so rekindled the divisive argument over Jewish defence work. On 29 April 1938, Gilbert approvingly quoted Josiah Wedgwood, MP, who said: 'It must no longer be thought that antisemitism can be stopped by improving the Jews.' Yet, when it was suggested that Jews were disproportionately numbered among doctors, lawyers and accountants, the *Jewish Chronicle* seriously considered whether 'It might be a good or a bad thing if Jews were to ration, if they could, their representation in the professions'. The proposition was treated with such gravity that in June 1939, the paper joined with B'nai B'rith in the establishment of a career guidance service.[62]

Once war broke out, coverage of Jewish life on the Home Front was continuously preoccupied by the persistence of antisemitism which has been so well documented and analysed by Tony Kushner. Irrespective of the declaration of hostilities Mosley and the BUF continued to campaign on an anti-war platform and made free use of antisemitism in their propaganda.[63] The role attributed to the Fifth Columnists in the Nazi conquest of Norway, Belgium, Holland and France provided the paper with a powerful weapon to strike back at antisemitic agitators whom it tarred (not always correctly) with Fascist and pro-German sympathies. 'Scratch an anti-Semite', it declared on 12 April 1940, 'and you will find a conscious or unconscious Hitler agent.'[64]

Antisemitism in Britain was not curbed by the internment of key Fascist personalities. In the midst of the Blitz newspapers printed stories that alleged Jewish cowardice lay behind the clamour to open underground railway stations for use as shelters. Following serious claims that Fascists were disseminating anti-Jewish propaganda in air-raid shelters and tube stations, the *Jewish Chronicle* detailed a special correspondent to report on the situation. His findings revealed that while some shelters had committees that worked to eliminate discrimination and discouraged prejudice, in others racism was openly displayed.[65]

The durability of anti-Jewish feeling made itself apparent also through the widespread identification of Jews with the black market. By the middle of 1942, this tendency in the press and in public perceptions had grown so worrying that the paper demanded action by the government and called for legislation against community libel.[66] Once again a defence debate broke out. Now the TAC, which admitted to a Jewish presence amongst the black marketeers, was pitted against the Board of Deputies, which preferred greater discretion.[67] Once more, the *Jewish Chronicle* offered a divided counsel. For example, in February 1942 it complained that 'It cannot be too strongly stressed that if there were only a single Jewish "racketeer", the dictates of Judaism and the minimum regard for the honour of Jewry would compel us to crush the miserable wretch with every power we possess.' Yet a month later an editorial stated that 'Our own community, and in particular its leaders, both appointed and self-appointed, has shown a tendency to discreditable panickiness under the attentions of skilful antisemitic picadors, because of the presence of a number of Jews, a tiny ratio of the whole Community, among the racketeers and reprobates.'[68]

This is not the place to discuss how the *Jewish Chronicle* reported the Final Solution, but it is relevant to consider how it conceptualised the Nazi persecution of the Jews during the war years. The paper obtained clear reports of conditions under the German occupation in Poland in 1939–40 and Western Europe in 1940–41. But the natural tendency was to make sense of German policy towards the Jews by placing it in a framework derived from the Jewish historical experience of antisemitism. The creation of ghettos and the use of the yellow star actually offered a comforting degree of familiarity to past phases of oppression, all of which had been surmounted by the mass of Jews.

For the first months after the German onslaught against Russia, in June 1941, the *Jewish Chronicle* supplied evidence of carnage on a huge scale, but in common with other news agencies could not conceptualise the scope or organised methods of the *Einsatzgruppen*. There could, as yet, be no inkling of a systematic plan of extermination. For example, in the retrospective for the Jewish Year on 19 September 1941, an editorial spoke of a 'crude policy of persecution' being carried out by the Germans in the Nazi-occupied countries and commented that for German Jewry, 'The *alternatives* [author's italics] seem to have been extermination or expulsion to the hopeless, starving, diseased Lublin Ghetto.'

To the consternation of the *Jewish Chronicle* the eventual revelation of the Final Solution and the exposure of the extermination camps did not discredit antisemitism. In May 1945, several Conservative MPs asked the Home Secretary when Jewish refugees in England would be repatriated. They were echoed in the press, and in the London borough of Hampstead a petition was circulated blaming refugees for the housing shortage. On 8 March 1946, the paper observed that 'One of the most astonishing phenomena of the times is that the martyrdom of the Jewish people, instead of being followed by universal sympathy and reparation, has begotten only a new spate of anti-Jewish feeling.'[69]

The experience of the war years had driven Greenberg deep into the Zionist Revisionist camp and his interpretation of events in Palestine was unsparing of British feelings. Jewish terror attacks on British troops in Palestine during 1946–47 raised the level of anti-Jewish feeling to something approaching that of 1936–37. Eventually, the paper's directors considered Greenberg's approach to be so inflammatory that in June 1946 he was sacked and replaced by the assistant editor, John Shaftesley (1901–81). Shaftesley took over under extremely difficult conditions, but could rely on the managing director, David Kessler, to proffer advice on how the *Jewish Chronicle* might ameliorate the situation. It was not long before they were put to the test. The hanging of two British sergeants in Palestine in July 1947, combined with economic hardship in Britain, led to serious anti-Jewish rioting in half a dozen cities, an all but forgotten incident which has recently been illuminated by Tony Kushner.[70]

Six months later the anti-Jewish agitation and violence in east and north London had become so serious that the paper warned: 'This is a time for plain speaking ... because the Jews of this country are aware that they are living in a social climate which is becoming increasingly stormy. Some are thinking in terms of emigration; and some of desperate flight, believing that even in Britain, with its great democratic and tolerant traditions, anti-Semitism is making such headway as to threaten seriously their well-being as Jews.' It showed great impatience with the communal leadership: 'For too long the humble backstairs approach has prevailed. Now is the time to reinforce it powerfully by action designed to ensure that the mass of British people do not become antisemitic.'[71]

As in the 1930s, young Jews formed groups to protect themselves, believing that the communal organisations were doing too little. The most aggressive, effective, and certainly most controversial of these was the 43 Group. The *Jewish Chronicle* condemned their behaviour, but it could not help but express sympathy for their motives. 'If our elected leaders do not make sufficient impression, it is only to be expected that the hot heads will get out of hand and discipline will disappear.'[72] During 1947–48, Sidney Salomon, secretary of the Board's defence committee, pleaded with Shaftesley to curb the publicity the paper was giving to the 43 Group. He even asked him to ban the advertisements which they placed in the paper. Shaftesley refused the request.[73] Although Fascist activity tailed off during the late 1940s, social antisemitism remained widespread. The *Jewish Chronicle* associated this with the pattern of racism in British society and began to take note of the colour bar operating in many pubs and places of entertainment, particularly after the Notting Hill riots in August 1958.[74]

Looking abroad the paper, like Anglo-Jewry as a whole, regarded the establishment of the Federal Republic of Germany (FRG) in 1949 with deep suspicion. As distinct from the rest of the British press, the *Jewish Chronicle* closely monitored the elections to the Bundestag and constantly drew attention to the existence of far-right splinter parties.[75] Since 1945 the paper had reported Soviet Jewish affairs with deep interest and pleaded with the Soviet government for a more open policy towards the

Jews. When the Soviet authorities began to suppress Jewish political and cultural organisations in 1949, the editorial attitude changed. It noted with anxiety that anti-Israel and anti-Jewish themes were becoming a staple element of Soviet propaganda, with similar trends visible in the Soviet satellite states in Eastern Europe.[76] The full extent of Soviet anti-Jewish policy only became evident after the 'thaw' began in 1956.

In 1958, William Frankel took over the editorship from Shaftesley and brought a new lease of life to the paper. He also gave the *Jewish Chronicle* a distinctly liberal inflection, particularly in its comments on race and immigration issues. Editorials during the 1960s frequently pointed to the links between antisemitism and anti-black racism, condemned racial violence in British cities, the colour bar and praised legislation on race relations. Reminding readers of the 1905 Aliens Act and the Jewish immigrant experience, the paper declared the 1962 Immigration Act to be a 'retrograde step'.[77]

At the start of 1960, neo-Nazi activity in West Germany found an echo in Britain in the form of swastika daubings on communal buildings, synagogues and tombstones in Jewish cemeteries and other acts of vandalism. Further waves occurred in the summer of 1962, 1963, and 1965. The *Jewish Chronicle* itself became the target for attack. The building suffered a broken window in January 1960 and was slightly damaged by a bomb in March 1963. Throughout this period it was the editorial line to counsel vigilance, although equally firmly to dispel panic and discourage Jewish vigilante groups. On the other hand, editorials accused the Board's Defence Committee of being 'rusty and antiquated' and observed that if the Board was seen to be acting decisively, public anxiety would be allayed.[78]

Although it maintained an impressive coverage of organised racism, editorially the *Jewish Chronicle* dismissed attacks on buildings and individuals as isolated incidents, the work of crackpots. The paper stopped short of the conclusion reached by black activists that racial attacks were symptoms of structural racism in British society. All the same, four in-depth articles on the exclusion of Jews from certain golf clubs in April 1960 produced disturbing results. 'The careful investigations conducted by our correspondents', the paper commented, 'show beyond any doubt that this discrimination is widespread.' It was a 'grave reproach to British fairness' and revealed 'a distressing symptom of the persistence of anti-Jewish prejudice in a particular economic and social section of the population'.[79] In February 1961 an inquiry into the application of quotas against Jews seeking admission to public schools had a similarly unpleasant outcome.

Under Frankel's guidance during the 1960s the paper took a consistent line towards each phase of antisemitic and neo-Nazi activity. It urged Jews to stay away from demonstrations, arguing that heckling and violence only played into the hands of right-wing agitators. But it castigated the lacklustre response of the Board of Deputies and, more importantly, the government: the absence of an effective riposte only encouraged independent action. The *Jewish Chronicle* wanted the authorities to use the Public Order Act more frequently to deny premises to neo-Fascist or neo-Nazi rallies and rejected the free speech argument as a reason for allowing the dissemination of inflammatory views.[80]

In December 1965, following a summer of arson and bombing attacks on synagogues all over London, a *yeshiva bocher* was stabbed by 'hooligans' in Stamford Hill. This provoked an editorial which typifies the paper's treatment of antisemitism at the time. It also uncannily prefigures current debates. The stabbing was held to be the result of 'mindless violence and hatred arising from spiritual starvation in an age of material affluence'.[81]

In the 1970s, several new elements entered the treatment of antisemitism. Feature articles in the paper by writers such as Max Beloff and Robert Wistrich identified a convergence of New Left ideology with advocacy of the Palestinian cause. They went on to suggest that this posed a threat to the survival of Israel and the Jewish people since this form of anti-Zionism was premised on the denial of Jewish difference.[82] The 1975 United Nations declaration that Zionism was a form of racism fuelled a fresh wave of anti-Zionist propaganda and activity that intentionally conflated Jews or Israelis with Nazis, so lapsing into a form of Holocaust Denial. Soviet propaganda had long used this canard, but now it became widespread in the West.[83]

From March 1974, the journalist Philip Kleinman was given a column in which to comment on the press, a feature which soon developed into a weekly catalogue of what Kleinman construed to be the anti-Israel bias and antisemitism in the British press and media. Along with a defensive attitude towards Israeli government policies it became increasingly common to identify anti-Zionism as a species of antisemitism. Although the theoretical grounds for this practice were questionable, the Arab boycott of Jewish businesses and the practice of banning Jewish societies on British campuses gave the claim all the substance it needed. A sense of paranoia and a siege mentality was, arguably, one result of these events and the way they were interpreted.[84]

Enoch Powell's 1968 'rivers of blood' speech, attacking non-white immigration, catapulted 'race' to the forefront of British politics. As the torch of racism was picked up and carried forward with growing success by the newly-formed National Front (NF), the paper warned Jews in Britain against the complacent belief that they were not as much the targets of organised racism as non-whites in British society. The *Jewish Chronicle* watched the advance of the NF with a sense of gravity accentuated by the worsening position of the British economy and the souring of the political atmosphere.[85] Against a background of industrial turmoil it warned in June 1974 that 'Extremism always flourishes in times of national emergency and political uncertainty and most especially when a nation seems to have lost its sense of purpose.'[86]

In the local elections in London in Spring 1977, the NF gained 10 per cent of the votes cast.[87] So, when Geoffrey Paul became editor of the paper that year, he immediately faced a defence debate that paralleled those of the 1930s, 1940s and 1960s in terms of the issues and intensity. The *Jewish Chronicle* insisted that the NF's success posed a real threat to the Jews as well as the non-white minorities. But should Jews join with Black and Asian groups, many of whose members were vehemently anti-Zionist?[88] One of the most effective anti-racist and anti-Fascist groups was the Anti-Nazi League: however to many Jews it was tainted by its association with the Trotskyite and anti-Zionist Socialist Workers Party.[89]

An editorial in the paper in October 1978 remarked that 'no issue in recent years has so divided Jewish public opinion as the argument for and against supporting the Anti-Nazi League Campaign against the National Front'.[90] While certain Jewish groups and individuals joined its work, the Board of Deputies hurled invective at it. In the May 1979 General Election, the NF won a mere 190,000 votes around the country, whereas in 1977 it had taken 119,000 votes in the Greater London Council elections alone. One reason for this decline was the success of the Conservative Party, led by Margaret Thatcher, in assuming the mantle of an anti-immigrant party.[91] By taking the heat out of the defence debate, Mrs Thatcher's victory was one of the less obvious blessings which she bestowed on the Jewish community.

In this survey, I have concentrated on the main threads running through the *Jewish Chronicle*'s interpretation of antisemitism. Of course, at various times, editorials, feature articles and book reviews have offered a wider range of explanations. I have dwelled at length only on editorial responses to antisemitism because this seems to me to say much more about how the paper perceived antisemitism than diffuse theoretical discussions, of which there were many.

In summary, what were the main attitudes projected by the paper over this one hundred-year span? During the nineteenth century, editors were convinced that anti-semitism was a mediaeval relic and that rationality would prevail were it not for the impact of Jewish immigrants. They thought that Jews caused antisemitism and if they altered the way they behaved, could prevent its spread. Under the two Greenbergs antisemitism was treated as an inevitable accompaniment of diasporic life and political powerlessness. Yet both were ambivalent and, in practice, tended towards an ameliorative policy which rested on the belief that antisemitism could be tackled rationally.

After the Holocaust, antisemitism was regarded as a continuation of Nazi Jew hatred or related to racism in gen-eral. Anti-Jewish feeling in the Third World or amongst Black and Asian immigrants in the West were new elements understood as a product of anti-Zionism, which tragically compromised resistance to the experience of racism shared by Jews and non-white minorities. The ambivalence towards joining with non-white minorities in the struggle against racism seems to reflect a sense that antisemitism is in some way *sui generis* and that, at the end of the day, the Jews stand alone. What is perhaps most interesting is that, since the 1950s, there has been almost no suggestion that Jews, or Israelis, give legitimate cause for antisemitism. To this extent, the century 1879–1979 saw a revolution in the reporting and analysis of antisemitism in the *Jewish Chronicle*.

NOTES

1. This chapter was first delivered as the 1993 Parkes Lecture at the University of Southampton.
2. Jacob Katz, *From Prejudice to Destruction* (Cambridge, MA: Harvard University Press, 1980), p. 260.
3. Colin Holmes, *Anti-Semitism in British Society, 1876–1939* (London: Edward Arnold, 1979), Chp. 1.
4. See the author's contribution to 'Anti-Semitism in the 1990s: a Symposium', *Patterns of Prejudice*, 25 (1991), p.13, and for a detailed and subtle exposition of 'Semitic discourse' the Introduction to Bryan Cheyette, *Constructions of 'the Jew' in English Literature and Society. Racial Representations, 1875–1945* (Cambridge: Cambridge University Press, 1993).
5. For background on these and subsequent editors and owners of the paper, see David Cesarani, 'The Importance of Being Editor: The *Jewish Chronicle* 1841–1991' *Jewish Historical Studies*, 32 (1990–2), pp. 259–78.
6. *Jewish Chronicle* (hereafter *JC*), 28 Nov. 1879, pp. 9–10; 5 Dec. 1879, p. 9; 19 Dec. 1879, pp. 9–10. For political analysis see *JC*, 27 Feb. 1880, p. 4. See also *JC*, 17 Dec. 1880 for analysis of racial antisemitism: 'The anti-Semites declare by their very title that they object to the race, and not the religion of the Jews.' For background see P.G.J. Pulzer, *The Rise of Political Anti-Semitism in Germany and Austria* (revised edn: London: Halban, 1988); R.S. Levy, *The Downfall of the Anti-Semitic Political Parties in Imperial Germany* (New Haven: Yale University Press, 1975), pp. 195–253.
7. *JC*, 14 Jan. 1881, pp. 9–10; 19 Nov. 1890, pp. 9–10.
8. *JC*, 16 Nov. 1883, pp. 9–10; 23 Nov. 1883, pp. 9–10
9. *JC*, 31 May 1895, pp. 13–14; 8 Nov. 1895, p. 5; 3 July 1896, p. 14. See analysis *JC*, 6 March 1896, pp. 7–8; 24 April 1896, p. 4. Cf. Pulzer, *Rise of Political Anti-Semitism*, pp. 156–63, 171–83; W.R. Weitzmann, 'The Politics of the Viennese Jewish Community, 1890–1914', in I. Oxaal, M. Pollak and G. Botz (eds), *Jews, Anti-Semitism and Culture in Vienna* (London: Routledge & Kegan Paul, 1987), pp. 127–30.
10. *JC*, 3 Aug. 1883, pp. 8–9; 17 Aug. 1883, p. 9.
11. *JC*, 8 July 1892, p. 9; 29 July 1892, pp. 11–12
12. *JC*, 22 Sep. 1899, p. 18; 9 March 1900, pp. 16–17; 23 Sep. 1900, pp. 16–17.
13. *JC*, 28 Dec. 1894, pp. 5–6. The most recent study of the Dreyfus case is J.-D. Bredin, *The Affair. The case of Alfred Dreyfus* (New York: George Braziller, 1986).
14. R.I. Cohen, 'The Dreyfus Affair and the Jews', in S. Almog (ed.), *Anti-Semitism Through the Ages* (Oxford: Oxford University Press, 1988), pp. 291–310; M. Marrus, *The Politics of Assimilation* (Oxford: Clarendon Press, 1980), pp. 196–242; D. Yellin Bacharach, 'The Impact of the Dreyfus Affair on Great Britain' (University of Minnesota, Ph.D. thesis, 1978).
15. *JC*, 18 Feb. 1898, p. 19, author's italics.
16. *JC*, 30 Sep. 1898, pp. 15–16.
17. Cf. Bacharach, 'Impact of the Dreyfus Affair', pp. 80–96.
18. *JC*, 6 Jan. 1899, pp. 16–17; 10 Feb. 1899, p. 20; 3 March 1899, p. 20; 21 July 1899, p. 15; Bacharach, 'Impact of the Dreyfus Affair', pp. 161–87.
19. *JC*, 27 Sep. 1878, pp. 9–10; 17 Jan. 1879, p. 4. G. Alderman, *The Jewish Community in British Politics* (Oxford: Clarendon, 1982), pp. 39–41.
20. *JC*, 26 July 1899, pp. 9–10; 13 April 1894, pp. 13–14; 9 July 1897, p. 14; 9 March 1900, p. 18. On the anti-usury campaigns, see G. Black, *Lender to the Lords,*

Giver to the Poor (London: Vallentine Mitchell, 1992), *passim.*
21. *JC*, 24 Nov. 1882, pp. 8–9; 20 Oct. 1893, pp. 13–14.
22. *JC*, 18 April 1884, p. 5; 2 May 1884, p. 9.
23. *JC*, 16 March 1888, p. 5; 12 April 1889, p. 6; 26 Aug. 1892, p. 6; 20 Oct. 1893, p. 20; 25 May 1894, p. 6. See S. Bayme, 'Jewish Leadership and Anti-Semitism in Britain, 1898–1918' (Columbia University, Ph.D. thesis, 1977).
24. *JC*, 22 Nov. 1895, pp. 10–11. See also comment on Lord Salisbury's Anti-Alien Bill, 18 Feb. 1898, p. 21. On anti-alienism and antisemitism, see B. Gainer, *The Alien Invasion: the Origins of the Aliens Act of 1905* (London: Heinemann, 1972); J.A. Garrard, *The English and Immigration, 1880–1910* (London: Oxford University Press, 1971); cf. D. Feldman, 'The importance of Being English: Jewish Immigration and the Decay of Liberal England', in D. Feldman and G. Stedman Jones (eds), *Metropolis: London Histories and Representations since 1800* (London: Routledge, 1989), pp. 56–84.
25. See B. Williams, 'The Anti-Semitism of Tolerance: Middle-class Manchester and the Jews 1870–1900', in A.J. Kidd and K.W. Roberts (eds), *City, Class and Culture* (Manchester: Manchester University Press, 1988), pp. 74–102.
26. Geoffrey Alderman, 'The Jew as Scapegoat? The Settlement and Reception of Jews in South Wales before 1914' *Transactions of the Jewish Historical Society of England*, 26 (1979) pp. 62–70; Bayme, 'Jewish Leadership', pp. 240–50.
27. *JC*, 26 June 1905, p. 8. The *Jewish Chronicle* was more robust in its response to the hostile Admiralty Committee report on *shechita*. It gave a good deal of space to the issue, including a special supplement in August and October 1904.
28. *JC*, 8 April 1904, pp. 7–8. See note 23.
29. *JC*, 1 April 1910, pp. 5–6: Lloyd P. Gartner, 'Anglo-Jewry and the Jewish International Traffic in Prostitution, 1885–1914' *AJS Review: the Journal of the Association of Jewish Studies*, 7–8 (1982–3), pp. 129–78.
30. *JC*, 29 Jan. 1909, p. 8; 5 Feb. 1909, p. 8; 23 Dec. 1910, pp. 5–6; 30 Dec. 1910, pp. 7–8. See also Jewish Research Group of the Edmonton Hundred Historical Society. *Heritage. An historical series on the Jewish inhabitants of North London*, 1 (London: Edmonton Hundred Historical Society, 1982), pp. 22–4; Donald Rumbelow, *The Houndsitch Murders and the Siege of Sidney Street* (Harmondsworth: Penguin, 1990); Colin Holmes, 'East End Crime and the Jewish Community, 1887–1911' in Aubrey Newman (ed.), *The Jewish East End, 1840–1939* (London: Jewish Historical Society of England, 1981), pp. 109–24.
31. *JC*, 19 Nov. 1909, p. 6; 17 March 1911, p. 7; Kenneth E. Collins (ed.), *Aspects of Scottish Jewry* (Glasgow: Glasgow Jewish Representative Council, 1987), p. 30; Andrew Rose, *Stinie: Murder on the Common* (London: Bodley Head, 1985); Holmes, 'East End Crime and the Jewish Community', pp. 111, 117.
32. For example, *JC*, 14 Feb. 1908, p.6; 22 Sep. 1911, p.10; 23 Aug. 1912, pp. 9–10.
33. *JC*, 31 Jan. 1908, pp. 7–8.
34. *JC*, 12 Aug. 1910, p. 14; 19 Aug. 1910, pp. 11–12. The *Jewish Chronicle* did a similar interview with Chesterton: *JC*, 28 April 1911, p. 18. Kenneth Lunn, 'Political Anti-Semitism before 1914: Fascism's Heritage?' in Kenneth Lunn and Richard Thurlow (eds), *British Fascism: Essays on the Radical Right in Interwar Britain* (London: Croom Helm, 1980), pp. 22–5.
35. Frances Donaldson, *The Marconi Scandal* (London: Hart-Dans, 1962), *passim*; G.R. Searle, *Corruption in British Politics 1895–1930* (Oxford: Clarendon Press, 1987), pp. 172–212; Bryan Cheyette, 'Hilaire Belloc and the "Marconi Scandal" 1900–1914: a Reassessment of the Interactionist Model of Racial Hatred' in Tony Kushner and Kenneth Lunn (eds), *The Politics of Marginality. Race, the*

Radical Right and Minorities in Twentieth Century Britain (London: Frank Cass, 1990), pp. 131–42.
36. *JC*, 18 Oct. 1912, pp. 7–8; 4 April 1913, pp. 13–14. See also *JC*, 15 Nov. 1912, p. 9; 20 June 1913, p. 9. For 'Greenberg's campaign against the Chestertons', see Dean Rapp, 'The Jewish Response to G.K. Chesterton's "Anti-Semitism, 1911–33" ' *Patterns of Prejudice*, 24 (1990), pp. 77–9.
37. *JC*, 25 Aug. 1911, pp. 5–6; 1 Sep. 1911, pp. 5–6. Geoffrey Alderman, 'The Jew as Scapegoat?' pp. 65–8 and *idem*, 'The Anti-Jewish Riots of August 1911 in South Wales' *Welsh History Review*, 6 (1972–3), pp. 190–200; cf. A.M. Wiener, 'Tredegar Riots' *CAJEX*, 26:1 (1976) pp. 17–26, 29–31.
38. *JC*, 18 July 1913, p. 12. Lunn, 'Political Anti-Semitism before 1914' pp. 20–40; Holmes, *Anti-Semitism in British Society*, pp. 63-88.
39. See David Cesarani, 'An Embattled Minority: the Jews in Britain during the First World War', in Tony Kushner and Kenneth Lunn (eds), *The Politics of Marginality*, pp. 61–81.
40. *JC*, 10 March 1916, p. 7; 28 Jan. 1916, p. 11; Feb. 1916, p. 13.
41. *JC*, 22 June 1917, p. 8 and also 16 Nov. 1917, p. 6.
42. *JC*, 5 Oct. 1917, p. 5.
43. *JC*, 28 March 1919, p. 7. See David Cesarani, 'Anti-alienism in England after the First World War' *Immigrants and Minorities*, 6 (1987), pp. 9–14.
44. *JC*, 21 March 1919, pp. 5–6; Sharman Kadish, *Bolsheviks and British Jews* (London: Frank Cass, 1992), Chp. 1.
45. Kadish, *Bolsheviks and British Jews*, pp. 120–1.
46. *JC*, 2 May 1919, p. 5 and subsequent weeks. Kadish, *Bolsheviks and British Jews*, pp. 120–34 and *passim*.
47. David Cesarani, 'Anti-Zionist Politics and Political Anti-Semitism in Britain 1920–24' *Patterns of Prejudice*, 23 (1989), pp. 29–40; Bernard Wasserstein, *The British in Palestine: the Mandatory Government and the Arab-Jewish Conflict 1917–1929* (London: Royal Historical Society, 1978), pp. 113–19; Martin Gilbert, *Winston S. Churchill: Vol. 4 1916–1922* (London: Heinemann, 1975), pp. 615–41.
48. *JC*, 14 May 1920, p. 7. Norman Cohn, *Warrant for Genocide: the Myth of the Jewish World Conspiracy and the Protocols of the Elders of Zion* (London: Eyre and Spottiswode, 1967); Holmes, *Anti-Semitism in British Society*, pp. 141–60; Keith M. Wilson, '"The Protocols of Zion" and the "Morning Post", 1919–1920' *Patterns of Prejudice*, 19 (1985), pp. 5–14; Wilfred Hindle, *The Morning Post 1772–1937* (London: Routledge and Sons, 1937), pp. 235–6.
49. *JC*, 22 Oct. 1920, pp. 5–6; 15 Dec. 1922, p. 7.
50. *JC*, 22 Jan. 1926, pp. 7, 15. Board of Deputies' Archives, London. BD minute book, Vol. 20, 17 Jan. 1926.
51. On Hitler: *JC*, 9 Nov. 1923, p. 5; 16 Nov. 1923, p. 7; 4 April 1924, p. 11.
52. Cf. Brigitte Granzow, *A Mirror of Nazism. British Opinion and the Emergence of Hitler 1929–1933* (London: Gollancz, 1964), *passim*.
53. *JC*, 3 Feb. 1933 pp. 7–8 and 24 Feb. 1933 p. 8. Nana Sagi and Malcolm Lowe, 'Research Report: Pre-War Reactions to Nazi Anti-Jewish Policies in the Jewish Press' *Yad Vashem Studies*, 13 (1979), pp. 388–93; Andrew Sharf, *The British Press and the Jews Under Nazi Rule* (London: Oxford University Press, 1961), pp. 6–41: Benny Morris, *The Roots of Appeasement. The British Weekly Press and Nazi Germany during the 1930s* (London: Frank Cass, 1991), pp. 2–10.
54. Compare *JC*, 8 Sep. 1933, p. 11; 8 June 1934, pp. 13–14; 24 Aug. 1934, p. 11 with *JC*, 5 May 1933, pp. 8–9; 24 Nov. 1933, p. 9.
55. *JC*, 30 Sep. 1932, p. 12; 7 Oct. 1932, p. 9. Cf. Robert Skidelsky, *Oswald Mosley*

(London: Macmillan, 1981), Chps 12–14.
56. Skidelsky, *Oswald Mosley*, Chp. 21; Richard Thurlow, *Fascism in Britain, a History, 1918–1985* (Oxford: Blackwell, 1987), pp. 106–11. On the defence debate, see Gizela Lebzelter, *Political Anti-Semitism in England 1918–1939* (London: Macmillan, 1978), Chp. 7; David Rosenberg, *Facing up to Anti-Semitism* (London: JCARP, 1985), pp. 46–60; Elaine R. Smith, 'Jewish Responses to Political Anti-Semitism and Fascism in the East End of London 1920–1939', in Kushner and Lunn (eds), *Traditions of Intolerance*, pp. 53–71.
57. *JC*, 5 June 1936, pp. 13–17.
58. See leading article 19 June 1936.
59. Central Zionist Archives, Jerusalem. A330/624, J.M. Rich to Joseph Leftwich, 14 Sep. 1936.
60. Board of Deputies' Archives, BD, 21 Feb. 1937.
61. See Laski's, *Jewish Rights and Jewish Wrongs* (London: Soncino Press, 1938), Harold Pollins, *Economic History of the Jews in England* (Rutherford, NJ: Farleigh Dickinson University Press, 1982), p. 190.
62. *JC*, 17 Dec. 1937, p. 8; 16 June 1939, p. 10.
63. *JC*, 20 Oct. 1939, pp. 14–15; 1 March 1930, p. 1; 24 May 1940, pp. 8–9. Tony Kushner, *The Persistence of Prejudice. Antisemitism in British Society during the Second World War* (Manchester: Manchester University Press, 1989), pp.16–22.
64. *JC*, 24 May 1940, p. 12. Thurlow, *Fascism in Britain*, pp. 181–32; Kushner, *Persistence of Prejudice*, pp. 78–105.
65. *JC*, 4 Oct. 1940, pp. 1, 8 and following issues. See Bernard Wasserstein, *Britain and the Jews of Europe 1939–45* (Oxford: Clarendon, 1979), pp. 116–20; Kushner, *The Persistence of Prejudice*, pp. 54–8, 65–77.
66. Reports and debate on black marketeers: *JC*, 27 Feb. 1942, p. 10; 6 March 1942, p. 10; 17 July 1942, p. 8. On antisemitism: *JC*, 18 Sep. 1942, p. 8; 26 Feb. 1943, p. 8; 9 April 1943, p. 8. Wasserstein, *Britain and the Jews of Europe*, pp. 119–20; Kushner, *The Persistence of Prejudice*, pp. 102–3, 119–22.
67. Kushner, *The Persistence of Prejudice*, p. 170.
68. *JC*, 27 Feb. 1942, p. 10; 6 March 1942, p. 10.
69. *JC*, 7 Nov. 1945, p. 12 on *The Times*; 19 Oct. 1945, p. 10 and 2 Nov. 1945, p. 10 on the Hampstead petition.
70. *JC*, 8 Aug. 1947; 15 Aug. 1947, p. 10; 22 Aug. 1947, p. 10. Tony Kushner, 'Anti-Semitism and Austerity: the August 1947 riots in Britain' in Panikos Panayi (ed.), *Racial Violence in Britain 1840–1950* (Leicester: Leicester University Press, 1993), pp. 149–68.
71. *JC*, 19 March 1948, p. 10.
72. *JC*, 4 Feb. 1949, p. 12. See Morris Beckman, *The 43 Group* (London: Centreprise Publishing Project, 1992).
73. Board of Deputies' Archives, C15/3/11/2, Sidney Salomon to Shaftesley, 13 May 1947; Salomon to Shaftesley, 24 Dec. 1947; Salomon to Shaftesley, 13 Sep. 1948.
74. *JC*, 7 May 1954, p. 18. Finchley Golf Club: *JC*, 10 May 1957, p. 18; 28 June 1957, p. 18. Notting Hill: *JC*, 12 Sep. 1958, p. 8; 10 Oct. 1958, p. 16. Colin Holmes, *John Bull's Island: Immigration and British Society, 1871–1971* (London: Macmillan, 1988), pp. 256–61; Geoffrey Alderman, *London Jewry and London Politics 1889–1986* (London: Routledge, 1989), pp. 108–9.
75. *JC*, 20 May 1949, p. 12; 19 Aug. 1949, p. 12.
76. *JC*, 13 June 1947, p. 12; 14 Jan. 1949, p. 12; 4 Aug. 1950, p. 12. See Benjamin Pinkus, *The Jews in the Soviet Union* (Cambridge: Cambridge University Press, 1988), pp. 145–54, 161–2.

282   *Cultures of Ambivalence and Contempt*

77. *JC*, 22 May 1959, p. 16; 20 Oct. 1961, p. 20; 7 May 1965, p. 7; 5 May 1967, p. 6.
78. *JC*, 15 Jan. 1960, p. 18; 29 Jan. 1960, p. 18.
79. *JC*, 8 April 1960, p. 28.
80. In November 1960 the paper called on young Jews to stay away from a meeting in Birmingham Town Hall which was to be addressed by Sir Oswald Mosley: *JC*, 25 Nov. 1960, p. 20. See also 6 July 1962, pp. 8, 20; 3 Aug. 1962, p. 16; 31 Aug. 1962, p. 16; 7 Sep. 1962, p. 20; 30 Nov. 1962, p. 24; 12 April 1963, p. 5; 3 May 1963, p. 7; 12 June 1963, p. 7; 23 July 1965, p. 6.
81. *JC*, 10 Dec. 1965, p.6.
82. Max Beloff: *JC*, 21 Nov. 1969, p. 7; Robert Wistrich: *JC*, 20 Dec. 1974, p. 15.
83. See Robert Wistrich (ed.), *Anti-Zionism and Anti-Semitism in the Contemporary World* (London: Macmillan, 1991).
84. Article by Robert Wistrich *JC*, 20 Dec. 1974, p. 15; 30 Jan. 1976, p. 18; 13 March 1976, p. 1; 2 April 1976, p. 24; 8 April 1977, p. 16; 11 Nov. 1977, p. 18.
85. On Powell: *JC*, 20 April 1968, p. 6; 3 May 1968, p. 6; 22 Nov. 1968, p. 6. On the NF: *JC*, 11 April 1969, p. 6; 30 May 1969, p. 6. See Martin Walker, *The National Front* (London: Collins, 1977).
86. *JC*, 21 June 1974, p. 22; 21 May 1976, p. 20; 9 July 1976, p. 18; 30 July 1976 p. 16; 8 Oct. 1976, p. 16; 12 Nov. 1976, p. 20.
87. *JC*, 4 March 1977, p. 20; April 1977, p. 20; 13 May 1977, p.18.
88. *JC*, 14 April 1978, p. 24; 10 June 1977, p. 16; 16 June 1978, p. 20.
89. For opposing views see *JC*, 6 Oct. 1978, p. 25: 20 Oct. 1978. p. 22.
90. *JC*, 27 Oct. 1978, p. 20.
91. *JC*, 20 April 1979, p. 18.

11

The Necessity of Antisemitism[1]

FREDERIC RAPHAEL

I hope that it will not seem churlish if I take as my subject tonight a book which perhaps ought to be, but certainly is not, in the Parkes Library. It is with no reproachful impudence that I draw attention to its unavailability. Its absence reflects discredit neither on the great Dr Parkes nor on those who cherish his example. I am as sensible of the honour of being tonight's lecturer as I am of myth in credentials as a student of Judaism and its relations with Christianity. In my ignorant circumstances, it is perhaps prudent of me to have chosen for discussion a book which no one can have read, since no one has yet written it. My tactics are taken, of course, from Jorge Luis Borges, though my manoeuvres may lack his elegant skittishness. I shall treat the author of *The Necessity of Antisemitism* as if his book had been accessible at least to me and I will ask you to trust me to epitomise and gloss him fairly. He will concede, in his preambulatory remarks, that some of what he says is compounded with an earlier essay, entitled *The Holocaust and Modern Memory*, of which the present work is a plump precipitate.

The title is, of course, reminiscent of Shelley's notorious pamphlet *The Necessity of Atheism*, which procured the poet's prompt eviction from Oxford. Had 'antisemitism' had any large sense at the end of the eighteenth century, a book with the same title as *our* author's would have led to no such rustication, even if advertised more blatantly than Shelley's shocker, which was, in fact, not as insolent as its title. A modern philosopher would soon see that Percy Bysshe was simply one more undergraduate making a logical distinction between statements about God – of their nature unprovable – and statements about physical events, which were susceptible of tangible proof. In the sunny confidence of the Enlightenment, young Percy assumed that he need only draw attention to the questionable status of the deity for the whole social and moral superstructure postulated on scriptural authority and divine primacy to collapse in dusty shame. The young imagine that the obvious has never previously been observed. Shelley's faith in the power of radical argument was seconded by a guileless belief both in the virtue of truth and in the universal freedom from superstition and humbug consequent on its proclamation. The Oxford authorities – most of them men of the cloth – thought it easier to get rid of Shelley than of the enabling structure on which their cloistered comforts and intellectual complacencies reposed. In my own undergraduate days, an editor was sent down from Cambridge for publishing a blasphemous work which accused God, in the early 1950s, of being too old for omnipotence.

Our author will remark on the tragi-comedy of Shelley's personal fate when he attempted to live according to his principles. Without gloating or jeering, he will point out that the secondary characters suffered more tragically than comically. Shelley demonstrated that liberation could be as destructive as it might prove exhilarating. It rarely occurred to him that good-heartedness was not automatically followed by good-headedness; he assumed that right feeling would always procure right action. The shrillness of his tone and the shambles of his actions need not wholly disqualify him from our sympathy. Our author will remind us that *The Necessity of Atheism* drew unfoolish, if unoriginal, attention to the absurdity – to use another provocative but not inept term – of theological systems.

A.J. Ayer was no less intent on rectificatory mischief when he spoke, in *Language, Truth and Logic*, of metaphysics as 'literal nonsense'. Although his polemic was prudent enough to procure him preferment rather than expulsion from the academic world, Ayer, like Shelley, was insisting that statements about God, and morals, were of necessity – by their logical nature – pseudo-propositions: they had the form of scientific assertions but were void of empirical content. They could be neither true nor false but were literally nonsensical, since they concerned matters immune to sensible observation. Any scrutinising ascent to heaven in order to verify how many angels danced in the pin-headed discotheque in the sky was embargoed by ladders which must always lack the required steps and were inevitably made of mundane stuff. Ayer's middle initial did not, you will recall, stand for Jacob; he neither wrestled with, nor gave much credence to, angels. He did not deny that God existed, which would have been a logical indiscretion, but he gave us to understand that attempts to guess or interpret the divinity's wishes or purposes, let alone to claim dogmatic access to them, were philosophically disreputable. In this, he was putting modern, positivistic dress on a view of the gods which Epicurus had, with sage agnosticism, propounded more than two millennia earlier.

In a fascinating – if tendentious – footnote, our author speculates on the possible motive for Ayer's iconoclastic posture. He observes that his first book was written just before the outbreak of Hitler's war, when the forces of unreason were loud with murderous purposes. Ayer, an Oxford scholar with Jewish origins, illustrates – in an insular mutation – one of the strategies, neither dishonourable nor – I dare say – conscious, by which Jewish intellectuals sought to find a way out of isolation by devising and advocating universalising doctrines: those whose common characteristic was that they applied everywhere and to everyone. The word 'scientific' was a badge pinned by their adherents on Freudianism, Marxism and Positivism. Our author may be accused of mere speculation, and of being side-tracked before he begins, but I detect consistent purpose in his taking Ayer as an emblematic instance, just before the Holocaust, of a certain kind of intellectual response to impending disaster. Our author will scrupulously point out that the ideas of the Vienna circle are neither validated nor damaged by the motives which may be said to underlie them. Here he prefigures a general point which applies throughout *The Necessity of Antisemitism*: the ascription of causal links between psychological circumstance and intellectual or barbarous notions is a needless and metaphysical intrusion. All that we can hope to do, our author tells us, is to discern patterns. His constant idea, as his argument unfolds, is to draw our attention to configurations, not to seek to hammer out a causal chain.

When A.J. Ayer embraced, with all the fervour of a convert, the notion of philosophy as the hand-maiden of science, he was of course suggesting a radical change of employment for a discipline which had previously seen service with God. Science, in the late 1930s, was the new universal deity. Ayer's dismissive attitude to traditional pieties was of a piece with that of his German-speaking teachers in Vienna, although it was spiced with a puncturing wit which was rarely their style.

The Logical Positivists never, so far as we can tell, supposed themselves to be addressing the Jewish

Question. They lacked Freud's self-probing fascination with motive. Their notions were systematically anti-personal: the value of what they had to say was independent of who was to say it, or why. 'Autobiography,' we were taught, 'is not a method in philosophy'. The Logical Positivists shared with Freud at least an impatience with any notion of exceptional cases. Their laws, like God's writ, applied without, so to speak, Andorran pockets where man was untaxed by the common rules. Freud never allowed that any male human being, under any social or moral circumstances, could escape the Oedipus Complex. One might as well imagine that by taking steroids a great sprinter could outrun his own shadow.

The Jewishness of the intellectuals who advocated these schemes of universal validity was, one might say, neither incidental nor determinant. It can be noticed; it is part of an undeniable pattern. What it 'means' need not detain us. 'Don't ask for the meaning, ask for the use', Wittgenstein advised, which will hardly deter us from speculation but reminds us that it may be more fruitful to examine what useful place antisemitism has in the logic of Europe than to seek its essential meaning. The distinction between deep anti-semitism, of the kind supposedly entertained by Céline, by Paul de Man, by Heidegger or by Ezra Pound, and the shallow prejudices of the *Français moyen* or of the Mosleyite bully-boy will, our author insists, turnout to be delusive, not because they all share the same taint or disease or delusion but because the whole idea of looking at each case as if it were more or less profound and so, in some way, more or less dignified is based on a medical or psychoanalytic model which misses the most important issue – the persistence, or necessity (if we accept our author's provocations), of anti-semitism as a useful, perhaps ineradicable, element of what we shall call the language of civilisation. Here we can recall Paul Valéry's paradox, *'la profondeur de la surface'*. Deep down, we might gloss him, language is superficial.

The eagerness with which brilliant Jews initiated or participated in homogenising, renovatory schemes does not, I repeat, cast doubt on – nor necessarily lend lustre to – them, but there is an undoubted tendency for them to seek, at least at certain stages, to slough off 'innate' particularism in favour of a voluntary (but necessary – because truthful) allegiance. Contingency – the lack of an obligatory logic – nauseated Jean-Paul Sartre's hero, Roquentin; it was hardly less repugnant to those who felt themselves arbitrarily cornered in a logic foisted upon them by a God in Whom they did not believe. A footnote will remark on Sartre's extraordinary post-war essay in which the Jew, alone of men, is exhorted to embrace the essence which his enemies – rather than God – choose for him and to wear their repugnant stars as if they were decorations. Here I should like to think that Sartre was remembering the minor French playwright who, on the day when the yellow star became obligatory, wore his in a fiacre which drove down the Champs Elysées. When he lit a cigar, his companion suggested that it might not be wise. 'My dear fellow,' he replied, 'this is no moment to hide one's light under a bushel.'

To resume: we need not postulate either cowardly purpose or covert treachery in the ambitions of those who – Jew or Gentile, Jew *and* Gentile – adopted a white-coated, impersonal posture. A.J. Ayer is an interesting local case for us, since he was under no great threat and cannot plausibly be accused of any fugitive purpose. He thought that he was enrolling himself in a truthful crusade to cleanse the world of windy dogma and obscurantist pretension. And wasn't he? Science was independent of personal opinions and advocated universal laws which incidentally rendered ridiculous those recently propounded at Nuremburg. Jewish intellectuals saw in the new economics, in the new physics, even in new music and art, universalising opportunities. By voluntarily relinquishing their particularism they would become united with all mankind; they would trade obsolete debentures for common shares in the future. Such ambitions may have been vain; were they ignoble? They combined immodesty (not always disreputable in men of genius) with humility (the discounting of personality, even in the arts, was programmatic). They hoped, one might say, to disappear in the public pool of humanity, although some of them wanted to do so with a bigger splash than others.

It is almost impossible for us to imagine ourselves in the situation of those who lived before the Holocaust. What was not avoided now reads as inevitable. The evasive efforts of statesmen and of intellectuals alike seem puny, perhaps fatuous; unforgiving condescensions are no less malapert. It is more useful to trace the patterns of response than to arraign individuals for their frailties. The fetish of biography has reached gross proportions in the contemporary world of books; I am disposed to read this as an indication of a regressive reluctance to examine history rather than the higher gossip. The Hellenistic Greeks, with categorical acumen, contrasted biography (worthless) with history (worthwhile). What interests our author is that the attempts to create a new class – of selfless scientific engineers – or to create a new classlessness – officered by initiates in dialectical materialism – were immensely seductive, if finally fruitless, to a variety of minds who thought, like Percy Bysshe, that faulty logics could be no sooner seen than undone. Every major intellectual and aesthetic movement of the twentieth century proposed to exchange old logics for new, imagining that such an alteration was self-evidently desirable and must – how man craves imperatives *and* freedom in the same breath! – *must* procure therapeutic consequences. Their prospectuses varied; their promises wore a singular uniformity: certain obstacles to truth had to be got rid of and the way to an undistinguishing millennium would then be open.

Bargaining, whether commercial or diplomatic (had not the Bolsheviks made the diplomatic archives public?), would be replaced by true and unarguable standards. Rhetoric would yield to equations. Ayer's great precursor, Bertrand Russell, once said that if we had certified proof that the elimination of the Jews (he did specifically exemplify the Jews), if the elimination of the Jews could guarantee universal and eternal happiness for mankind, then there could be no sustainable reason for not doing away with them. Now it is no part of my purpose to put Russell among the antisemites, let alone among the fools, but I ask you to file this plausible folly in your minds, not in order to be armed against Russell but in order to notice the temptation, even in a great and, on the whole, right-thinking man, to embrace murderous possibilities, if the terms are good enough. How odd, to put no finer a point on it, for Russell to look for divine guarantors for a solution to earthly misfortune which, although offered in the form of a scandalous paradox, does not finally differ from the one proposed by Adolf Hitler! Let us not labour this point, but note it well: Russell could imagine without repugnance a God who offered those kinds of terms. The disappearance of the Jews, self-effacingly proposed by Positivists, Communists and other universalisers, was – I mean to remind you – a common feature both of benign and of malign blueprints for the future. It is impossible for me to believe that Russell could ever have accepted the small print of the diabolical contract offered by God, but his provisional agreement is there on the paper. This marginal episode serves to illustrate one simple, perhaps banal, point: even the cleverest men, and perhaps *particularly* the cleverest men, will endorse theories of elimination (either gleefully or, as in Russell's case, with reluctant unselfishness) without any serious consideration of what the bloody specifics of the matter will involve. If he goes on to ask what Russell's attitude would be to, say, a mere millennium of universal bliss on the same terms, our author may be accused of squeezing more juice from a freak fruit than one can well swallow, but is he not right to emphasise the 'eternal seductiveness', as he rather winsomely puts it, 'of Lady Macbeth'? Just one little death and the crown is on the right head! One sacrifice and utopia is our common address! Our author asks us to share the temptations of the prospect before we froth our indignation. Where Russell fell, we should not disdain at least to falter, although we may concede that this particular wedge has no thin end.

Before leaving the chestnut stall, we may recall George Bernard Shaw asking his neighbour at dinner whether, at 1920s prices, she would go to bed with a man for a hundred pounds. When she showed some interest in the deal, he asked whether she would do it for half a crown. Bridling, she said, 'What do you take me for?' Shaw replied, 'We've established what you are; it simply remains to discover your price.' Shall we be equally severe with Russell's lapse as with Julius Streicher's obscene rant? Do they both 'mean the same thing'? Is it merely a question of establishing their price? Yes? No? Yes *and* no? 'Say it if you like', John Wisdom used to advise, 'but be careful'. Be *very* careful. How? Quite.

Our author's next chapter seems disjunctive from the foregoing. He proceeds to ask why it is that the *Shoah* has proved indigestible both in the history and in the literature of the post-war years. Theodor Adorno famously remarked that there could be 'no poetry after Auschwitz', but do our bookshops not bulge with slim volumes? Have birds ceased to sing or novelists to be short-listed? Our shelves may be ominous with silences, of which Paul Célan's, self-imposed, is not the least loud, but on any commonsensical reckoning, poetry rhymes on. We may revert to this apparent refutation of Adorno in due course. For the present our author elects to distinguish between what can be digested and what can be assimilated. Assimilation denies uniqueness; it denotes the likeness of one thing to another.

Here another notable intellectual figure becomes paradigmatic. Since I am not a German-speaker, I hope that I do not travesty him when I take Ernst Nolte to have argued, in a number of influential texts, for the assimilation of Hitler's war against the Jews with other campaigns, whether Stalinist or Hitlerian, in which populations of dubious loyalty were either transported or massacred. Nolte, if reports are to be trusted, recoils from endorsement of Hitler's methods, but does not find his policies devoid of prophylactic sense. Affecting dispassionately to repair a black hole in German history, Nolte can scarcely prevent himself from being dragged into it. The language of obscenity has hydratic muscles: cut, they come again.

There is a certain courage in the historian's determination to stitch regular words over an abyss more commonly stepped silently around. Nolte darns where others have preferred, often briefly, to damn. By using the old historical vocabulary to cover the *Shoah*, Nolte means no harm to the Jews. As a good German, we are assured, he means well to the Germans: he wants to give them a history *comme les autres*, with highs and lows, but without unfathomable lacunae. The lakes he wishes to drain are, it may be, full of blood, but it is old blood and perhaps can scarcely be distinguished, after all this time, from spilt milk. Such reclamation is now a sociable, even overdue, act of cultural ecology and patriotic renovation. The new Germany – with reunification in mind – needs a history which builds over the past. Being in the same place as other nations furnishes a curious alibi.

Nolte's arguments for the declassification of his fellow countrymen from eternally tainted demons to people with an unfortunate but un-unique history are neither stupid nor malevolent, though they are spiced with an aggressive self-pity which we should properly hesitate to ascribe to innate characteristics. I remarked of Nolte just now, 'He means well'; I hope I spoke unsarcastically, but I ask you to apply Wittgenstein's formula and ask not what he means but what the *use* of his protracted work turns out to be. Never mind the motive, what pattern is being woven? One of its elements is that Nolte and his faction are obliged to re-eliminate the Jews in the process of their sanitary engineering. This act of re-elimination has nothing in it of savage nostalgia; we need not question that the main intention is to bury Nazism and spoil it of the glamorous uniqueness which might inspire its resurrection or at least its cult. The irony is that Nolte's act of ponderous sepulture – of deep-sixing, to use a less fancy term, requires the banalisation of the *Shoah*, its down-grading from singularity to yet another great pity: in brief, its assimilation to other routinely regrettable procedures.

Our author will insist here on the indigestibility of the Jewish experience. He does so, he would like to believe, out of no desire to pre-empt forever the supreme tragic role for Jews alone. This kind of morbid vanity has its uses, as Mr Begin used embarrassingly to remind us, but it derives from a mystique rather than from history (but then what is history?). Our author's belief that he is not involved in special pleading may be a delusion, but the discerning of patterns is not necessarily rendered self-serving or misleading because a man may incidentally figure in them himself. Indigestibility is not a boast, but a fact, and – in our author's estimation – a significant one. It would, he is willing to agree, be no unquestionable misfortune for the Jews if their history could be assimilated to that of other victims of murderous malevolence. It just happens to be the case that this assimilation fudges the issue. Here he recalls Sir Lewis Namier's notorious remark when asked why he did not deal with Jewish history: 'The Jews do not have a history, they have a martyrology'. Namier did not deny his Jewishness, as we know, and was a fervent Zionist, but that fervour was, so he thought, independent of academic purposes.

A fat footnote (my favourite kind, as long as it is at the bottom of the pertinent page) will observe that the methodology of which Namier was a pioneer – his reductionist analysis of political parties in terms of the interests, social and economical, of their particular members – appears to be in direct opposition to the universalising (often determinist) schemes of the Marxists, the Logical Positivists and the Freudians, but it is of a piece with them in this at least: it deconstructs the antique model by unclotting group interests through the rigorous revelation of individual motivations. It may seem that this is counter to the homogenising strategies of others but it too has the consequence, *as if by chance*, of questioning existing categories: if groups are best and properly analysed in terms of their atomic rather than their molecular structure, so to say, then we are right to think that there is no typology of man which *necessarily* links him with any allegiance larger than the one to which his own interests – in either the genial or the mercenary sense – incline him. It requires no large effort, in our author's view, to see that Namier was dissolving old configurations and assimilating all men, at least those under his minute scrutiny, to a common model, however discrete its monistic manifestations. There is, you might say, lumping up and lumping down, but all lumping is assimilatory, systematic, universalising. When Namier exempted the Jews from history, he grudgingly, even charmlessly, relegated (or promoted) them into a special category, just as Arnold Toynbee, a constructionist of megalomaniac confidence, did when he referred to Judaism as a 'fossil religion'. As Hugh Trevor-Roper points out with mischievous accuracy, this procured Toynbee great prestige in Arab countries. Well, it would, wouldn't it? But the observation is not rendered void on that count.

Vain men can still tell the truth; the modest too can be tendentious.

We may object here – and the paradox is central to our considerations – that the notion of antisemitism, so far from being 'necessary', appears largely irrelevant to the evaluation of the historians we have mentioned. Trevor-Roper, like Namier, is a Zionist, although unlike Namier he is not a Jew, but his attacks on Toynbee do not depend on any ascription of antisemitism to that polymath windbag, nor does Toynbee's estimation of the Jews greatly vary, in categorical terms, from Namier's. Jewish self-hatred – that boring charge, which can hardly be distinguished from Jewish intelligence or even, perhaps, from Jewish self-importance – cannot explain away Namier's irritated dismissal of what the cant calls 'his own people' as a historical topic. There was, he seems to be saying, – if not *with* Toynbee certainly not *against* him – something tiresomely unique about the Jews. They play, one might say, a monotonous character-part on the historical stage and cannot, with conviction or success, be enrolled for any other. With one bound, our author jumps back to indigestibility.

We are, as Brillat-Savarin gastronomically observed, what we eat. We are also, one might add, what we do *not* eat. The literal and the metaphorical run, at times, on parallel lines which meet and do not meet at meal-times. The indigestible may be killed and even swallowed, but it fails to become us; our system refuses it. It is not a matter of appetite or personal preference when a cow refrains from *foie gras*. Such abstention is neither creditably humane nor discreditably puritanical. The herbivore's abstention is not a moral matter. With man, it is rather different. Killing and eating are, we are promised, natural to him. But – as Walter Burkert emphasises in *Homo Necans* – man knows he kills, just as he knows, to his disastrous and unique distress, that he dies. He has to eat; does he have to kill? He excuses himself and blinds himself to what happens in the abattoir by saying that what is digestible is natural; what does not come up again has, as they say, gone down all right. Nevertheless, as anthropologists note-takingly insist, menus vary; they are hot and cold, they include or exclude fish, fowl and red herring. Red herring is perhaps one of the most interesting dishes, much more commonly consumed and much more sustaining than the scornful proverb suggests. Man kills and eats; guilt and innocence sit constantly with us at table. We have blood on our knives, most of us, if not on our washed hands. The sacrificial and the utilitarian share facilities, though one or the other aspect may cloak the logic of our bloody consumption. Eating the evidence is often the best way of getting rid of it. You will remember the old joke about the secret so secret that its recipient was instructed 'Swallow before reading'. The act of swallowing is a form of obedient credulity no less than it can be one of solemn communion. We swallow stories as well as food; they too become part of us.

Our author suggests that the uniqueness of the Jews, which need hardly be attributed to innate qualities or divine selection, is due, at least in part, to their equivocal status, literally and metaphorically, in the routines of social consumption. Jews sometimes do and sometimes do not eat with others; they may approach the common table, but they often sit at it either uncomfortably or with uneasy showiness. It is not simply a matter of whether there is *jambon de Parme* in prospect, nor is it entirely a metaphorical matter. To put it shamelessly, the Jew takes the missionary position in the old New Yorker cartoons: he is not sure whether he is to eat or to be eaten. The grammatical slippage between the alternatives alerts us, as any first-year Freudian would notice, to the structural ambiguity of the supposed antithesis. The Jew is at home with the series of trick choices of which 'Heads I win, tails you lose' is the chestnuttiest. If assimilated, he becomes indistinguishable;

if he insists on being indigestible, he sticks in the throat of the world, as George Steiner, *philosophe* and gastronome, has memorably put it. Can he expect a better fate than to be coughed into the dustbin? Words too are food; they have their dietary significance. Even the most ordinary phrase has its poisonous freight. Man kills; words – as Norman Cohn reminds us – give him his bloody warrant.

Our author points out how what is, in some sense, a fate determined by others is often rigged to be the consequence of a choice on the part of the victim. The sacrificial heifers at Athenian festivals were offered their favourite food as they reached the altar, in order that, in lowering their heads towards the delicacies, they might give the nod to their own slaughter. The condemned man's breakfast procures a not dissimilar acceptance of the sacrificial role. Nadeszhda Mandelstam remarks on how rarely human victims scream and struggle in the face of death and injustice. If she rightly sees no necessary virtue in brave reticence, the choice of mute resignation, on the part of victims, is perhaps their last luxury, in that it is defiantly *chosen*. Mrs Mandelstam had the right, God knows, to suggest that it was at least as honourable to embarrass one's killers as to deny them the satisfaction of witnessing one's fear. It is a point on which those of us who have been spared the horror should perhaps have the modesty not to pontificate.

How does our author propose to illustrate the indigestibility of the *Shoah* in particular in the European or perhaps the world-scheme? How, in due course, can he link this with what he dares to call *'The Necessity of Antisemitism'*? He may begin with a dry example of how societies which either engendered or acquiesced in genocide both have and have not acknowledged the scandal. Before that, I might remark that a recent correspondent of mine was full of furious reproach when I used the word 'scandal' with regard to the *Shoah*. It made him think of

Christine Keeler, he said. Well, we can only use the vocabulary available to us (the limits of our world are the limits of our language, which is why silence can recommend itself as a fitting figure for the unspeakable). 'Scandal' has been debased, like so much of our vocabulary, but its root meaning involves 'an affront to religion'. It is, one can argue, not inappropriate, once again bearing in mind the ambiguities available in the definition, to call the *Shoah* a scandal; not only, I mean to say, does mass murder cry out for a merciful God and, in the face of His helplessness, throw amiable notions of divinity into scandalous question, but – and this 'but' is scarcely adversative, as we shall see – but/and the fact of the *Shoah*, that it took place, jars so painfully with established notions of divinity no less than of humanity that, in order to save the logic by which, for better or worse, Western civilisation (in particular) proposes to continue living, it turns out to be necessary to mount a two-pronged operation which has as its secret and single purpose the *de*-scandalisation of the *Shoah*, its eviction from crucial centrality in the relations between man and his sacred machinery. The issue is crucial indeed: as the matter of the Carmel of Auschwitz implies, The Jew must, if nothing else, be denied a supplanting cross, a crueller, trumping Calvary.

The Irishman denies that he stole the bucket and adds, by way of further mitigation, that it had a hole in it anyway. On the secular as on the theological level, Europeans are driven, without malice or conscientious callousness, to deny that they had any responsibility for the Holocaust and, when goaded beyond patience, can suggest that the Jews are tiresomely vain, not to say cashing in, when they maintain that the *Shoah* was a unique and unredeemably scandalous event. The holes in the bucket, the seriously vexed suggest, were partly self-inflicted and go to show what kind of merchandise certain people are in the business of peddling.

We shall resist the urge to lampoon or to ascribe consciously blinkered motives to honourable men. We shall limit ourselves to taking vigilant note. In this context, observe that what happened to the Jews between 1941 and 1945 at first had no descriptive term in any public record. The Battle of El Alamein was never merely 'something that happened in the desert'. Yet the survivors of the camps were long known to us, almost anonymously, as 'Displaced Persons'; no one asked what their place was, or would be: they could neither go back nor go forward. 'D.P.' might as well stand for Damned People. They continued to have numbers (which had to be reduced) but they had no names. Ernest Bevin, who is still touted as a Great Foreign Secretary, remarked that he was 'not 'aving the Jews push to the front of the queue'. In his lovable way, he was one of the first, as the Greeks used to say, *sozein ta phenomena*, to hold appearances together by cleaving to the concepts which had served the old order and could thus sustain those continuities on which recovery – covering up again – seemed to depend. Bevin's orderly vulgarity, in denying precedence to notorious queue-bargers, however desperate their case or loud their mouths, served early notice that no large homage would be available to those with hard-luck stories. *Vae victis* was a slogan that extended even to victims who declared themselves on the victorious side. 'How many divisions does the Pope have?' was Stalin's dismissive response to moral suasions. (It turns out that he has, to say the least, more than dialectical materialists cared to count.) 'How much clout do the Jews have?' was Bevin's loudly unspoken question, 'And how much does anyone want them to have?' was the equally brazen supplementary.

We may qualify our veneration for good old Ernie, but it would be foolish to sneer too promptly. Our author counsels us to try to imagine what could conceivably have been the right and appropriate response to what the Allies found in the heartland of civilised Europe. It is one of the uneasy oddities of the 1939-1945 war that the vast majority of the fighting forces, at least of the Western allies, discovered just what they had been fighting for, or against, only when they were all but victorious. In this respect, the effect preceded the cause; here again, the pattern proves more evident than the motivation. I once had a tense evening with a decent man, who had gone right through the war in a Guards Regiment, no contemptible record, and who promised me that it had been fought on behalf of the Jews. This was, I felt, to do them too much honour. His remarks were made without rancour, perhaps with a sense of righteous purpose, but the ambiguity which irritated my over-sensitive susceptibilities is surely undeniable. The Jews were, in the Guardee's decent blue eyes, both literally and figuratively the reason for Britain's involvement. Thus they were, albeit without any such intention, responsible for Britain's expenditure, in men and treasure, and – not quite the same thing – they were the sole beneficiaries of the Allied effort. By the same token, they could hardly have any reproachful claim, could they, against their selfless saviours? An officer and a gentleman thus impersonated sentiments of a decidedly – what shall we say? – Jew-conscious order. We may hesitate here to speak of antisemitism, as if it were a clinical condition, with a regularly identifiable pathology, and our hesitation will be, in my view, wholly proper. And yet, can we deny that there was, in the Guardee's guileless candour, the symptoms of a defensive-accusatory bias – balance perhaps – at the centre of his perception of events in which he played a gallant part?

Our author, with his penchant for digressive procedure, will contrast the notion of a war fought 'to save the Jews' with the steady resistance which Winston Churchill encountered when he sought to honour certain Jews' desire to fight under their own flag, and in an exclusively Jewish regiment, against the Nazis. Here again, no charges of malice are necessary (although some are warranted) in order to see how the idea of Jewish soldiers was as alarming to their supposed champions as that of defenceless and incurably civilian Jews was contemptible. The 'Heads you lose' syndrome rears its ugly tail. (And what shall we say of Israel's fundamental reluctance to conscript its Arab citizens? Is that different? How different? Comfortably or uncomfortably? Should these questions not be put? Why?)

In academic circles, the indigestibility of the Jews finds an equally ambivalent crux in an apparently nominalist context. The extermination of six million Jews at first had no specific descriptive or denoting term at all. El Alamein, you will recall, was one thing, with a place in official history, but the camps and their lethal factories gave no opportunity for crossed swords on official maps. Martyrs have no battle-honours; the death of fossils is not honourable.

Already, in 1945, in my first quarter at Charterhouse, very thin boys were nicknamed 'Belsen'; but Belsen itself formed no part of the curriculum. When the term Holocaust began, thanks – I think – to Elie Wiesel, to be applied to the attempted genocide of the Jews, grammarians sought to limit the damage to the verbal stock by seeking at least to deny the term a capital letter when applied to the *Shoah*. Etymologists winced at the appropriation of what should, as they were prim enough to insist, have entailed a *wholly* burnt offering, to what was, at best or worst, only a partially successful operation. The Jews had to be warned off from the tactless appropriation of one of *our* words in order to describe, without proper linguistic certificate, *their* particular misfortune. We might note that 'holocaust' does not, in its etymology, imply that all the conceivable victims were burnt. A holocaust of oxen would scarcely have implied the simultaneous incineration of the entire bovine population. Shall we see any symptomatic significance in a pedantry which becomes so compulsive as to itself verge on a howler? Why not? I have, as you will notice, accepted the term publicised by Claude Lanzmann in the title of his film, in order to designate the mass murder of the Jews. It may well be best to use the Hebrew term, but the reluctance of Europeans to delegate a term of their own vocabulary remains an indication of the duplicities involved and of the phenomena that had to be saved, or salvaged.

We are by now aware that our author trades – perhaps revels – in ambiguities. He sees the Jews as both like and unlike other men, both part of Europe and external to it, both assimilable and indigestible. He may still claim here that he is simply trying to clarify a situation, not to propose an aetiology, yet he will be disappointed if we have not picked up several clues as to what is to come. Surely we are supposed to recognise an attempt at least to indicate why antisemitism is not a sad contingency or even a disagreeable contagion, but a constant and essential working part of Europe's sombre and unreformed logic. The reluctance of philologists to concede a single stick of their linguistic furniture symbolises, without exaggeration, how reluctant are the lords of the word to lease or release a single item of their basic inventory. It is all, we begin to see, part of a set; this set has mythical significances which render it unbreakable, in every sense, although the myth itself cannot be disclosed. In the elevated charades of duplicity, we must know that there is a hidden term, said and unsaid, implicit and explicit, but we cannot – without rendering the world's game unplayable, without 'blowing it', or the whistle – be told what it is. We cannot be told because the other players, even those who rule the court and watch the lines, at best only half-know; they know and they do not know, just as Heracleitus' Supreme Being both wishes and does not wish to be called Zeus.

'Forgetting too is a kind of conservatism' is the cryptic quotation our author chooses to alert us to the tenacity with which men prefer the old language to any recognition of the new thing. 'Through a glass darkly' will always be preferable to seeing things face to face. The magic of words, of formulaic utterance, derives from their place in mythical procedures from which – and here our author presages a new theme – man again and again supposes himself able to emancipate himself, as Shelley exemplifies, only to find that the shadow is stronger than the substance; reality is systematically ignored in order that the myth remain intact, untouched like the Ark of the Covenant, any contact with which – however well-intentioned – was necessarily punished by death, not because the culprit had done anything wicked, but because he had done something unforgivable. Taboo has no appeal court. The *Shoah* has not *accidentally* suffered a double eviction; its discounting sustains continuities which no 'injustice' can be suffered to curtail. By double eviction, our author alludes to both assimilation – which seeks to disperse the Jewish clot by analogising their fate with that of other unfortunates, and so removes them from hermetic consideration – and, for egregious instance, to their literal transportation to Israel. The desire of Zionists to leave does not affect the larger, different logic of *why*, despite all the obstacles, their departure was part of a process which they themselves imagined they were decisive in ending forever. The Athenians, classicists will recall, having killed the sacrificial beasts, tried the executioner's axe for murder and then flung it into the multitudinous seas. The Europeans – so a hyperbolic argument might maintain – went through a supplementary routine, having disposed of some of the axe-men: they repudiated the surviving victims and flung them into Asia. It is a matter of mythic obligation, no less than of sorry contingency, that the resulting state, supposedly the realisation of a Jewish dream, was destined also to become a pariah altogether unlike the other *parvenu* post-war states, however shameless in their corruption or their murderous practices. We have all heard of the West Bank, but how many have heard of East Timor?

The reason that it is argued that studies of motivation, on the Namier-esque model, cannot be decisive – although they may be sociologically of great interest – is that we are seeking to understand the unspeakable roots of a tragic enactment which can never be analysed without remainder through the articulation of any single logic, however subtle. Duplicity involves more than one variable. Certainly, we cannot atomise the issue by reducing it to a matter of the vile ambitions of a Gauleiter or the almost understandable reluctance of an Auschwitz guard to exchange his hellish office for a freezing billet on the Russian front. The sorry ironies parasitic on the *Shoah* go so far as to include the documented dilatoriness of certain mechanicals in the full implementation of the Final Solution, lest its success should lead to their assignation to a fighting unit. Poor unpardonable bastards! Among them are to be found those axes which Europe accused of unique bloodiness and threw away, the better to attain freedom from miasmal guilt and to procure that unity on which, with truly admirable hypocrisy (the Greek word involves dramatic performance), the new solidarity is based. All foundations have blood in them somewhere, as readers of René Girard will not need to be told.

In view of such men (there but for the grace of what is left of God go some at least of us!), we can see that the noblest tragedians – Aeschylus or Racine – could never begin, even with the equipment of genius, to encompass the gross muddle of tragic and comic ingredients which lead us, when taking the Nazis as seriously as their crimes, to flinch from recognising their grotesque and almost pitiful absurdity. The unspeakableness, which Adorno was honouring when he spoke of the death of poetry, has its shallow as well as it bottomless end. Can we even begin to conceive of a purging, a cathartic logic in which the *Shoah* could be disgraced as, for instance, slavery was disgraced – rendered indefensible – by Wilberforce? Has any new, disembarrassing formula begun to be given? What would it be for a new Shelley to find a way, however naive, of removing – by clearly describing – the strategies of malice and distinction by which Europe persists in conducting its morality? What new language could conceivably, conceptually, render the old charades unrepeatable, unplayable? What poet, to come to Adorno's point again, could displace, decentralise Ezra Pound and T.S. Eliot, the canonised good and baddish fairies of the modern Parnassus? Even now our author will dread being misunderstood; he will implore his readers once again not to suppose that he is blaming anyone or everyone for what is implicit in the language: the unlaughable comedy of the situation is that we cannot quickstep our way away from partnership with the shadows, which are also ourselves, and with whom we are sentenced to dance or limp through any conceivable future.

Here is the nature of the necessity which makes antisemitism Europe's elastic, agile, weightless companion, as necessary to its articulations as is the negative to its vocabulary. For modern Europe, our author will say, the Jew is 'not'. It is what Hitler wanted to be able to say; he was denied, but with no decisive denial: we shall be reminded that throughout the *Shoah* – even when it was no kind of a secret – not a single allied broadcasting station, and not the Vatican either, ever uttered a single inexpensive word of *warning* to those who were mounting the trains in accordance with Eichmann's lethal timetable. The repetition of the fact becomes, as they say in philosophy, a mere lament. Its futility does not, however, imply that the sacrifice of the Jews, whether or not they were wholly burnt, was not in accordance with the logic of European thought and that their elimination – their being thrust over the *limen* or threshold – was not part of a mythically inspired scheme to be rid of their damnable witness, their martyr role, to be done with impudent alternatives, with the Pascalian witnesses who now, to Christianity's shame, outranked God in the ghastliness of their suffering. It is here that we see the rupture of those continuities which James Parkes, in his industrious decency, wanted to emphasise. Fearing, yet preceding, the *Shoah*, he can hardly be derided for failing to take it into account. But we must now be conscious of being and not being in the same tradition as Christianity, and it is with this situation – in the centre of a once excluded middle – that any plotting of our present moral chaos must seek to deal. The Jews, our author will tell us, are marginal to Europe's history and to its apparent confidence in its future, which will be built over its past. There is unacknowledged but reinforcing blood in the foundations of the old continent's new harmony, just as Jimmy Hoffa's body, we are told, underlies certain steel and concrete investments by the Mafia. The Jews, our author insists, are the margin which runs down the middle of the page. The caesura they announce is a loud blank, but it speaks and will always speak louder than the words with which, in furtive reasonableness or honest exculpation, in Christian apology or in pragmatic shamelessness, historians and apologists of all kinds will hope to drown it.

'The Jews and Antisemitism', our author dares to conclude, 'are shadow and substance; one cannot be effaced without the other.' Is this rhetoric or is it fact? Can there be rhetorical facts?

What do you think?

Notes

1. This paper was first presented as the first Parkes Lecture in 1989, to mark the 25th anniversary of the deposit of the Parkes Collections at the University of Southampton.

Afterword:
Liberalism and Toleration

James Parkes was a great man and the essays in this volume are a fitting tribute to his life and work. The University of Southampton has managed to put the Parkes Collections (his library and related Jewish archives) on a proper footing, and the establishment of the Parkes and Karten Fellowships, together with the Marcus Sieff Lectureship and the Parkes–Wiener Chair, have projected the University and the Parkes Centre into the forefront of Jewish studies both in the United Kingdom and internationally.

Reading this volume is a powerful reminder of many things, but two issues on which I want to dwell very briefly are the richness and dynamism of Jewish identity and the fragility of the circumstances under which that identity has been able to flourish. There is a problem here which is a central one for western liberal societies. We are seeing a growth in what might be called the politics of difference, which involves a positive evaluation of the ways of life and traditions of particular communities and the narratives which hold them together and give them distinctiveness.

There are all sorts of pressures which are encouraging this process but probably the most important is globalisation and its accompanying standardisation and homo-genisation of economic goods. Individuals are bound to look to the local and traditional sources of their own identity to give them a sense of meaning and security in a fast-changing but also increasingly homogeneous world. So, paradoxically, it may be that the growth of a dynamic market economy will play a central role in encouraging the politics of difference and the importance of the distinctive life of particular communities.

This trend is exacerbated too by the growth of a post-modern approach across a whole range of academic disciplines and cultural forms. In opposition to Enlightenment standards of general rationality and reason, which owe little to tradition and indeed are frequently hos-tile to it, the postmodern approach rejects a general stan-dard and norm of reason in favour of seeing ideas like rationality, justification and legitimacy as being relative to a particular way of life with its own standards and values. The encouragement of such ways of life and their narrative forms is the other side of the rejection of 'meta' concepts of reason, of history and of narrative.

This move to emphasise the indispensability of the richness of community life and communal narrative for a sense of identity and indeed of rationality and judgement is in many ways very welcome. There is, however, a potential down side. The constitutional arrangements of a liberal society, which seem to be a necessary condition for the flourishing of diverse forms of community life and identity, require justification. Diverse forms of community life can only flourish in security within a constitutional structure which secures mutual tolerance, mutual non-coercion and mutual respect. The difficulty, though, is that if we go too far in terms of linking an individual's sense of self and self-worth to community membership alone, we shall find it very difficult to develop the intellectual resources to justify constitutional arrangements which have to stand above different forms of community and ways of life. Thus, the arguments to legitimise such arrangements have to be non-specific to particular communities.

It would be far too simplistic and syncretic to assume that all the diverse communities of western societies can somehow – out of their different intellectual, cultural and religious traditions – find similar ways of justifying the constitutional arrangements of a tolerant society. These ways of life are too discrete and conceptions of the good and of what gives life its meaning are too diverse. This problem is exacerbated in the context of toleration since communities in their religious aspects believe that they know the truth and thus may not wish to be tolerant of error.

We cannot just assume that liberalism is the best or most appropriate way of coping with moral and religious diversity and particularity. Indeed, one hardly needs to draw attention to this fact in a book about James Parkes, since Fascists saw their own views and theories not as a way of accommodating social diversity, but as a way of overcoming it. So it would be facile to believe that liberalism is somehow uniquely appropriate to the circumstances of diversity. Liberal toleration has to be justified and legitimised, not just taken as given. The problem then becomes how to determine general moral resources for legitimating the basic constituents of liberal citizenship when so many cultural pressures encourage a retreat from the general to the particular, for the reasons I have tried to sketch. It is at our peril, however, that we reject the general principles on which liberalism and toleration have to be based. These cannot be the property of any single community in a diverse society.

A good deal of Anglo-American political thought is now concerned with the links between citizenship, value pluralism, the role of the community and the possibility of achieving what might be called neutral justification: that is to say, an argumentative strategy which could be endorsed by members of quite diverse religious and cultural communities as a way of securing a common constitutional framework within which to live. It seems to me that the Jewish community can play a major role in seeking to preserve the idea of the general principles of liberal citizenship in a world of growing particularity partly, of course, because the Jews have suffered in many ways more than anyone from the fragility of toleration. Surely they more than any others need to sustain the principles which could underpin a tolerant society.

But equally important are those universalist elements of the Jewish tradition itself. While of course Jewish tradition is rooted in law and covenant and even theodicy, nevertheless we have to be alive to the universalism of that tradition which believed that God's judgment lay on everyone, not just on Israel. The prophets were not just covenant mediators, vitally important though that was to them. Amos, Isaiah, Jonah and other prophets had a message for the nations as well as Israel. Prophecy was not just for the community which shared in the covenant and whose identity was bound by that; there was a concern too about how Israel and the nations should live together and the norms that would allow this to happen. These norms go beyond the covenant and embody a more universalist sense of natural law. This point has been made particularly strongly by John Barton in his essay 'Ethics in Isaiah of Jerusalem', in which he argues that Isaiah had a concept of natural law embodying a general standard of morality which was valid for all people, a point which is also insisted upon by James Barr in *Biblical Faith and Natural Theology* and by H.H. Schmid in *Gerechtigkeit als Weltordnung*.[1] It is important, it seems to me, that we have a broader recognition of this appropriate balance between the affirmation of the vitality and importance of a community life and a concern for the general and the universal, particularly in relation to a justification of tolerance. If we do not, we may find that the justification for tolerance between communities has been swallowed by the specific moral understandings of each of those communities with little chance for public discourse between them. We must preserve the public forum and this cannot be collapsed into patterns of community life, however rich and varied.

Raymond Plant

NOTES

1. John Barton, 'Ethics in Isaiah of Jerusalem', *The Journal of Theological Studies*, 32, 1 (April 1981), pp. 1–18; James Barr, *Biblical Faith and Natural Theology* (Oxford: Clarendon, 1993); H.H. Schmid, *Gerechtigkeit als Weltordnung* (Tubingen: Mohr, 1968).

Select Bibliography of Major Works Referred to in this Volume

Berger, D. (ed.) (1986) *History and Hate: the Dimensions of Anti-Semitism*, Philadelphia: Jewish Publication Society.

Cheyette, B. (1993) *Constructions of 'the Jew' in English Literature and Society. Racial Representations, 1875–1945*, Cambridge: Cambridge University Press.

Davies, A. (ed.) (1979) *Antisemitism and the Foundations of Christianity*, New York: Paulist Press.

Everett, R. (1993) *Christianity Without Anti-Semitism: James Parkes and the Jewish-Christian Encounter*, Oxford: Pergamon.

Eriksen, T. (1993) *Ethnicity and Nationalism: anthropological perspectives*, London: Pluto Press.

Gager, J. (1983) *The Origins of Anti-Semitism: Attitudes Toward Judaism in Pagan and Christian Antiquity*, Oxford: Oxford University Press.

Gilman, S. and Katz, S. (eds) (1991) *Anti-Semitism in Times of Crisis*, London: New York University Press.

Jones, S. (1997) *The Archaeology of Ethnicity: Constructing Identities in the Past and Present*, London: Routledge.

Katz, D. (1982) *Philosemitism and the Readmission of the Jews* to England, 1603–1655, Oxford: Clarendon Press.

Katz, J. (1980) *From Prejudice to Destruction: anti-semitism, 1700–1933*, Cambridge, MA: Harvard University Press.

Kushner, T. (ed.) (1992) *The Jewish Heritage in British History: Englishness and Jewishness*, London: Frank Cass.

Lazare, B. (1967) *Antisemitism: Its History and Its Causes*, London: University of Nebraska Press.

Langmuir, G. (1990) *Towards a Definition of Antisemitism*, Berkeley: University of California Press.

Moore, R. (1987) *The Formation of a Persecuting Society: Power and Deviance in Western Europe, 950–1250*, Oxford: Basil Blackwell.

Rubinstein, R. and Roth, J. (eds) (1987) *Approaches to Auschwitz*, London: John Knox Press and SCM Press.

Stern, M. (1974–84) *Greek and Latin Authors on Jews and Judaism*, 3 Vols, Jerusalem: Israel Academy of Arts and Sciences.

Thorowgood, T. (1650) *Jewes in America or, Probabilities that the Americans are of that Race*, London: W.H. for the Slater.

Tovey, D'Blossiers (1738) *Anglia Judaica or a History of the Jews in England*, London.

Wood, D. (ed.) (1992) *Christianity and Judaism*, Oxford: Blackwell.

Select Bibliography of James Parkes

Sidney Sugarman, Diana Bailey and David Pennie (eds) (1977) *A Bibliography of the Printed Works of James Parkes with select quotations*, Southampton: University of Southampton, which is available through the University of Southampton's Special Collections Division, lists 329 works published between 1930 and 1976. The selection below highlights some of the key books published by James Parkes throughout his distinguished career. Those books published under his pseudonym, John Hadham, which deal with more general theological matters, are not included here:

The Jew and his neighbour: a study of the causes of anti-Semitism, London: Student Christian Movement Press, 1930.

The conflict of the Church and the Synagogue: a study in the origins of antisemitism, London: Soncino Press, 1934.

Jesus, Paul and the Jews, London: Student Christian Movement Press, 1936.

The Jew in the medieval community: a study of his political and economic situation, London: Soncino Press, 1938.

The Jewish Problem in the modern world, London: Thornton Butterworth, 1939.

An enemy of the people: antisemitism, Harmondsworth: Penguin Books, 1945.

The emergence of the Jewish problem, 1878–1939, London: Oxford University Press, 1946.

Judaism and Christianity, London: Victor Gollancz, 1948.

A history of Palestine from 135 A.D. to modern times, London: Victor Gollancz, 1949.

End of an exile: Israel, the Jews and the gentile world, London: Vallentine Mitchell, 1954.

The foundations of Judaism and Christianity, London: Vallentine Mitchell, 1960.

A history of the Jewish people, London: Weidenfeld and Nicolson, 1962.

Antisemitism, London: Vallentine Mitchell, 1963.

Prelude to Dialogue: Jewish-Christian relationships, London: Vallentine Mitchell, 1969.

Whose land? A history of the peoples of Palestine, Harmondsworth: Penguin, 1970.

Index